Walking Each Other
Home Again

*A young Peace Corps Volunteer in Niger,
1960's, and her return 30 years later*

A memoir by

Laurie Oman

Library of Congress cataloging-in-publication

Color photographs and other information available at:
www.facebook.com/peacecorpsmemoir

Contact author at walkinghomeagain@gmail.com

Cover Design by Stephanie Noble and Colin Williams

ISBN: 978-0-578-81697-5

To the memory of
Sarkin Dariya and Richard Lehtinen
With thanks for all the laughter

ACKNOWLEDGMENTS

My sincere thanks go to Abby Wasserman, my writing group leader at O'Hanlon Center for the Arts in Mill Valley, where I wrote many chapter first drafts, and who was one of several editors. More editing and organizational guidance kudos go to dear friend, Stephanie Noble, who created a logical flow for the narrative, helping me tie up many loose ends. She and her husband, Will Noble, brought 60's photos back to life. Much gratitude as well to Mike Tauber, Mike Tauber Photography, who took wonderful photos of my return to Aguié, and to Jerry Koloms, co-volunteer, whose photos he generously shared. Beth Smith offered helpful guidance as did Marleen Roggow, Paula Helene and Gayle Reid. Linda Siegel, (technology4life.org) gave me gentle tech guidance throughout and did all final formatting. Thanks too to my nephew, Colin Williams, who created maps, edited photos, and helped to design both front and back covers. My son, Zachary Lehtinen, constructed the "Walking Each Other Home Again" Facebook page, and to my sister and chief exhorter, Frances Oman.

I feel much gratitude for Maimouna and all my friends in Aguie, Niger, for their forbearance, friendship, guidance and for their warm and generous welcome upon my visit thirty years after the Peace Corps two-year stint.

Last, **and** foremost, I am grateful to my husband, Bryan Gould, who encouraged my 1999 trip to Niger, supported me in every conceivable way, gave me faith in my story-telling, and did the first several rounds of editing, enduring years of my on-again, off-again writing spurts.

TABLE OF CONTENTS

Niger in Context

Pronounced "nee-zher"

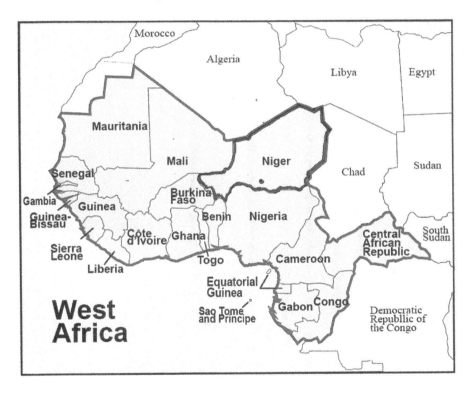

PROLOGUE

Maimouna took my hand as I turned to go, saying, "I'll walk you as far as town center." As we left, hand in hand, I was reminded of the many times, thirty years before, we had walked each other partway home after work. We'd get to my house first. I would then turn around and accompany her halfway to her house. On other occasions, we'd arrive at her house from some mission of ours, the market or a home visit, and she would turn with me towards my house and join me halfway. It was a lovely Hausa tradition which I was delighted to be re-enacting: walking a friend partway home before parting.

Of course the title has a meaning beyond our simple walks: metaphorically, Maimouna and I, half a world apart, have been walking parallel lives, into our elder years. Thirty years earlier, I was the self-appointed do-gooder coming to improve lives in a third world country. Now I'd returned to re-discover friends and see what changes three decades had made. The intertwining of our lives almost certainly enriched me far more than the impacts of the helping hand I extended for two years in Aguié.

1999 | *EN ROUTE FROM PARIS TO NIAMEY, NIGER*

I had been too excited to sleep the night before, so as soon as the plane was in the air I drifted off, waking to look down on the Mediterranean Sea. As we began to fly over the Sahara, I felt my body relax in a sense of homecoming. But it was still a long way to go across Algeria to the southwesternmost corner of Niger. I stared down at the wind patterns on the vast expanse of dunes, fascinated by the all the shapes sand can take, from gently curved mounds to pock-marked, indentations like dry riverbeds with many tributaries, deep craters, areas white with salt, and then, out of nowhere, perfect deep green circles, obviously crops, but with no discernible community around them. That vastness was all that stood between me and the realization of a dream more vivid than any I'd ever known.

Hours of flying over the desert gave me plenty of time to think. I challenged myself to reach as far back as I could in my memory to identify how my life took such it's dramatic turn, so different from my Mill Valley beginnings.

When, in the '60s, the Peace Corps was created under Kennedy's administration, I loved the idea of it. I had always been encouraged by my parents to think in terms of a global community. But to identify the exact moment when my life pivoted toward joining, it would be one evening in 1964 when I was washing pots and pans.

I was then a freshman at Sonoma State College. The cooperative dorm kitchen assignment roster paired me with another student: an attractive, athletic and funny junior named Rich. While scrubbing, rinsing and drying, we hit it off and quickly became a couple. Even after he graduated and even when our various volunteer commitments kept us apart for months, we stayed together. But when Rich applied and was accepted by the Peace Corps, they had concerns about investing time and energy training someone who might pine away for his sweetheart in the U.S. while on his two-year tour.

Rich was even more concerned about his upcoming eligibility for the draft. Serving his country by joining the Peace Corps and being a force for good in the world made much more sense to him than Viet Nam.

The solution seemed obvious: We'd marry and join up together. He proposed in October 1966; we married in December and were in Peace Corps training in the Virgin Islands by Easter 1967. I remember how the Peace Corps psychologist on St. Croix suspected that my commitment was weak, that I only joined because Rich wanted me to. He grilled me again and again, trying to catch me in ambivalence. He failed. I was, by then, totally committed to my marriage *and* to going to Niger, (pronounced with a French accent, nee-zher.)

It's not as though I lacked the gumption. At 19 I had taken a nine-month leave from college to join Caesar Chavez in the farmworker struggle to unionize. I was ready for more adventure and opportunities to contribute, but because I hadn't graduated yet, I didn't think the Peace Corps would accept me. They did, and there I was, alongside my new husband, launching a whole new life full of unknowns. Had I known how much I didn't know, I might never have boarded that plane.

Rich had the window seat. I was recovering from an emergency tonsillectomy after our three-month Peace Corps training in the Virgin Islands, so I slept, leaving Rich to his window and private wonderings about what we had gotten into. Because of my tonsillectomy we were arriving a month later than our training group.

JULY 1967 | NIAMEY, NIGER

When the door of the plane opened, we were enveloped in a blast of hot air so thick I felt I could lie down on it. Certainly, lying down was all I was interested in after our long flight from Paris. I was so used to being strong and healthy, (the spirit in which I signed up for the Peace Corps) but here I was arriving for duty in less than tip top shape, still convalescing from the tonsillectomy. I wondered if I'd made a mistake.

Our greeter and chauffeur, Hamidou was dressed in Western clothes except for his multicolored embroidered cap. He picked us out easily from the mostly African passengers, and led us expertly through baggage claim and customs. He spoke to us slowly in French. Clearly, he had a lot of experience with new Peace Corps volunteers. Rich and I held hands in the back seat as he drove us into the capital, peering out the windows, soaking in our first impressions of Africa. There were late-night corner stands lit with kerosene lanterns where a few people gathered, smoking and talking. I was struck with all the walls lining the road to town: long and short, concrete and mud brick, fancy and plain. An unlit area of mostly one-story mud commercial buildings gave way to office buildings, banks and storefronts. Eventually, Hamidou stopped and told us to wait in the Land Rover. He was back in a few minutes. *"Vous êtes a votre hotel. Descendez-vous ici."* (You're at your hotel. You get out here.) More welcome words had never been spoken. He helped us with our luggage and saw us settled into a small room in a central courtyard of the dimly lit hotel before quickly departing, promising to return at eleven in the morning to take us to meet the director. Thanking him, we fell into bed and were asleep within minutes.

We woke to someone pounding on our door. Rich groaned, got up, muttering to himself, and opened the door to a blast of morning light and a barrage of urgent French. Because I was slightly more fluent, I got up and joined him. A man with a very-full keychain in his hand and a tool-laden utility belt around his hips, very slowly repeated for us in French, "T-h-i-s h-o-t-e-l i-s c-l-o-s-e-d. We are remodeling. Look. Construction. You must leave. We are not open at all."

Wondering how this could be happening, we showered, dressed, collected our bags and waited for Hamidou in a hot, dirt courtyard under a sparsely-leafed canopy of trees, where I was startled by a big red and blue lizard scuttling up a trunk.

"Here we are," I said, "not even twenty-four hours in, and we're already having a misadventure and have also just seen our first exotic animal."

Rich laughed. "Not bad for having only been awake twenty minutes! I hope Hamidou doesn't forget us." Nothing could squelch our excitement about being on this adventure together. Niger was the quintessential assignment, rated by the Peace Corps as five (most challenging) on a scale of one to five.

A number of factors earned Niger its 'extremely difficult' rating: The very hot weather, the difficulty of getting around or communicating with anyone outside one's village, the scarcity of fresh fruits and vegetables, the necessity of communicating in two foreign languages, French and Hausa, and the challenge of overcoming huge cultural differences without much guidance. Niger volunteers, we learned, especially 'bush vols' like we would be, were left pretty much on our own. Were we up for it? Only time would tell!

Before long, Hamidou drove up and asked, *"Avez vous faim?"*

"Oui!" we exclaimed in unison, suddenly starving and looking forward to our first in-country meal.

Niamey's streets teemed with many more pedestrians than cars. We passed tiny shops with droll signs depicting different styles of hair braiding, and street vendors with their wares on grass mats laid out on the sidewalks. We came to a stop in front of a small kiosk. Hamidou recommended the fried egg sandwich. Soon we were eating a very oily hard-fried egg smashed into a section of baguette. In our ravenous condition, it tasted fabulous! At the coffee stall, we were disappointed to see that the coffee was powdered. "Nescafé, on a continent known for its coffee!?" The coffee was served in a bowl and the only cream available was sticky-sweet concentrated milk. I was grateful to be a black-coffee drinker.

At headquarters we met the Peace Corps Director, Dr. Frank Beckles, and the deputy director, Jim Garrett. We were excited to find out where we'd be posted. Unfortunately, they said, we had to temper our expectations, explaining that the rest of our training group had already filled all the established sites. Additionally, it was proving difficult to find a village that would be appropriate for both our skillsets, public health education and peanut cooperative work. They begged us to have patience.

They weren't kidding! Over the next four weeks, we became increasingly frustrated on our frequent visits to their crowded, three-room office, for news of our assignment.

Meanwhile, we lived at the Peace Corps hostel where volunteers, casually referred to as "vols," stayed whenever they came to the capital. Our delay did allow us to get to know the vols who were posted there. While in their company, we were given new names that they felt would be easier for Hausa speakers to pronounce. So Rich became Ibrahim. He liked it and it suited him. But I kept my name Laurie. None of the alternatives the group came up with, sitting around drinking beer, felt quite right to me. I wasn't in a big hurry to change it, and figured I'd wait and see what was right, when at last we got assigned.

Our longer than expected stay allowed us to become adept at getting around town despite the confusing street configuration. We were able to find the open air market, the museum, the zoo, restaurants, places that served ice cream and ones that featured live music; a hotel with a swimming pool, roadside food stands, and where to buy cigarettes.

One day Rich and I were asked to give President Hamani Diori, Niger's first president, an English lesson. His chauffeur picked us up, along with another vol named Gilbert, in a slinky black Mercedes with tinted windows and a small Nigerien flag flying from the antenna. We rode beside the Niger River and into the countryside, then spiraled up a small hill and through a guarded gate, stopping at the Presidential Palace. A highly correct and well-dressed civil servant greeted us at the door and ushered us into a room with several spacious seating areas. Gilbert, a regular at the palace, was far more fluent in French, so we expected to be mere observers. But when the President entered the room and was introduced to us, he was very interested in our experiences in his country, and asked us lots of questions, not in French but in English. He was as impressive and handsome as the pictures we had seen of him. He wore a well-tailored African suit; a matching, loose-fitting, pajama-like shirt, slacks of light grey cotton, and dark glasses that he took off to converse.

President Hamani Diori.
Photo by Ron Kroon, Dutch National Archives

The President had English classes with vols six nights a week, had been studying for at least four years and was quite fluent. We spent an enjoyable hour reading a play to him. He would repeat each page after us, and then we'd correct his pronunciation. The play was full of swearing and slang, and several times I got the giggles hearing him put strong emphasis on *'Damn them! Damn them all to hell!'*

After the lesson Mrs. Diori, Aissa, swooped in, her head wrapped in a bright print scarf that matched her ultra-chic version of the traditional long, wrap-around skirt and top. She urged us all to come into the garden for something to eat and drink. The garden lay on a slope overlooking a field where servants fired off shotguns to scare off birds, which, much to my dismay, they continued to do throughout our visit.

After strolling through beautifully landscaped flower and vegetable gardens, Mrs. Diori invited us to pick strawberries so sweet and juicy they were almost inebriating. Since we hadn't been able to find strawberries in the market, this was a real treat. We were also served lemonade with ice in it. It was like a dream, so very different from what was available in the city, just a mile away.

I returned so often to the open market, and at such a leisurely pace, that I believe I could have been led into it blindfolded and known exactly where I was, based on smell alone. There was the fetid odor of the fly-populated butcher's area, the acrid stench of the leather-workers aisle; the sweet scents of fresh fruit and vegetables in the produce section, and the mouth-watering aroma wafting from the cooked foods alley where onion, tomato and garlic simmered together with a whiff of smoke. One of my favorite areas featured all kinds of dried herbs, roots, and barks, both culinary and medicinal. Stopping to rub a leaf or substance between my fingers and giving it a sniff, the vendors generously explained their uses. Sugar was sold in solid light-brown cones, and there was a lovely looking taffy-type candy that exuded a molasses scent and got stuck in my teeth until it dissolved. Even the racks of fabric emitted the odor of dye and sizing. But I would never want to be blindfolded at the fabric stalls, when there was such a bounty of brilliant colors and diverse patterns. Though most of these fabrics were destined to become clothing, the Peace Corps doctor's wife tipped me off to buy lengths of cloth for bed sheets. She also tipped me off about the spelling of Nigerien(m) and Nigerienne (f), meaning from Niger, as distinguished from Nigerian, from Nigeria.

Niamey market

Though tourists were few, vendors lurked near hotels, banks and the post office, displaying their carved calabash bowls, leather work, wood and ivory statues and woven goods laid out on grass mats.

Lepers begged, thrusting out their deformed hands. Never having seen leprosy, our immediate reaction was both repulsion and curiosity. But after the initial shock, compassion set in. We learned to keep small change in our pockets to ward off feeling heedless and heartless.

For our future village home, we bought pots and pans, bowls and utensils, bedding and some foodstuffs we were told wouldn't be available elsewhere: jams, popcorn, packets of dried soups and puddings, and cigarettes, all imported from France. We knew with our obvious foreignness and our lack of language skills, we'd never be able to pay the same price locals paid. But we quickly learned we'd get no respect if we accepted the first price mentioned. One was expected to counter with an impossibly low figure. The vendor would then act insulted and extol their product's virtues, announcing their final price, which wasn't final, of course, and so the bartering went on, each side alternately impassioned and sullen until, at last, a middle ground was reached. An African would have paid much less, which we thought was as it should be.

Since we seemed to be stuck in a holding pattern regarding our assignment, we took the opportunity to learn as much as we could about our new country. We visited the *Musée Nationale*, studying maps that showed the regions of Niger inhabited by over twenty ethnic groups. We saw full-sized models of traditional houses and examples of regional crafts.

At the *Musée,* a Djerma man from the westernmost part of Niger sat on the ground with a back-strap loom, his legs straight out in front of him, his hands swiftly alternating between small bobbins of red, black and white cotton thread. We watched as he created a three-inch narrow, striped band which would eventually be sewn to another band, and then to many more bands to form a blanket. Since we needed bedding, we splurged and bought a Djerma blanket in the museum gift shop. Leaving the *Musée* boy approached us, holding up a black and white kitten. Having promptly fallen in love with it, we agreed to take it and gave the boy two coins, approximately ten cents.

We knew that Niger was a fledgling democracy, having achieved independence from France just seven years prior to our arrival, with a president, legislature and provincial elected officials. Curious to find out about local governance, we learned about cantons and sarkis, both ancient traditions held over from before colonial times. Now the *Sarki du Canton* meted out land and privilege and administered justice, functioning very much the way they had for hundreds of years. Would we be meeting one of these sarkis?

A full month after our arrival "in-country," we finally received good news at the Peace Corps office. Jim Garrett announced it was time to find us a site. Arriving at the hostel the next morning, in a Land Rover, he had a cowboy aura, and seemed as eager as we were to get out of the city and into the countryside.

"Alley-oop! I bet you guys are more than ready to get out of here. Got everything? Enough water? Good. 'Cause we're not turning back once we clear the city. Say, what's in that hat?" Jim's patter put us at ease, and Rich, ever the joker, answered that we were planning to fatten up the cat for our first wedding anniversary dinner.

In Niger, no one dared travel into the backcountry without a well-trained, resourceful and equipped chauffeur. Since there were no service stations, he needed to be able to fix anything that might go wrong along the way. Ours was Hassan, a young Djerma man, dressed all in khaki with dark glasses and a turban of white gauze. He helped Rich load our luggage and household goods into the back of the Rover: mosquito netting, kitchen utensils, our Peace Corps-issued medical kit and carbon water filter. After a short delay while he prayed, he flashed us an understanding smile, got behind the wheel, leaned on the horn, and said in English, partly to us and partly to the Land Rover, "Let's go!"

Jubilant, we hopped into the back seat, and settled Kitty snug in my hat, along with a jar of milk and a medicine dropper. Jim sat up front with Hassan. We were finally ready for our big adventure.

Rich and I finally hit the road with our kitten

It turned out that Jim didn't actually know where our post would be. We headed eastward on the *Route Nationale*, stopping at towns along the way to see if any of them could work out for us. "It sounds crazy," Jim said, "that post and work arrangements weren't made before your arrival, but our small staff had just placed forty new volunteers, and managed this without benefit of telephone communication, since most towns have no phone service." Adding to the challenge, he explained, we were *two* volunteers needing jobs in the same town. He went on to explain that Peace Corps policy dictated that the town had to have a hospital for me as a health educator, and also a peanut cooperative market for Rich. "A difficult bill to fill. But at least you're on your way!"

While looking quite small on the map of Africa, Niger is about the size of Texas. The National Route, (the only east-west highway) is a relatively straight line going from the capital in the far western region of the country, to Zinder, about two-thirds of the way to Lake Chad on the far eastern border. The road paralleled the southern border with Nigeria most of the way across the Sahel, the semi-arid region between the Sahara and the tropical regions to the south. The Route goes through the only arable portion of Niger. The remaining four-fifths to the north is the Sahara Desert.

We were comfortable for the first one hundred miles. After that, the grand-sounding "National Route" became just a deeply rutted dirt road. The incessant hammering over its washboard surface rattled our teeth, bruised our derrières, and made every delay feel like a blessing.

"You'll toughen up," said Hassan in purposely slow French. Laughing, he added, "This is luxurious compared to the way you'll be getting around from now on: on the tops of loaded trucks most likely."

There were a few low hills, and very few lakes or stands of trees along the seemingly endless straight road. We couldn't see much of the villages we passed because everything was hidden behind walls. Occasionally there were people walking beside the road, some with loads of firewood or sheaves of millet stalks on their heads, some with their load on a donkey. One group was of mostly women, elegantly dressed, walking barefoot in a single file, each with a large bundle balanced on her head.

"It's a wedding party taking the bride and her dowry to the home of her new husband," volunteered Hassan. Some of these groups seemed to be in the middle of nowhere. We asked where they were coming from and going to. "Most of the villages are very small and off the Route, so they're not visible. But people do walk long distances in this country."

Occasionally we'd see a small camel train, the master swathed completely in dark blue homespun clothing and turban—the kind that winds around the whole head, leaving only a space for the rider to see out a narrow slit. Some were riding and some walking, leading their camels, which were loaded high with burdens. "Many ethnicities share this country," said Hassan. "Some of them are nomadic, like these Tuaregs."

Tuareg on his camel

The first night en route we stayed in a small, dark room rented out by the owners of a Vietnamese restaurant. Vietnamese restaurants in Niger were not uncommon, since both Niger and Vietnam had been French colonies. We had a fabulous meal in which I was introduced to thin cellophane rice noodles. We washed our food down with Nigerian beer, which Rich asserted tasted like camel piss. Our room had two narrow, lumpy beds, but after a day on the washboard road, we slept like logs.

In the early afternoon of the next day, we wobbled to a halt within sight of a very small village. We had a flat tire. All the boys and men who were not otherwise employed came out to watch the excitement. Hassan, Jim and Rich all set to work jacking up the car and cranking off the wheel. The Land Rover had nothing so luxurious as a spare. They removed the tire from the wheel and the tube from the tire. The first patch didn't work. The process seemed to take forever, with the fierce heat and no shade.

A group of women and children ventured closer, eyeing us with shy curiosity.   The kitten in my hat offered an immediate transcultural connection. One of the women gestured an invitation for me to come with her into the village to get a drink of water. We wound around a few of the conical-roofed grass huts, then into one of them, stooping to enter the dark, smoky interior. It was very neat, with grass mats for sitting, and hollowed-out calabash bowls hanging from rafters in grass nets. I'd been told in training that the small villages of Niger had no refrigeration, electricity, running water, toilets or stores, but this was my first glimpse of what that really meant. I barely had time to register the reality of what life would be like for us in the next two years, because I was so enchanted with my first contact with village Nigeriennes. We pantomimed and laughed and tried to coax the youngest children out from behind their mothers. *Ooo*-ing over our kitten turned out to be the same in both our languages. The older children took turns holding him.

One of the mothers picked up a toddler and brought her face up close to mine. The child looked terrified, twisting and clawing at her mother to be let down. The women all laughed uproariously. It took all my tender self-esteem to realize that it wasn't that I was so frightfully ugly, but that the child had never before seen anybody with skin so pale, as if all the color had been drained away.

Probably none of them had ever been this close to an *anasara*, which translates as Nazarene; i.e. Christian, and is applied to all white people, regardless of religion. We were equally exotic to one another. This visit to a village whose name I never learned, the first of many times that I had to risk insulting a host by dropping an iodine pill into the water and waiting until it dissolved before drinking. But they stared and smiled, and I smiled back.

"WE'LL TAKE IT!"

We were weary of the ride and the various ways village leaders had politely refused us, or when they welcomed us, how Jim made the determination it wasn't the right fit. So we had little hope left in us when Hassan veered off the National Route yet again, bumping along the track leading into another village.

"This is Aguié. It has about a thousand inhabitants," Jim told us. "Small as it is, it's the center of the Canton of the same name, Aguié."

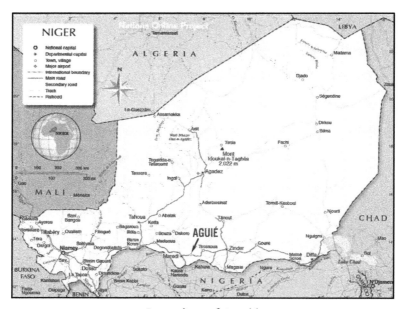

Location of Aguié

Faces filled with curiosity popped up from behind walls to watch our progress. Ours was the only vehicle around. Hassan brought the Land Rover to a halt in the center of town under the shade of a huge Neem tree. Rich and I descended from the back seat, joints askew, encrusted in road dust and smelling of sour milk from trying to feed Kitty in a bouncing vehicle.

Exhausted from the seemingly endless search, Rich was only half joking when he said, "This looks like a good town. We'll take it."

But, of course, it wasn't up to us. We had learned to wait and see if Jim and the village chief agreed. But in this case, we weren't greeted by the village chief, but by the *Sarki du Canton*.

Indeed the front of Sarki Brazaki's palace was impressive by village standards, decorated with geometric designs in bas relief plaster, stained with bright colors now sun-bleached to faint pastels. The design over the door reminded me of an owl face. A child skittered into the doorway of the house as if into the mouth of the owl, and then the Sarki and a small retinue of advisors emerged from the owl's mouth.

Facade of the Sarki's palace

The Sarki was short and thin, with a strong jaw and burnished dark-brown skin. Atop his shaved head and slightly protruding ears sat a multi-colored embroidered kufi hat. As he took our measure, I noticed his eyes were warm and piercing. His face, like the others in his retinue, had dark scarification, with a leaf-shaped pattern on his cheeks that curved from the edges of his mouth nearly to his ears. He recognized Jim from a previous reconnaissance visit, and welcomed Rich and me with smiles and handshakes. Our dialogue was translated from Hausa to French and back again.

Aguié didn't have a hospital to use as a home base for my work, but it did have a peanut cooperative for Rich. Jim knew from his earlier visit that Sarki Brazaki would welcome a married couple. So, two out of our three requirements were met. Though the Peace Corps policy was to put health educators only in towns with hospitals staffed with doctors and nurses able to meet the community's medical needs, this town did have a dispensary and a nurse. Perhaps that would be enough? I hoped so. Squeezing each others' hands, Rich and I silently agreed that we felt good about this village. The Sarki had a quiet power in his manner and posture as he gave intense attention to each one of us in turn.

A serious negotiation ensued, with the assistance of Hassan. The town hosted an annual cooperative peanut market with an infrastructure that Rich could plug into, but Jim said that it was imperative that both of us find work. Ideally, I would be allowed to train a village woman as my Public Health counterpart. Then the Sarki turned to us and said formally, "We in Aguié would like you to choose to live here. We have a very tranquil village. A friendly village." To Rich, he said, "I have a house for you and a horse if you need it, and you and your wife would be very happy here."

A vibrant young woman breathlessly stepped up to the group. The Sarki motioned with his arm for her to join us, introducing her proudly as a girl who was educated and could work with me. She had obviously taken a few minutes to clean up and put on her best clothes. Her willowy body was as skinny as my own, and I judged her to be about my age. She had knobby shoulders and well-muscled arms, a toothy smile betraying a playful humor, and eyes that stepped right up to meet mine. A beguiling modesty couldn't disguise her curiosity and excitement at having been summoned. I was impressed when she spoke to me in French that was more polished than mine. Her name was Maimouna.

Things progressed from there with amazing speed. It was almost as if we were in a play and Maimouna had been waiting backstage for her entrance cue. The Sarki had scoped out the situation perfectly, producing Maimouna as the offering that clinched the deal to secure Rich and me for Aguié.

He showed us a storage compound across the square from his palace. We could see that with a lot of work, it could be transformed into our living quarters. Though we were disappointed not to move in right then, we were relieved to have finally found our posting.

We piled back into the Land Rover and continued east towards Tessaoua, where Jim left us at the home of Connie, a volunteer we had trained with in St. Croix.

CRASH COURSE IN MIDWIFERY

While Rich soon returned to Aguié to oversee renovations of our new home, I took the opportunity to shadow Connie, who had been at her post for several months. She was only a couple years older than I, but much more mature. She had short blond hair and bold black-rimmed glasses that lent her an air of authority, the kind exercised by efficient secretaries—a place for everything and everything in its place. She no doubt thought I was a naïve and privileged youngster with few practical living skills. True enough, I had to admit.

She taught me a lot about the language, the food, the culture and the work I would be doing in Aguié. Tessaoua had a true hospital with a French doctor and trained nurses. Connie was developing her health education program there. Her French was far superior to mine, making it easy for her to make friends with the doctor's wife and a cadre of French Militaire secondary school teachers. They were very social; frequently we were invited to delicious French meals.

Since there was no hospital in Aguié, I expected I would be called upon to attend births. In training, we had seen a movie of a birth. It had been a hot day and Rich was standing in the back of the room. He fainted when the baby was born on screen. I recalled thinking that this was a very appropriate reaction: being in the presence of the amazing miracle of birth could easily cause one to black out!

But I had never attended a birth in person, so I figured it would be good for me to take the opportunity to do so, should one be born while I was there.

Meanwhile, the doctor encouraged me to spend time at the Maternité to observe how midwives helped expectant mothers. I was struck by the differences from U.S. hospitals. This one wasn't fancy enough to have a kitchen, so patients had to have family members with them to bring them food and attend to their other needs. Many of the patients came in from surrounding villages, so family and friends camped all around the outskirts of the hospital buildings, lounging, cooking on small fires, washing dishes and tending children.

A genial, buxom midwife took me under her wing and showed me how to palpate an alarmingly firm, round abdomen, and to feel the position of the fetus. She demonstrated ways to interact with women in the last stages of labor. In one case, she demonstrated how she pushed here and there and put her gloved hand up into the vagina. She explained all the signs she was tracking, noting that the baby had dropped into perfect position to descend into the birth canal. The water sac had already broken and the baby would be coming very soon. She took the mother's temperature and pulse and listened to her belly and her heart. She invited me to listen and I was thrilled to hear the baby's heartbeat. Everyone else was so casual about all of this, but I was filled with expectation and excitement.

Surprising only to me, the woman then got off the examining table and joined her family outside, but it wasn't long before she was formally admitted into the labor room. I hovered outside the open door, entering each time the midwife motioned me in. Checking now included a gloved hand up into the birth canal to examine the dilation of the cervix. Then the woman was up walking again, around and around the table, her sister at her side, stopping during each contraction to brace herself against the table. Soon the midwife directed her into the delivery room where she paced around and around the delivery table, her sister still at her side. At the very last minute she hauled herself up onto the table and, within minutes, the top of the baby's head was visible. The mother obviously experienced discomfort, but no screams or prayers escaped her lips. She was stoic and concentrated, pushing whenever the midwife urged her to. The baby's head started to crown, black, wet and slippery. After the head, only two more energetic pushes and the shoulders and torso emerged. Hind-end, legs and feet slithered out.

The new baby was now exposed to the air, our prying eyes, and the indignity of being slapped and weighed. "It's a boy, Allah be praised!" said the midwife. The umbilical cord was cut and he was swaddled and delivered to the waiting arms of his resting mother. The sister came in to admire the baby. It surprised me when, soon after the placenta emerged, mamma sat up, placed her bare feet on the floor, stood and, wrapping her skirt around her hips, walked out of the delivery room carrying her precious new family member. I watched in awe.

I was in an altered state after witnessing the emergence of a new human being from the belly of his mother. No gurneys, painkillers, sterile drapes or theatrical lighting here; no special recovery room. I felt I had participated in a sacred rite of initiation. I floated back through town in a trance-like state. The mystery surrounding childbirth had disappeared, and in its place was an astounding and visceral sensation: the honor of belonging to a long line of women who had given birth or had helped others give birth through the ages.

NESTING

While I immersed myself in midwifery in Tessaoua, back in Aguié Rich had been making the house livable and supervising the renovation. This included hitchhiking back and forth to Maradi for materials. Occasionally trucks went by on the road and made a little side money picking up hitch-hikers. There were no vehicles in the village itself. Even the Sarki was not wealthy enough to own a car. Ownership of a horse conferred status to a man. The chief had several and made a deal with Rich to loan him a beautiful white stallion with grey mane and tail. Rich named him Doikie which is Hausa for horse.

The Sarki had given us full permission to make the spacious compound livable. The six-room storehouse had floors of rammed dirt. It was a complex of three attached units, two rooms deep, that were being turned into our interior living spaces.

Looking at it from the street entrance, the far-left corner of the building was to be the shower room with our bedroom behind it. The two middle rooms were the living room facing out into our yard with a dark storage room behind it. On the right side was the kitchen with the pantry behind it.

The door from the street opened into the compound, with a traditional round grass hut on the right corner, which was not ours. It was used on occasion by the oldest son of the Sarki, Ibrahim, who would eventually inherit this compound.

Rich preparing for concrete floors and patio

By the time I arrived back in Aguié, there was a latrine hole in the ground at the side of the house next to the kitchen, four interior doorways connecting the front three rooms with the back three, a cement floor, a shower pan in the bathing room, and a big poured patio on front.

The wall of our compound formed one side of the large open village square with seven streets leading off into separate areas of town, each neatly delineated with thick, brown walls masking multiple dwellings behind, all unseen except for the upper portions. Diagonally, across the square from our compound stood the imposing front of the Sarki's palace.

Our compound

The three masons had never worked with anything other than traditional mud bricks from the clay soil quarry nearby. And to add just a little challenge, they were all deaf. Their names in Hausa identified them as such: Kurama Daya (*kurama* means deaf; *daya* means one) and his two partners, Kurama Two and Three.

Though we assumed their deafness would be a drawback, we soon learned that communicating with deaf masons was easier than speaking Hausa, since they were accustomed to getting ideas across without verbal language. We could act out what we wanted to say with fewer misunderstandings.

This nonetheless had its complications. I asked Kurama Daya to make a window on the back wall of our new bedroom. He balked. I was impatient with his hesitation. I felt the room would be much too dark without a window. This was our first home as a married couple, and we'd be living in it for two years. So I gestured emphatically that yes, I want a window exactly here on this wall. We'd been over all this the day before; why the delay?

So, dutifully, Kurama Daya started hacking at the mud wall. I left the room. When I returned a half-hour later, he was breaking through to the other side. I watched eagerly as a larger and larger patch of light shone through an expanding opening. Dust filled the air, covering our clothes and getting into my nostrils and eyes, but I was too excited to care.

At last Kurama stepped aside so I could look out our new window for the first time. To my amazement, what I saw was a round smiling young face and two dark brown eyes looking curiously up into mine. Tal Hadji, our nine-year old neighbor girl, was standing in her family's compound on the opposite side of our bedroom wall. All at once, I realized my mistake. In one fell swoop we had obliterated our own *and* our neighbor's privacy by doing what no one ever did: put an opening in a wall into another family's compound. So this is what Kurama had been trying to tell me!

Behind me I heard his distinctive guttural noises. I turned and saw on his broad face a mixture of amusement and exasperation. His long, low, non-melodic notes wove in and out of his hand gestures. I didn't need Hausa or sign language to understand he was saying, "Didn't I try to tell you? But you wouldn't listen."

Luckily, our visual trespass opened into the part of their family compound where they tethered their horse, as well as Rich's Doikie, and fenced in their goats. I made partial amends by hand-sewing a curtain to mask the offending aperture.

That ill-conceived window episode was an embarrassment, but we were graciously forgiven for that and for many other blunders we made in our new home as we got to know our neighbors, Akwiya and Mazadou, his brother Neino, other relatives, adults and children, and especially Tal Hadji and her little brother Muman.

Soon the Peace Corps delivered our basic furniture. The two single iron beds with mattresses fit exactly into the tight, windowless part of our bedroom, flush on three sides against mud brick walls. We draped our bed with the red, white, and black Djerma blanket we had bought at the National Museum in Niamey, then hung the double mosquito net from the ceiling.

Along with the beds came a sturdy cardboard book locker that opened to become a three-tiered bookcase, promising many entertaining and enlightening evenings ahead. We welcomed the arrival of a small propane refrigerator and stove with canisters of fuel. Even with an oven, the stove stood only two and a half feet tall, so we had the Kuramas build a mud brick platform to bring it up to normal stove height. The delivery also included a metal armoire for food storage and two wooden chairs. All we needed was a dining table, and luckily Rich was handy enough to have built one with lumber and tools he had bought in Maradi while I was training with Connie in Tessaoua.

With the settling-in money the Peace Corps provided, we had a buying spree in Maradi and bought a shower bucket, water filter, bedding, a dowel and some rope to create a "closet" in the bathing room, and lumber for shelving and counter tops. Finally we installed all that we had brought with us from the market in Niamey: pots and pans, utensils and china, lanterns, a wash tub, and fabric for curtains.

Before leaving our U.S. homes, each Peace Corps volunteer received lengthy instructions on what to pack and what not to pack in our one trunk each that was not to exceed a certain weight. Among the things to bring were a two-year supply of deodorant, sanitary napkins, lotion, toothpaste, underwear, our favorite spices, dried soups and puddings; a good cookbook and a pressure cooker. Rich and I had dutifully packed our two trunks.

Only one ever arrived. But in it, thank God, was *The Joy of Cooking*, which even described how to kill, pluck and gut a chicken, instructions I had no use for at home, but which would come in handy here. Fortunately, the delivered trunk also contained the pressure cooker. We managed perfectly well without that second trunk, but without *Joy* and the cooker, I would have been completely lost.

Fortunately, I was spared the job of cooking any of the victims of Rich's hunting exploits. While I was away in Tessaoua, Rich had fashioned a crude bow and arrow for himself and began walking out to see the countryside in all directions beyond town. As he told it to me, he never got close enough to any game to have a chance at hitting it, but he enjoyed learning the lay of the land. By the time I returned from Tessaoua he had already established a reputation as a would-be hunter; and as a comic. He would re-enter town pretending that he had a Guinea hen stuffed in his shirt. This created opportunities for fun; his friends would congratulate him on his catch. Or, if they'd seen him leave town, a friend might stop by the compound while he was gone and, from the doorway, urge me to get out the cooking pot, because Ibrahim would soon be back with dinner.

Not long after I returned to the village, while we were still settling in, I was visited by a contingent of dignified matrons. Rich was at work at the peanut cooperative and I was alone. Each woman was dressed head to toe in matching cloth: a long, patterned, wrap-around skirt, tight bodice and headscarf, an ensemble proper for important occasions and holidays. Each held a gift for our household: a bottle of peanut oil or a live chicken hanging upside down grasped by the feet.

I had no notion as to the protocols on how to receive such a delegation, and I probably violated them all by simply thanking them profusely and sending them away. I learned much later that gift-giving is like banking: what you give a person is eventually returned in kind. And, it turned out, my welcoming committee was made up of the wives of the wealthiest and most influential men in Aguié, and their offerings were valuable gifts. By the time I learned what was proper, I had forgotten who had come and what they had brought. At that moment, I was only concerned with what to do with three upside-down squawking chickens!

The hens addition to our household occasioned yet another hitchhike for Rich the 19 miles into Maradi to purchase lumber and wire to build a coop for the "girls," an extra bother but clearly worth the trouble. They promised a steady flow of eggs.

I was beginning to get used to hearing only Hausa, so I couldn't believe it one day when I heard voices in English calling 'Hello? Hello!' at our door. It was the couple who ran the Sudan Interior Mission school about a half mile out of town. They introduced themselves as Millie and George. They had been in Nigeria and Niger for sixteen years and spoke fluent Hausa with a broad American accent. They generously offered to give us some corrugated metal for our doors, and extended an invitation for lunch the next day.

One morning after our surprise bedroom window greeting, Tal Hadji appeared in the compound doorway and clapped her hands, meaning, "Hello...anyone home?" She had thickly-calloused bare feet, dusty legs, and a still-colorful skirt and scarf of faded, well-worn cloth. A toddler was wrapped at her waist, clinging tightly to her and straining to direct her back to the street. He clearly didn't want to come any closer to the strange-looking pale person. Tal Hadji ignored his twistings, and, when I welcomed her to come on in, she approached the new patio where I was having a cup of coffee. The baby hid his face ferociously in her neck.

Though we had already learned each other's names, Tal decided that a proper conversation on her first formal visit should begin with proper introductions, exchanging names. With the language barrier, it seemed like a good place to start.

"My name is Tal Hadji. His name is Hadu. Your name is Laouré." I repeated after her many variations of these sentences until she was satisfied that I had mastered them. I liked the way Tal pronounced my name: Laouré -- two syllables with a swift, strongly accented *ré* at the end. I liked it so much I was impatient for Rich to get home so I could introduce him to his new wife.

"Where is Ibrahim?" Came the next salvo, and away we went, teacher and student, climbing into a semblance of understanding. Little Hadu peeked from the safety of her neck, never unclenching his hold on Tal. Babies of carrying age, (two and beyond) are never clothed, covered only by their carrier's clothes and sling.

There came a time, however, when Hadu needed to defecate. I watched curiously while Tal Hadji continued with our lesson while deftly untying Hadu's sling and pulling him around in front of her. How she knew he was ready is a mystery. She sat on the ground with her legs straight out, straddling Hadu between her legs, facing away from her. Almost immediately he produced both pee and poo. She had found a twig to wipe him, then used it to scoop up the waste into a sandy pile. Using a piece of broken calabash I gave her, she tossed it over the wall onto the street.

MY LITTLE TEACHER

The effervescent Tal Hadji and several of her younger siblings became regular visitors. Her little brother, Muman, was able to go to school each morning, but Tal Hadji, being a girl, wasn't allowed, so she had time to hang out with me and still fulfill her responsibility of caring for any toddlers in her extended family. Her baby brother Oumarou was not as easily terrified as his cousin Hadu had been, so he often came with her, held closely on her back or hip with a cloth sling.

She was determined to teach me Hausa, and started right in. Pointing to her head scarf, she enunciated clearly, "*kalabi*" and I repeated, "*kalabi.*" She pointed at her skirt and said "*zani*". I pointed at mine and said "*zani*". She shook her head frowning, and I could see it wasn't because I was pronouncing it incorrectly, but because what I was wearing was not the long skirt worn by all the women in town. But she went on, pointing at a bowl and drilling me until I said *kwano* correctly; and so went my lessons. I learned to answer questions about the location of an object with the word *chung*, meaning "over there", while pointing my chin in the direction of the object in question. I noticed that often people didn't bother with the word itself, and just jutted their chin in the general direction.

Many times, she would keep repeating a word or phrase, and I would replicate what I heard, but to her ear there was something out of kilter.

"No. Like this: *kiale*."

"*Kiale*," I'd repeat faithfully.

"No. Like this: *kiale*." This word, which meant *to be quiet*, required a "k" sound matched by an explosion in the back of the throat, similar to an English "k" but quite elusive in the mouth of a Westerner. Sometimes she would fall to the ground laughing at my hopeless attempts to sound just like her. The fact that she was *my* teacher may have given her a sense of power and permission to be more directive and honest than if it had been the other way around. A sweet intimacy quickly grew between us.

It seemed that nothing escaped my young friend's curiosity, though she was not always sure how to express it. I'd see her struggling with a request, not wanting to ask directly. When her lips would purse way over to one side while she eyed our refrigerator, I'd know she'd come to the end of her patience and could not stand it *one moment* longer. I would then open the fridge, take out one of the diminutive ice trays, and pop out a cube of ice for her. This she would hold first in one hand, then the other, then pop it into her mouth for a few moments, trying to make that tiny miracle last as long as possible. Then the cycle would begin again. When she asked the inevitable, "How does it work?" I was at a total loss to explain in English, let alone Hausa, how the kerosene flame visible beneath the fridge could possibly make water turn into something hard and cold.

Such curiosity was not confined to Tal Hadji. New women friends were fond of coming over and politely coaxing me to produce ice from this inexplicable novelty. They'd heard that ice could fall out of the sky and asked if I'd ever seen that happen. I said I had, yes. Not only that, but sometimes the ground would become completely covered with white and the air was colder than they could imagine. At this, their eyes grew wide.

Word of the ice rocketed out to all the kids in town. *Glace! Glace!* Curiosity and desire overcame even the most timid child, who for any other reason would have lacked the courage to approach our compound. Countless little hands opened for the magic of *glace*. The first few times this happened, Rich and I both enjoyed handing out ice to the rapt children, but then the requests became too frequent and invasive. We somehow came to an understanding that ice would be special and infrequent. Peace was thereby restored. After that, to my delight, as I went about town children, even those I didn't know, would greet me on the street saying wistfully, "Laouré, *glace*," perhaps repeating it a couple of times. They seemed to take pleasure in pronouncing the first part of my name slowly, sliding down to the o and then finishing it off quickly with an uptone ré, with a rolled r; (la o ray). They were unable to forgo the possibility that I might produce the coveted prize right there in the street. "Laouré, *glace*," became a refrain that linked me to children all over town.

Another puzzling but delightful innovation for them was popcorn. They were familiar with corn, grown mainly for animal food. But to see me pour kernels of corn into a heavy-lidded pot and open it up minutes later, full of delicious popcorn was more than they could fathom. Word of popcorn spread like wildfire and even grown women would come and visit, hoping to be offered this amazing treat. It was fun to sit on mats on our living room floor with three or four women, all of us marveling and delighted with this miracle.

Along with minding family babies, Tal helped the family by selling food prepared by her mother, Akwiya. She would balance a tray of warm millet pancakes on her head. Her first sale of the morning was frequently at our house. Rich and I often finished off her whole tray, shaking off the sprinkle of hot pepper flakes and eating them with butter and ersatz maple syrup I made from sugar, water and maple flavoring. She would take our coins of payment and tie them tightly into the corner of her skirt.

She often accompanied me to the open market. She could be so mischievous, sometimes skipping ahead of me, her bare soles tough as shoe leather, to preview what market offerings she might find and claim as a surprise for me. She knew I was always looking for things I didn't recognize—something new and tasty I could learn to cook. Sometimes she would forge ahead and then run back to me, tugging on my skirt to come see what she'd found, maybe a small pyramid of browning limes, a treat she knew I'd want to buy. She undoubtedly hoped that I would mix their tart juice with water and sugar and give her some with ice in a cup. She would then go home and report it all to her curious family who no doubt laughed in amazement at Laouré's peculiarities.

Tal Hadji, my little teacher

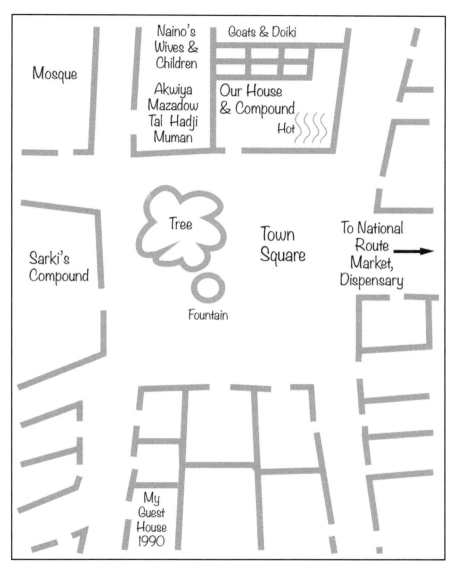

Village orientation

MODESTY A MUST

During the first few weeks in Aguié, I wandered through town wearing my Western knee-length skirts and no head scarf on my head, not realizing how serious the religious and cultural strictures were on women about showing the head and legs. Yes, our Peace Corps trainers had tried to teach us to pay attention to cultural norms, but I was oblivious to the fact that for a man to see an unrelated woman's uncovered head or legs was *totally forbidden*. I assumed it was just a matter of style, but came to realize that it was just plain arrogance of the young, ethnocentric, American woman I was.

Once I realized my egregious faux pas, I had to quickly learn how to dress appropriately, especially if I was to earn the trust of the villagers so I could be effective in sharing health information. But it wasn't easy! I purchased a length of cloth that constituted a *zani,* the traditional long skirt worn by all the village women. But how to wrap it and secure it was beyond me. One day Tal Hadji noticed how I was struggling to tie my *zani* and she hauled me next door for her mother to help me. Akwiya was almost a head shorter than I and a bit broader, but the *zani* accommodated all shapes and sizes. I paid close attention as she made her special tuck. But when I tried to emulate hers, mine fell apart right away. Getting the hang of it was crucial since it would fall off if it wasn't secure. I pictured myself walking through town and my skirt dropping off. Now that would give the villagers something to talk about for years to come.

Over and over again Akwiya bunched up a handful of fabric and then tucked it into her waist just so. And over and over again my attempts failed. The other women in the family compound encircled us with unabashed guffaws. I could tell that Akwiya was trying not to laugh, but she and I abandoned the attempt at the same time and surrendered to a group hoot.

Once I achieved a crude but at least secure version of the zani tuck, the women showed me the many different ways to tie my matching square cotton scarf could be folded and worn: with a high crown or low on the forehead, always with the ends tucked in.

AGUIÉ'S FIRST SHOWER

One day Tal Hadji clapped, then slipped into our compound through the doorway that linked to her family's. She'd heard about our newest project and was certain it required her personal supervision. This project had been going on for several days and was quite a puzzle to her and everyone else. Following the edicts of our Peace Corps handbook on proper waste and water disposal and wanting to set a good example, Rich and I had employed the Kuramas to dig a three-foot deep by three-foot wide hole just outside our shower room. This was designed as a sump for our shower water. After they had cemented our inside shower pan, the next step was to punch a hole in the mud wall for the shower water to exit and drain into the sump. According to our book, we were supposed to fill the hole with rocks, creating a seepage system for our shower water.

However well-intended, this effort did not prove practical. First of all, there was no running water in the village. Every drop of water we used had to be carried to us on someone's head from the village well. And secondly, there were no rocks to be had! No quarries, no rocky riverbeds, no rock outcroppings. *No rock.* The entire village, canton, nay, country consisted of sand. Water sunk instantly into the ground, leaving no trace. What need did we have for rocks?

Our shower bucket was designed to be lowered with a rope to the floor, filled with a mixture of hot and cold water to the desired temperature, and hoisted up overhead. Many little holes were punched into the bottom. Inside, covering the holes was a sealed disk that acted like a plug, so when you stood under the bucket and pulled the chain connected to the plug, voila! A not-so-instant, not so long, but oh-so-blessed shower.

The three Kuremas with the sump hole

Tal Hadji and most everyone else in the village either saw or heard about each of our strange projects. As if our rock sump idea was not exotic enough, there was also the stool we had built over the latrine hole. The villagers had heard of latrine holes, though only four people had them: the teacher, nurse and two agricultural agents, all government employees. But no one had ever heard of a stool over a hole. When they needed to relieve themselves they went out into the fields where the sand and sun absorbed and dried out the leavings to dust.

Although we were adapting in many ways to local customs, when it came to this basic human function, I needed a toilet. So we sketched out our idea on a piece of paper, but the Kuramas had never worked from drawings before. They peered at one another, perplexed, but eventually, with the help of hand gestures, figured out how to turn the two-dimensional lines on paper into a three-dimensional object. Through trial and error, the mud brick pedestal slowly grew to a satisfactory height, and was capped off with a concrete finish resembling a toilet seat. Rough on the posterior as it was, I had many occasions to appreciate this improvement.

Our little mud home became an oasis of safety, rest and relative cool where we could relax, read books, have easy conversations in our native tongue, and feel free to complain about the heat and the flies. As newlyweds, with all the usual difficulties that attend building a life as a couple, we also needed that time alone together. And we felt fortunate to have each other to share our bewilderment and triumphs as we ventured forth into the community to carve out work for ourselves.

Rich's job with the agricultural coop was much more clearly defined than my challenge to create something new and unheard of in Aguié: a health education program. But even so, we were both learning Hausa from scratch, having studied only French during our three-month training. Though we did need French in our work, Hausa was crucial to communicate with most of the villagers. We were out of our element, doing work we'd never done before in languages that were not our own. So yes, we gladly took refuge in our humble abode.

That said, it was the people who truly made us feel at home. The Sarki stopped by on a regular basis to check on our building progress, always urging me to come over to visit his wives. Neighbors were friendly and let us know they welcomed us. We loved Aguié, the neighborhood, the weekly market and the green fields of mostly millet and peanuts on every side of town.

Many of those fields were worked by the villagers, each for their own family's needs. But the Sarki had many fields, and it was customary for the men in the village to pitch in to work them as well. If there was a drought, the Sarki had a stockpile to help provide food and seed for everyone. It was the African version of crop insurance. In our first week in town, we noticed all the men in the village heading out to work on the Sarki's farm in a parade with drums, through town and to the fields. The drumming went on all day and into the night.

THE DISPENSARY

The dispensary was located a few hundred yards off the National Route, a sandy five-minute walk from our home. It was a three-room concrete structure with a covered porch across the front. The main room was large for what it contained: a single desk and chair. The small second room had an examining table used exclusively for dressing wounds. The third room was little more than a closet, where medicines were stored and shots given.

Mustafa, a plodding fellow whose job it was to dress the wounds, was also the janitor and watchman. Every morning he took the pan of used needles and syringes around the back of the building to sterilize them in boiling water over a wood fire, making them ready for use again, day after day. The needles got pretty dull over time!

Somaila was the nurse. He was young and unbelievably handsome. His face was not animated, but his dark eyes set between dark eyelids with long, thick lashes, were full of expression and life. He never had to speak his amusement or scorn; they were right there in his eyes. When he smiled, he revealed a row of very white straight teeth -- a movie-star smile. He was single—it was very unusual for a man who could afford a wife not to have one—and he dressed in stylish Western clothes. Attractive as he was, he also had more than a touch of arrogance that I found difficult.

At first, feeling my way, I took my time setting up a formal health education program per Peace Corps guidelines. I couldn't implement it until I learned the language and understood more of the culture. To that end, Maimouna and I met together a few mornings a week.

Rich and me with nurse, Somaila, mosque tower in background

I spent the other mornings at the dispensary, seeing the kinds of health problems that brought people in, listening to the ways people described their ailments, and observing what Somaila did for them. Since I had no medical training, and wasn't expected to as a health educator, and just the beginnings of being able to communicate in Hausa, this was all a steep learning curve. But day by day I improved and gained confidence in my ability to communicate and be of service in some way.

We saw people with malaria, schistosomiasis (snail fever) and infected injuries; babies with severe conjunctivitis and many undernourished children with diarrhea. Very often it was difficult to diagnose what exact ailment a patient had due to their use of general terms like *zahi*, which meant heat, and corresponded to the English use of the word "cold" to describe the same symptoms of nasal congestion and sneezing. *Chiwo n chicki* meant stomach ache.

When I started working at the clinic, I was grateful that Somaila welcomed my help with administering quinine to small children who balked at taking the bitter liquid from a cold, shiny spoon. It was a way for me to win the trust of the mothers who would become my main students. I was also flattered when he taught me how to give shots. Very hesitant at first, I quickly became a pro. He had me administer shots to all the female patients who needed them, a change that was welcomed by him and by the women too. But our honeymoon period was short. Somaila refused to understand that my role in the dispensary was one of a health educator, not his personal medical assistant.

If we were having a slow morning he would simply say, "*Sai anjima*"-- "See you later"-- and wander off, leaving me in charge while he strolled through town with a friend.

My position was awkward. Because I worked at the dispensary, it was natural for people to assume I was a nurse or doctor. When asked, "Are you a *likita*?" I explained that I was more a teacher than a nurse, that I was in Aguié to teach people about staying healthy. This was confusing to them. Why was I alone in the dispensary if not to diagnose their ailments and dispense medicine?

When I began to notice that Somaila saved most of the rationed antibiotics for his friends with venereal diseases, while other villagers were told there were none, my irritation with his absences turned into a lack of respect. I felt emboldened to assert my independence in ways that made him annoyed.

Meanwhile, Maimouna was working out extremely well. Since she spoke both French and Hausa, she could both translate for me and teach me Hausa. I soaked up as much useful terminology as I could, jotting down phrases and vocabulary in the school notebook I carried with me everywhere.

I was grateful she was so bright, perceptive and willing to take the initiative. With her help, I was sure I would be able to create a well-baby clinic, healthy-living demonstrations and make home visits. These were the three main education tools I'd been taught in Peace Corps training, and which I, in turn, wanted to impart to Maimouna. Once the program was in place, I hoped to be able to free myself from Somaila's dominance.

Training session, in our compound

It was a major transgression for a woman to talk to men outside their family, but though I had made many concessions to custom, I felt strongly that I had to break that rule. Though most of the men who came into the clinic were treated by Somaila, if I was the only one there, of course I had to speak with them. When I felt it was important, I sometimes spoke to fathers about providing money to buy a bit of liver or an egg for an ailing child. I would tell a father that his child might recover, or gain weight after an illness, more quickly, and the extra expense was necessary. My being *anasara* seemed to give me special status and privileges. He might give more credence to my explanations, and be more likely to give his wife extra money for special purchases, than if she asked him herself.

But I didn't limit myself to speaking out of medical necessity. I spoke with friends and neighbors, regardless of gender. Self-censorship was a big step beyond changing my clothes to suit local custom, and I couldn't do it. I stubbornly refused to do it. Fortunately my foreignness allowed me a certain freedom from the strictures.

The tradition of local midwifery was still in full swing in Aguié. I was only aware of one time that a woman was evacuated to a hospital to give birth, and that evacuation was affected after a long, arduous labor which was beyond the scope of a local midwives. Her husband went out to the National Route and flagged down a small truck and away they went, bumping along to Tessaoua. So much for an ambulance.

One morning soon after we moved in, I had just finished breakfast, sipping my instant coffee and having my first cigarette of the day when a man came clapping at the doorway. I recognized him as a neighbor. He indicated that his wife was in childbirth, would I please come. I followed him across the square and into a dark hut where a circle of women were attending to the mother. When my eyes became accustomed to the dark, I took my place next to the mother and repeated what the other women were saying to her: to relax between contractions, to not give up hope, to drink tiny sips of water. Her contractions were obvious agony. There was no way for me to tell why the child wasn't coming forth into the world. So many possibilities and I had none of the knowhow to help with any of them.

It was a truly helpless feeling, especially with so many hopes riding on my arrival.

It wasn't long before I knew what was needed: they would have to call the nurse. I knew their reluctance to have a male present. I argued that Somaila might be able to save at least the mother's life. Someone was dispatched to go find him. When he arrived, he gave her an injection and instructed me to massage her abdomen, and quickly departed, to everyone's relief except mine.

I stayed and did the massage. After an hour or so, I passed the job on to the other women, then went back to our house. Only a couple of hours later, I heard a loud wail from the direction of the birthing woman's home. Then another and another, until the heart of the village was saturated with the incessant keening of the household women, mourning the death of their sister. The lamentation went on for at least half an hour. I was to hear this sound a number of times in our two years. Each time I stopped what I was doing to feel the thin thread between life and death, and to appreciate the keening tradition for fully expressing and sharing the loss, something so lacking in my own culture.

TIBIRI FESTIVAL

The second-year volunteers had emphatically encouraged us to come to Maradi for Tabaski, a Muslim high holiday. So when we arrived I wasn't surprised to find Mark's house strewn with the travel satchels belonging to other volunteers. Mark, indulgent, never complained about having to step over our sleeping forms on his way to the bathroom. We arrived on Saturday because we'd be getting up early Sunday morning to travel twenty kilometers northwest to the town of Tibiri.

Rich and I had been finding excuses to hitchhike to Maradi as often as every other month. There were hardware stores, restaurants, bars and a movie theater, a large daily market and huge weekly market on Fridays. Our Peace Corps stipend was a pittance, but there was no way we could spend it all in Aguié where meat, fruits and vegetables were scarce; and bread, instant coffee, beer and wine were non-existent.

On this day, the bustle in the streets of Maradi told of the impending major holiday. Women hurried home from the market with bundles on their heads; many sheep were tethered next to doorways; and children buzzed excitedly on every street corner.

We looked forward to going out for dinner to our favorite bar that served the highly spiced *poulet a la tomate*. As evening approached, we gathered a group of hungry pals and walked to our destination. It was exciting being with other English-speakers who were enduring and enjoying and persevering and coping and learning a lot of the same things we were. There was plenty of time to drink too much bad beer because the chickens for our meal had to be caught, killed, plucked and cooked to order, or so it seemed, and the meat came out tough but so very tasty! We staggered home happy, drunk and ready for some music making, which put us to bed very late.

The Maradi Gang: Rich, Cathy, Tom, me, Richard and Jerry drinking red wine directly from the jug

But at the crack of dawn we piled into bush taxis that were lined up and heading south to the parade grounds in Tibiri, the seat of the Gobirawa branch of the Hausa people. The Gobirawa people have different facial markings from the Katsinawa branch in the Aguié region, but they are all Hausa.

Even though the National Route, running east and west, was unpaved, it was at least haphazardly maintained, but the road south was a lumpy dirt track, and our bush taxi's shock absorbers had absorbed their last shock long ago. The windows were open because of the heat, and we arrived at the parade grounds covered with dust.

We were dropped off at the edge of a vast field where hundreds of Hausas in their finest, brightest clothes, formed a thick oval around a large open space. We had donned our finest traditional costumes as well. Rich had bought a highly embroidered, light blue grand boubou from the sarki and looked very handsome. I had borrowed a pedal sewing machine with which I had fashioned a simple dress. Women wore every cotton print I'd ever seen in the market, yellow with black and gold, green with red and yellow, and my favorite, batiked with light and dark blue on a white background. Scarves framed the women's glistening faces, and children were cocooned on their backs or tucked by their sides. Men in more conservative pastel colors, some on horseback, gathered at one end of the field.

Almost as soon as we arrived, we heard what sounded like multiple horns, medieval fanfare slicing deeply into the ambience, quieting the crowd. The six musicians wore identical red and green boubous. They stood in a line on a slight rise, each blowing a long metal horn, its bell resting on the ground about eight feet in front of him. The unison notes, long and haunting, caused an immediate hush. Turning with the crowd, I spied a large floating umbrella, striped with colors matching those of the horn-blowers. Sitting in its shade in a sedan chair carried by eight men, was the Emir of the Gobir nation, his turban enlarging his head to double its size. Middle-aged, wearing sunglasses, he looked enormous in all his regalia, and seemed comfortable in his entitlement.

His retinue of elaborately decorated horses, riders with sabers across their chests, in front and behind him, made its way slowly through the crowd. All activity halted for the traditional prayers to Allah and the ceremonial killing of the first sheep, representing the one God asked of Abraham after being satisfied that he would have sacrificed his son.

When the parade moved on again, circling the parade grounds, our small group, the only whites in the crowd, walked along slowly to keep the Emir in view. In the crush, someone accidentally stepped on my foot and broke my sandal. So there I was, in the hot sand with one bare foot, wondering how I was going to get through the day with only one shoe. Distraught, I hopped along, hanging onto Rich's shoulder.

Somehow, the Emir himself noticed my predicament. He said something to one of his attendants, who was at my side in a minute, presenting me with a beautiful new handmade pair of Tuareg sandals. He indicated that it was the Emir I had to thank for them. I looked up and the Emir nodded to me and gestured for me to put them on. As I did, I flashed him my biggest smile and shook my fist, which in Hausa means "right on." He smiled back. Rich later said that he was sure the Emir was flirting with me.

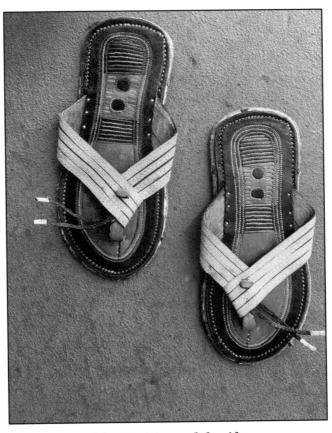

The Emir's sandals gift

The Emir stopped his procession at the far end of the field, and drumming commenced. The crowd formed into an oblong, about the length of two football fields, with the Emir at one end. Horsemen lined up abreast at the other end. The crowd hushed. The Emir gave a wave of his hand and the horsemen all took off, lashing their steeds with whips. Faster and faster they galloped toward the Emir until, just before they would have run over his entire retinue, they reined in their horses and reared them up in homage. Shouts and ululation arose from the crowd. A second tier of horsemen readied themselves at the far end of the field, and with drumming fanfare, commenced their own gallop.

After the horsemen, men on camels lined up. These mounts were more skittish and less well behaved than the horses. But at the signal, they too galloped towards the Emir, lumbering on their long, knobby legs faster than I would have imagined possible, getting in each other's way, ungainly and rowdy, but stopping short in front of the Emir. A great cheer rang from the crowd.

After an hour, the crowd began to disburse in a disorganized way. We were hot and hungry. The dust on my eyelashes was heavy and my legs were tired. Despite the discomfort, we were satisfied to have witnessed the unique ritual. A German anthropologist in our group explained that camel racing is an ancient tradition brought along with Islam from the Arabian Peninsula, and that this version was mainly a show of obeisance, not a race with a winner.

We waited a long time for seats in one of the trucks heading back to town, grateful that we had thought to bring canteens. People were obviously curious about us, some of them (mostly men) stopping to greet us and exclaim over the glorious day. I was able to tell a couple of bold women about my sandal breaking and the small miracle I had experienced. They expressed their delight by placing their palms in front of their faces while breathing in quickly through their mouths.

A tepid shower and a tepid beer were like manna after our dusty ride back to Maradi. My sandals and my tale were much admired by our compatriots at Mark's house as we relaxed and shared stories of the day.

We stayed up late listening to The Beatles' new album, *Sgt. Pepper's Lonely Hearts Club Band,* which another volunteer had received in cassette form. I remember thinking that the whole album was odd, but with repetition, I began to love it.

VILLAGE JUSTICE

During our initial weeks in the capital, we had noticed all the volunteers in Niamey had what were commonly called "houseboys". They were stewards who took care of household chores, marketing and guarding the house when the vols were away. Bill, a seasoned volunteer, advised us to hire one when we settled in.

Rich was prepared to go the houseboy route, but I balked at the idea, arguing, "Two grown people should be able to take care of their own housekeeping needs, for heaven's sake." I meant it. But I quickly learned that housekeeping activities in Aguié demanded a great deal of time. Just washing clothes took up one day a week. Shopping, sweeping, cleaning up dishes, all were more difficult and took longer than in the US. We simply couldn't work full-time and manage our housekeeping; it was that simple.

So when a young man with a charming smile came clapping at our doorway, offering his services in broken French, I remembered Bill's advice. Sali was tall and thin and wore a dirty white cap. He said, "I worked for a Frenchman in Zinder. I'm an experienced houseboy and can do anything you need done. You need me."

Rich and I decided to give him a try, and we agreed upon a salary, duties and hours. He was there bright and early the next day. Since I enjoyed shopping and cooking, we didn't need him for those tasks, but with no running water or even a sink, I was grateful to have him take the dishes outside to wash them. He took our dirty laundry away and brought it back clean and dry. I could feel my misgivings peel away. He didn't work full time, so he wasn't seriously underfoot, and I accepted his comings and goings as part of our routine.

Then, one month we came up missing cash that we kept in an unlocked trunk in the shower room. We began to suspect Sali. We spoke of it to Sarki Brazaki. He asked around. The villagers reported Sali had been out spending money like a rich man. The Sarki lost no time. He sent one of his men to bring Sali to him and ordered him to get out of town and stay out. We were glad to be rid of him, but dreaded taking on all the chores again.

The next day, another young man showed up at our door. But this one came with the Sarki's recommendation. Though he had no prior houseboy experience and spoke no French, we had learned enough Hausa to communicate. From that day forward Issaka took on our houseboy duties.

Issaka had a face like a changing exhibit. When he was happy it shone, and when he was worried, his brow furrowed deeply. His eyes took on a smoky, puzzled look when he wasn't sure what we were asking him to do. His mouth scooted over to one side of his face when he was skeptical about anything, and his chin jutted out when he was thinking. Over a period of weeks, we came to trust him entirely. He took good care of our compound, house and belongings and we learned to rely on him for advice about many aspects of life in Aguié.

Near our kitchen beside the compound wall, we stored large terra-cotta water jugs, and this is where Issaka did the dishes. The wall had a drain hole to the street, a convenient way to dump wastewater. It was among the town's informal dumping places. Roaming chickens scratched there and enterprising children mined it for treasures. Vultures hung out on our wall, hoping for a scrap of something tasty.

Though at first sight, I had complained, "Just what we need: a garbage dump on the other side of our wall creating a stink," in fact it didn't smell. People had little to throw away. Very few could afford to buy canned tomato sauce or condensed milk, the only tinned things for sale in the one tiny store. Those few cans kids turned into toys. Glass bottles were never thrown away. They were treasured for storing homemade peanut oil. Most people had just enough to eat and any leftovers were given to the Koranic students who came begging at the doorways every evening. The weather was generally so dry that stinky things that weren't eaten by the vultures or rolled away by dung beetles dried out and became desiccated, dissipating any odor, and wastewater sank instantly into the sandy soil.

One morning, while Issaka was washing the breakfast dishes, I heard a commotion on the street just the other side of the wall. We both stood on tiptoes to see what was happening. It looked like a small parade. In the lead was a man, bent forward, carrying several sheaves of millet on his back. Trailing behind him was a group of villagers shouting, chanting, and shaking their fists at him. People came to their doorways and watched as they went by.

"Issaka, what's happening?" I asked.

He looked amused and explained, "This man was caught stealing millet from another farmer. They are making him return that millet to its owner and are giving him a lot of trouble on the way."

This town had no need for a police force. The citizens publicly humiliated him through the streets, while letting everyone know that he's not trustworthy.

"He won't steal again," said Issaka. "At least not soon." His eyebrows expressed approval.

Earlier, I had learned another lesson in village justice. Maimouna and I were on our way to a home visit when we came upon a man and woman arguing in the street. They were shouting and gesticulating, almost coming to blows. We stopped at a safe distance. Neighbors were peering out their doorways and over their walls, interested to see and hear the dispute. Maimouna explained then that husbands and wives were forbidden to fight inside their compounds.

"If they can't settle something peacefully, they must take to the streets to air their argument in public."

"How ingenious!" I exclaimed. "What a way to temper marital disputes!"

As the quarrel became even louder, Maimouna told me, "If you make a threat or raise your hand, there will be multiple witnesses, and also helping hands if things get violent. Arguments that don't get settled in this way are brought to the Sarki."

I pictured Sarki Brazaki in his low sling chair in the shade of the huge tree in the main square, between our compound and his palace, often with his deputies discussing politics, sharing news and telling stories.

Sarki Nouhou Brazaki with one of his sons

"Citizens with disputes can come to him for a judgment," Maimouna explained. "If the person with the complaint comes alone, the Sarki will often hear him out. Then he will send for the other people involved. He listens carefully to both sides and then makes a decision.

"One's word is really important. If you have an agreement with a mason to build a house or a tailor to sew a new suit of clothes, you need to trust one another."

Since all contracts were verbal, I could see that misunderstandings would surely come up. "Sarki Brazaki's judgments are final," she said, "unless the parties can afford to go to Tessaoua and go before a provincial judge. That can get expensive and time-consuming." I wasn't privy to any of these local deliberations, but the Sarki had great respect among his people, and in all of his dealings with Rich and me, he was wise and fair.

I wondered about the *village* chief's role. Though Sarki Brazaki was a central figure in our lives, I had come to know the *village* chief only slightly. You wouldn't pick him out of a crowd as anyone special. His dress and demeanor were similar to the other farmer/husband/householders on any street in town. But I learned that his title as chief of the village was inherited through all the generations of fathers and forefathers, going back to the son of the original chief for as long as the village of Aguié had existed.

He lived on a back street in a slightly larger compound than most. His three wives had thirteen children between them. Though his authority in town was overshadowed by that of Sarki Brazaki, chief of the whole Canton of Aguié, he still garnered much respect.

But I had other more pressing questions for Maimouna:

"I've never seen a woman at the Sarki's chair. Do women get a fair deal?" I asked her, wondering if she would feel comfortable answering honestly.

She didn't seem bothered by my question. "In a dispute between a man and a woman, the woman usually loses. A man can divorce a woman simply by taking her before the Sarki and saying to her, 'I divorce you, I divorce you, I divorce you.' His wife has no such right. A woman is required by Muslim law to remain married unless her husband decides to divorce her. A woman goes back to her parents' home."

Maimouna sensed my shock at this inequity, but she just rolled her eyes as if to say, "Yes, I know it's different where you come from. But that's just the way it is here and there's nothing you or I can do about it."

I understood. There were rules and traditions that Rich and I were wise enough to know we couldn't change. The status of women was one of those. Still, I could fairly say that I was involved with changing the status of one woman—Maimouna, the only townswoman to receive a salary. For now it was from me, but I hoped that the government would make her pay and her position permanent, that she would take my place when my tour of duty with the Peace Corps ended.

Because she received pay, she could in turn pay other women to collect her firewood, pound her millet, make her peanut oil. She could pay a water carrier, and even sometimes have other women cook for her family. She had become respected as a teacher beside me, and I hoped she would carry on the work when I left. I allowed myself to imagine that if she had daughters, they would have a better chance to go to school. Her example might encourage her siblings, friends and neighbors to envision new kinds of futures for their girl children. Change always starts slowly. I envisioned Maimouna's career echoing over time and having an impact.

RHYTHMS OF DAILY LIFE

Mornings started early with the cock's crow. It might be from the far side of the *quartier* or just next door. Very soon an answering rooster would assert himself, and the concert would begin in earnest.

The same pattern was replicated by women pounding millet in the pre-dawn, their wooden pestles thudding in mortars made from sections of hollowed tree trunks. One of the beats came from just a few feet outside our bedroom window, from Aisha, Neino's new wife. I could picture her pounding spot next to her snug round hut as I felt the vibration of her strong strokes through the ground and walls of our bedroom. The regular beat was sometimes accented with a little half-beat on the upstroke when she tapped the inside of the mortar before raising the pestle above her head to ram it down once again. Often more than one woman in a compound was pounding at the same time, and the rhythms would align, then syncopate, and cross back again into unison among themselves and with others down the street, and distant muffled riffs far off towards the edge of town.

The sound was so reassuring that it would sometimes lull me back to sleep for an extra hour or so. Clock time fell away. Like everyone else in the village, we arranged our activities by the rhythms of the village and the position of the sun in the sky. On the day we noticed that the battery on Rich's watch had died, we didn't need it anymore.

With each sound, I woke a little more, then dozed back to sleep to be woken again, perhaps by the sound of Neino talking gently to Doikie as he fed and groomed him outside our bedroom window. Or by Kitty meowing for breakfast. Or by the quiet footsteps of Issaka sprinkling water to tamp down dust before sweeping. He had no qualms about entering the bedroom while I was sleeping, so intent was he on his chore.

When I woke in this way, responding to a gentle rhythmic invitation from the community, I felt energized and ready to greet the day.

Hausa is a tonal language, and because of this, stories could be shared by drum. The changing pitch matched the tonal ups and downs of the language closely enough for a native speaker to understand. So too, the women could drum in their mortars with more or less force, shorter or longer spaces in between thrusts. These could convey greetings or more complicated messages over walls.

One day Maimouna and I were walking up the main street toward the dispensary when suddenly she let out a squeal of delight. She laughed, looking to the left where there was only a high mud wall. I turned to her with a perplexed look. Still laughing, she explained that her friend who lived behind that wall, had heard us talking as we passed by, and she, busy with her pounding, had pounded out a funny greeting to us. I suspect Maimouna didn't translate it to me in its entirety, but it was something like a friendly tease: "It doesn't look like you're in a very big hurry to get to work this morning."

I remember one morning while I was walking near the outskirts of town, I came upon a group of girls working at the communal mortars and pestles. They sang as they pounded the seeds off the millet stalks, adding interest to their work by tossing their pestles high in the air and inserting quick claps of the hands before catching them again for the next downward plunge into the deep wooden bowl. After removing the grain from the stalks, they poured the grain from one basket to another, allowing the breeze to carry the chaff off while the heavier grains fell straight down into the lower basket. They were colorfully skirted girls, some with babies tied onto their backs, singing, clapping and pounding together. All of a sudden, I imagined their mothers, grandmothers and so on back before memory, at this same place, singing these same songs and playing the same clapping games. It was a continuity that, with so much rapidly changing technology and lifestyles, rarely occurred in my own country anymore. Seeing and hearing these young women made me wistful for American folk traditions of an earlier era.

The village quieted down in the evenings. We could hear the muezzin's call from the small mosque across the street from us. Men gathered silently for prayers, leaving their shoes lined up outside the mosque door. Then families came together for the evening meal. Men ate first, then women and children. Later on, at the last muezzin's call, men who lived nearby again gathered, shed their shoes and entered. Those who lived farther away gathered in their neighborhoods, and, since there were no cars in Aguié, unrolled their grass mats in the street. They could be seen carrying a small plastic pot of water for their ablutions of washing their face, hands and feet; then they prayed together facing the Kaaba shrine in Mecca. They'd kneel, bend down to touch their foreheads to the earth twice, praying quietly. Women, who were not allowed inside the mosque, did their praying singly in the privacy of their homes.

Some evenings, for reasons we couldn't always discern, we were treated to the rhythm of the talking drums. These were small, hand-held drums with an hourglass shape. Leather tension cords attached the two leather heads, bottom and top. These cords would be squeezed between the player's arm and body, causing the pitch to sound higher or lower.

After prayers and eating, men would typically stroll out on the streets smoking cigarettes, or cluster in small groups around a friend, who by day was a farmer but some evenings sold single cigarettes, matches and *goro* nuts from a tray with raised edges. He might have a kerosene lantern, but then again, kerosene was expensive and so were wicks. The men would squat, tell stories and talk about the crops and weather for an hour or two. Groups of younger men might hang out at the main road and hunker around a radio owned by an enviable friend. When Rich went out to join the men after dark, he would often come home wishing he knew Hausa on a deeper level than he needed for his work. He began to realize that the men's story-telling technique often involved only telling the story's punch line. It was assumed that everyone knew the rest of the story, much like we might say 'a stitch in time,' and know that our listeners would understand. He realized no amount of mastery of the language would fill in the backstory of a shared cultural heritage.

Eventually the men returned home and the deep silence of night settled the village to sleep.

NEVER DONE

Preparing millet required as many as three different poundings: one to get the seed off the stalk, a second to get the husk off the seed. These first two processes would typically be done with communal mortar and pestles just at the edge of town, where the mess could be left to filter back into the fields rather than have to be swept up in their compounds. No doubt, such work was more pleasant in each other's company.

Then, on days she wanted to prepare the millet over an open fire, a woman would cook the whole grain and then pound it one or two times depending on what she was making. For *tuwo*, a porridge-like dish, she would use a coarser grind of millet with a sauce flavored by goat meat, cracked bones, dried tomatoes and thickened with dried okra, served usually as the evening meal.

For *foura*, usually drunk for breakfast and lunch, she had to make the flour fine enough to stay in suspension when mixed with liquids. A mixture of millet, soured milk, water and hot pepper, *foura* is definitely an acquired taste and I did, eventually, like it, though I never did pound my own millet, or have any ambition to do so.

Beside hulling, pounding and preparing millet, most women's days were full of tasks like carrying water, gathering firewood, minding the younger children, feeding and herding the goats and sheep, feeding, plucking and cooking chickens, washing clothes and the large earthenware cooking pots, nursing and washing babies, shopping, cooking, making peanut oil; not to mention planting, cultivating and harvesting with their husbands. A woman could delegate some of these tasks to older children, but she bore responsibility for them all.

Woman pounding millet

Just as in my US community, the tidiness of the home was a source of pride. A good housekeeper, I became aware, saw to it that the compound was always swept. This was done daily with a short broom, a bundle of some kind of reed.

One housekeeping job was infrequent and communal. When Neino built a new hut for Aisha, his new wife, she invited her women friends to come and help her pound the floor. They beat and sang while they worked, sprinkling water lightly and smoothing the floor, creating a nice solid surface.

Once it was dark, women finally got a chance to slow down from the myriad activities of their daily duties, and do less energetic jobs like hulling peanuts and playing with children.

MONDAY MARKET

Monday was market day, the only day to buy meat other than chicken, and it required rising early. Many villagers greeted me on my way, and frequently I was followed by a troop of children for whom it was a lark to watch me at my purchases. At the butcher's tree a goat carcass would be hanging after its proper ritual slaughter by a *mallam,* a Muslim cleric. At my request the butcher would cut whatever part I wanted, usually the fillet and part of a leg, while I stood by. Since Rich and I had a refrigerator, the only one in town, I could buy meat to last several days. Goat was not my favorite—it was good for stew and not much else—but it was the most plentiful. Beef was only regularly available during the peanut-market month, when lots of people came in from the bush. No one in Aguié raised beef for eating, and oxen were kept for hauling loads. Cattle were herded by semi-nomadic Fulani herdsmen who sold cheese, butter and soured milk and, on occasion an animal for slaughter.

Sometimes I thought back to when Rich and I had spent time in the market in Naimey while waiting to be posted, and tried to negotiate with the vendors, mostly unsuccessfully. Now that I was no longer a tourist but a village resident, even though an *anasara,* I wanted to develop my bargaining skills. In the first few months in Aguié, Maimouna would accompany me to the market. I studied her techniques as she took over for me with the butcher for my favorite cut of goat, the fillet. She would say, "You've jacked up the price just because you think Laouré doesn't know what that meat is worth." And then, incensed, she added, "Give me a reasonable price or we'll go elsewhere for meat." (This was a weak bluff, since it might be that only one butcher killed a goat on that day). "We'll find a chicken across the way," she threatened, starting to lead me away from his booth. At this point the butcher, weighing the fillet in his hand and pondering dramatically, threw out a new price. Acting insulted, Maimouna again took my arm and started to walk away, offended by being asked for such a ridiculous amount. It took a few rounds of bartering before Maimouna let me take out my money and seal the deal. I learned from her and Tal Hadji, and I took to market bargaining like a goat to head-butting. It was a way that I could fully participate early on before I had learned very much Hausa. I quickly learned the numbers and coins and market language so I could have a full and complete interaction all in Hausa.

Aguié Market

Lots of personality, both mine and theirs, came to life, along with a good deal of humor. There was play-acting on both sides. I would point to an object and ask, "How much for three of these?" The vendor would say, "two hundred francs." "I'd say, "A-ee!" in a high voice, shaking my right hand to the side to indicate "You've GOT to be joking!" I'd then counter with, "A hundred and fifty francs is what they're worth." And then it was his turn, either to laugh, grimace dramatically, or look away in disgust. Then, I might begin to leave his booth, and he might let me take a few steps before I'd hear him say, "Oh well, then, a hundred and seventy-five, last price." At which point I would take out my purse. We both ended up feeling respected and satisfied that we'd played our parts well.

I loved to walk the market perusing each stall. The goods were usually arrayed on grass mats on the ground with the vendor on a separate mat, sitting under a rustic shade structure. The green, unripe-looking guavas hid a sweet juicy, pink interior which I came to love. I bought limes when I could find them, usually brown, displayed in small pyramids; brown or not, they still had juice. All year long I saw large bowls of dirty-looking salt crystals, others containing dried henna and a great variety of other dried green herbs, dried tomatoes, white twists of cane candy, small dried peppers, manioc, rice, and black, knobby roots used as incense. On a good day I might score a ripe papaya or small yellow mangos.

Very few items were imported and even those, by being sold within the town by a townsperson, contributed to the wealth of the whole. Aguié was an almost entirely self-sustaining community. For example, if I bought a millet pancake from Tal Hadji in the morning, she would give the coin to Akwiya who made the cakes. Then Akwiya might use that money to buy some stew bones for dinner, and the butcher would then be able to buy a new embroidered hat he'd been wanting. The artisan who made the hat could pay a builder to repair his granary and buy a gift of fabric for his new wife, who would have a local tailor make her blouse. And so it would go, the money traveling around and around within the community, providing occupation and promoting dignity.

CAUGHT UNPREPARED

In Aguié, as in most of Niger, each wife had a hut and her children slept there with her, her husband (if he was polygamous) rotating nights in some fashion from one wife's hut to the other. Families slept together and when there was a birth or a death, they were all close by, even the children.

As I discovered in my midwife training period at the hospital in Tessaoua, pregnant women worked right up to the time when labor started and even then, didn't lie down. They walked, sat and talked. The only difference was that the women of Aguié had no choice but to have a home birth. As their time got close, a family member was sent out to fetch the midwife, often the same woman who had presided over the birthing mother's own birth. Most local women would have felt awkward going elsewhere. In Aguié they had mothers, aunts, sisters and experienced midwives; most births were uncomplicated.

We had not been in the village long when early one morning a woman came to our compound door, speaking quickly and loudly, imploring me with her arms to follow her. I didn't understand what she was saying, except that it was an emergency, so I obeyed. I grabbed my headscarf and followed her rapid steps through the winding streets. At last she led me into a labyrinthine compound I recognized as that of the village chief. I followed the woman around the side of a mud and thatch hut. There, squatting between two women, was the chief's sister-in-law in the midst of giving birth. The baby was more than halfway out, but breach, its head still inside the mother. There were flies and sand on the baby's body and great distress on the mother's face. She was obviously tired and frightened.

Feeling entirely inadequate for such a dire situation, I asked the midwife how long the baby had been half-delivered. She said it had been several hours already. I was their last recourse. They didn't even consider asking Somaila since he was male. Even though foreign, at least I was female.

I was aghast at the lack of hygiene in this horrifying tableau. I asked the midwife for a clean *zani* which I placed under the mother and dangling infant. Then I urged the mother to push. Almost right away, the baby's head slipped out, followed soon by the umbilical cord. The women all sent up a communal "Allah be praised," as I took the cold, inert infant into my arms and proceeded to administer artificial respiration. There was shock and dismay on the faces around me. Someone tried to restrain me, but I couldn't have lived with myself without having tried to revive this baby.

I'm sure they had no idea what I was doing. They could see that the baby was dead. I didn't know how long to work at my grizzly task, but I just kept trying. The baby's chest would rise with air and then expel breath. Wasn't there still some possibility that life could be breathed back into this tiny motionless body? Everyone but my stubborn self knew that this baby was lost. At some point, a tailor came and momentarily got in my way, an intrusion I didn't understand until later. He was measuring the little body for a shroud.

I left that scene distraught. I felt I had failed and was overcome with sadness. During the following week, however, it got back to me from several women how grateful the women of the chief's family were. The story that circulated was that my arrival and the clean *zani* were what had made the difference. They had known there was no saving the child. All they'd hoped for was the baby's head to be freed from the birth canal to ensure the survival of the mother. From their perspective, my arrival had precipitated the exit. What I had been considering to be a failure they held to be little short of a miracle.

In retrospect I could see that when the midwife came to get me, the birthing mother, knowing that someone had gone for help, stopped struggling and had rested until I arrived. By that time, she had recovered her strength and was able to give a really energetic push when I asked her to do so.

The whole experience has given me nightmares ever since. But it also gave me, earlier than most twenty-one-year-old American girls, a first-hand experience of life's fragility. Furthermore, it made me realize that the Peace Corp policy against placing health workers in towns without hospitals was well thought out. I was in an untenable position in Aguié. I could see that I would continually be called upon to help in situations that were far outside my expertise.

Decades later, I still tear up with compassion for that younger self who had signed up for an African adventure that stretched her beyond her ability to cope professionally and emotionally. I *did* cope and gave it my best. What else could I do? Although Rich tried to comfort me, there was no one to help me overcome the traumas of the many life and death dramas I was drawn into in Aguié.

WELL BABY CLINIC

My arrival in Aguié was a major turning point in Maimouna's life, but she already had an unusual trajectory. She had been allowed to stay in school longer than any other girl in Aguié ever had. She had made it through the middle of sixth grade before her father finally arranged her marriage, luckily, to a young, handsome man she knew and liked, and one who had no wives yet. This forced her to quit school at the age of fourteen to become the cook, farmhand and wife to Konko. By the time I arrived, she was eighteen and still had no children. This was considered a tragedy for her, but for me it was good fortune. It meant that she had the freedom to work with me. I suspect that her father and husband frowned on this sudden shift away from domestic duties, but the Sarki had decreed that she would be my assistant, and that was that.

Maimouna's new job released her from the typical woman's daily toil. Since our work together didn't start until nine in the morning, she had the early morning hours to do some housework, but soon I started giving her a contribution out of my small Peace Corps monthly stipend so that she could hire others to gather wood, carry water and perform other chores.

Mornings, Maimouna would come to my house, stand at the doorway and clap her hands. Then her slender form, swathed in a full-length wrap-around skirt with a sleeveless blouse to match, her flip-flops clicking, slipped into the compound. Her matching scarf, wound snugly across the middle of her forehead, tied and tucked in the back, made her appear very elegant.

We'd sit on our two kitchen chairs, sharing information and getting to know one another. She had poise and a self-confidence which, mixed with her intelligence, made our interactions flow easily. You would not have known who was training whom; we both had much to learn. I was almost completely ignorant of Hausa village customs and language, and she, for example, had never heard of birth control or germs that carry illness. We drank Nescafé out of bowls as we talked and absentmindedly swatted flies away. Kitty would wander by and rub our legs, then lounge nearby.

I laid out my plan to start the well-baby program, which would include demonstrations, home visits and eventually, an actual weekly clinic day to serve all the babies and mothers in town. Pretty soon Maimouna picked up on the important concepts. Once she learned what I was trying to teach the women, she went ahead and spoke for me. And when we initiated the program, in no time she became the lead teacher while I continued to learn on-the-job vocabulary by listening to her. We made a great team. This was what I came to Niger to do. Somaila soon got used to my absences from the clinic, though he was unhappy about them.

Maimouna accompanied me everywhere as my guide and translator and learned essential material as we went along. The material wasn't very complex: 1) There are germs on flies and in dirt; 2) The food we give to children should be protected from germs; 3) Solid foods should be introduced to babies gradually, with special mild, nutritious foods to be the first foods a baby is given; 4) During pregnancy, women need to eat more protein than normal; 5) A child with diarrhea should be given special foods to make the diarrhea stop; 6) Children should be given quinine once a month to protect them from malaria.

Maimouna introduced me to her sisters and then to her friends and neighbors. At first, we had only friendly visits, no teaching. I admired their children, worked at remembering their names, sat and chewed *goro* nuts, and mostly listened to them chatting, picking up new words each day.

Her friends and I asked each other polite questions with Maimouna as our intermediary. They wanted to know how old my children were and how long I had been married. I answered, "I'm

twenty. I've been married almost a year. I don't have any children."
This last was a problem. Because I myself wasn't a mother, my
credibility was suspect. How could I know what was proper to make
their children thrive? How could Maimouna? We were two childless
women telling them how to be mothers.

Working with mothers and babies all the time, and having all
the appropriate hormones, I wished that I could have a child, but
Peace Corps policy was clear: get pregnant, get out of country. The
Corps didn't want the liability of a pregnant volunteer way out in a
small town with poor health services and no phone or transportation.
So I would just have to earn the women's trust.

In order to start a well-baby clinic at the dispensary, I
desperately needed the Peace Corps to provide a baby scale.
Somehow, a scale proved difficult to obtain, despite numerous
urgings. When after a long, frustrating time, it eventually arrived
from USAID, Maimouna and I were off and running.

The town was divided into *quartiers,* so I decided that each
week, on Wednesdays, we'd hold the well-baby clinic for one fourth
of the town. Early that morning, I would ask Tal Hadji to find the
griot, the town-crier, and ask him to come to my house. I would pay
him to walk all the streets of the first *quartier* with his drum, calling
out in a loud voice to remind the women with babies that it was clinic
day. They must bring their *fiche* (visit record), and not forget to bring
their own metal spoon. I hoped too that if the *griot* announced baby-
weighing day, it would be more official and legitimate, and would
overcome the natural reluctance of their husbands who might resent
their wives' escapes from home.

The women came in twos and threes, usually around mid-
morning, dressed in their bold, colorful print zanis, matching tops
and headscarves. The mothers seemed to enjoy waiting in line. They
reminded me of a flock of brightly colored birds as they chatted
together. I'd hear: "Hadiza, did your sister have her baby yet?" And,
"Oh, what pretty fabric!" And, "Are you feeling better yet, Aisha?"

Maimouna and I would give each baby a spoonful of quinine to prevent malaria, and then lay them on the cold, hard baby scale. Most screamed, writhed, flailed and kicked, but one way or another we usually succeeded in completing both procedures. Often we'd gently pinch the child's nose so he had to open his mouth to breathe, and that's when we'd slip the spoonful of quinine in. It seemed cruel, but the quinine saved babies' lives, so we figured it was worth the trauma we put them through. We'd then write down the new weight on each mother's *fiche* and on the one we kept for our records.

The babies were invariably naked except that many of them had grigris on braided thongs around their waists or necks. These were koranic verses sewn up in small leather amulets; charms that were never removed until they dropped off. Babies had an uncanny way of signaling their mothers about needing to pee or poo. Usually there was time to unwrap the otherwise back-pappoosed child before there was an accident.

Me, Maimouna and Somaila at well baby clinic

The conversation we had with each woman would be instructive, so we asked our questions loudly, hoping the other women would overhear. We'd ask Habu's mother, "Did Habu have any diarrhea this month? Did she have any other illness? Is she walking? Are you beginning to wean her yet?" If yes, "Have you introduced egg or goat milk into her diet?"

If we noticed from one clinic day to the next that a child's weight hadn't increased normally, like Habu's, we'd ask the mother if she'd consent to a home visit.

I enjoyed home visits. They provided an excuse to see a new compound and get to know a mother better. Once a woman had a chance to spend time with me, I hoped she might begin to consider me a friend, and be more likely to follow the suggestions I was making, even if at first it was done only to make me happy. If in pleasing me, her child thrived, she might tell her friends how her child's chronic diarrhea went away, and those friends would be more likely to try our suggestions.

Typically, when Maimouna clapped at the door in the compound wall, only women and children would be home. We might find baby Habu's mother pounding millet in her free-standing mortar. Or she might be cooking millet in a large round-bottomed clay pot over a tripod of rocks at the open fire. She would put out grass mats in the shade for us to sit on and offer us some water or a *goro*. Our visit often attracted all the kids in the compound, and sometimes the other mothers as well.

We'd make light conversation and then look at the child's *fiche* together. "Habu's weight hasn't increased the way it should at her age," we'd say. "It's really great that you bring her to the clinic so that we can keep track of her weight, and so we can talk over anything else that might be a problem. Is she still having diarrhea?" Dehydration caused by diarrhea was a grave concern. If the mother answered yes, we suggested that her diet be changed to long-cooked, soupy rice. "Can a portion of the *foura* you're making for the family be made without hot pepper?" Most babies didn't like the peppers and had trouble digesting it.

Sometimes, unbeknownst to me, what I was trying to teach the women was culturally unacceptable. One day walking home from clinic, Maimouna diplomatically asked me, "Have you noticed the women's reaction when you tell them to feed their children eggs?" I hadn't. "They believe that if they feed their children eggs, they'll grow up to become thieves. They think that if a child is taught that it's alright to take an *egg* from under a hen, then wouldn't they think it's alright to steal absolutely *anything* when they get older?"

"I can certainly see their point of view!" I answered. "But it makes it so much more difficult to feed their kids the necessary protein." This was an instance where custom clearly got in the way. Everyone had access to eggs, while meat, such as liver, cost money and was, therefore, much more difficult for mothers to obtain. Prepared baby food was a foreign concept. Children were nursed for several years and then had adult food introduced into their diet gradually as they became interested in it.

The husbands, meanwhile, were not getting the same education from us as their wives, and it was often difficult for a woman to ask her husband for extra money for liver, for example. So I sometimes found myself talking to the husbands to convince them of the necessity of special foods. I never knew how convincing I was, but it was definitely worth a try.

Maimouna and I also gave demonstrations, using a storyboard with pictures. For example, the first picture would show a fly landing on some feces. In the next, the fly landed on some uncovered food. The last picture showed the food now covered so that the fly no longer had access. Naturally, we'd spend time explaining that there were bugs in the feces, impossible to see with the naked eye, and that the fly unwittingly carried them onto food. This was difficult for them to comprehend: invisible bugs?

Another type of demonstration taught a mother how to make healthy baby food by preparing it right there with her at her home. We might cook chicken liver, or cook an egg in the millet porridge to make it more nutritious.

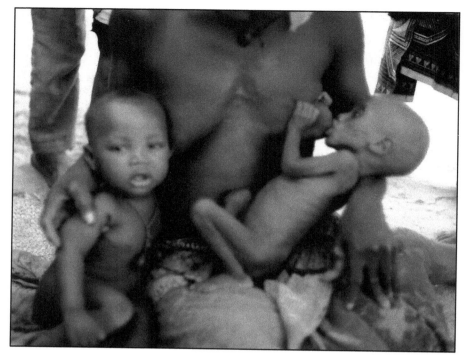

Baby at breast

We usually gave the demonstrations at individual compounds to small audiences, because when large numbers of women gathered at our well-baby clinic, Maimouna and I were both too busy to do demonstrations.

Wednesday became my favorite day of the week. On that day, my purpose in Aguié was clear to me and to others. I could hold and interact with dozens of babies (which made me even more desirous of my own). I got satisfaction from seeing so many healthy breast-fed babies and talking to their mothers.

Early on, as I was learning Hausa, I could listen in and begin to understand Maimouna's conversations with the mothers without having to conjure all the right phrases myself. I also began to build friendships with some of the moms. And working with Maimouna in that busy environment was a real pleasure.

WORKING FOR PEANUTS

Rich's work in the nationalized peanut co-operative (UNCC) was linked to the rains and the growing season. He was the assistant to a well-educated Nigerien named Abarshi who was posted year-round to Aguié. Abarshi wore ochre slacks and a pajama-style collarless shirt with big buttons and two large pockets. Short and stout, with a round face, close-cut hair and remarkably broad shoulders, he resembled a lion. His manner was serious and professional, and Rich, who spent long hours with him, liked and admired him. Though he was always pleasant to me when we met, his life was peanuts and mine was babies, and so we had little to say to one another.

Rich's agricultural education consisted solely of what he received in Peace Corps training. Like me, an important part of his job was educational. But instead of teaching about germ transmission and hygiene, he taught the latest Western ideas on best farming practices, with the aim to increase crop yield.

He would ride Doikie out to remote communities, sometimes on a four or five-day circuit, always accompanied by a villager who knew the way and could help translate, as well as take charge of Doikie's care. Rich and Abarshi would lead meetings to disseminate information about all aspects of peanut farming.

Though millet was something all farmers grew and ate as their staple, peanuts had been introduced as a cash crop by the French in Colonial times, recognizing that peanuts love sandy soil. In the last few decades, families had gone from being subsistence farmers to having a crop to take to market for money. With this money they paid taxes, married, bought cloth, paid tailors to make their clothing, purchased cooking pots, tools, animals, and gifts for weddings, births and holidays. Before the advent of peanuts as a cash crop they would have relied more on exchanging goods and services, as well as their own fabrication of cloth, pots, bricks, roofs, mats, and other needed items.

All farming in the area, until then, had been done by hand with no mechanization. The farmers' most useful tool was the *daba*, a heavy-duty, short-handled hoe.

As a peanut cooperative agent, Rich encouraged farmers to pool their money so they could purchase expensive but more efficient farm implements and work animals that their extended family could share. These small groups bought donkey-drawn plows, human-powered peanut seeders, or teams of oxen for plowing, hauling harvests, and carting just about anything. Rich taught the use of pesticides and fertilizers, how to buy on credit, and how to read the peanut scale so that farmers were less likely to be cheated by the weighers at market.

He taught farmers the method of planting peanuts two to a hole, and to use a small amount of pesticide powder on the seeds. He figured the best way to show the efficacy of these techniques would be to develop a demonstration farm. He went to Sarki Brazaki and asked for some land for us to use. It was granted, but the plot was almost a mile out of town.

Rich worked out a simple experiment, dividing the field into roughly equal quarters. In one, we sowed one peanut per hole; in another, we sowed two peanuts per hole. The last two quarters were one and two peanuts respectively but with the addition of pesticide.

In Niger, it was hard to know exactly when to plant. You had to wait until the rains started, but if you jumped the gun and planted after the first good rain, and then it didn't rain again for several weeks, you would lose your seed and have to start over again. Village men gathered on corners or near the mosque arguing and prognosticating, each with an opinion about when to plant, or sharing a memory of a former year when the weather was similar. There was no way to irrigate, so during the growing season farmers needed regular rain. Most years they got it, but there were terrible stories about drought years when crops failed and many villagers died.

That's why the Sarki had huge granaries for storing peanuts and millet, to feed the town in case of drought, or if the farmers were caught by a false rain and had used up all their seeds. For such insurance, villagers willingly worked their designated days in the Sarki's fields.

Most Sundays we'd rise early in the morning, grab a canteen of water, shade hats, a packed lunch and our tools to make the trek out to our farm. Even early in the morning it was hot.

We were intrigued by a small, old farmer we passed on our way. He wore a loin cloth and a brimless cloth hat as he worked his field. His body, a collection of knotted muscles, glistened with sweat. Unlike neighboring fields, his small parcel was fenced. He grew only manioc, a long tuberous root with shoulder-high branches. The fencing was made of thorny branches and briars piled up against an anchored framework to keep goats, sheep and cattle from trampling or devouring his plants.

Rich had more physical stamina than I, and when the afternoon heat exhausted me, I would lie in the shade of the lone tree in our field and take a nap. One time he took a photo of me resting there that he forever after would often pull out to show friends, telling them this was typical of "Laurie working at the farm."

Our peanuts grew beneath the surface with green foliage above ground. When they were ripe, we went through the rows with our trusty *daba* and scooped deeply to unearth the cluster of peanuts, then left them on the ground for a few days to dry out. This was traditional. And traditionally herders in the area were careful to keep their cattle from wandering through and snacking on the tasty piles of nuts.

But sometimes the cattle would have their way, and so they did with our harvest. Oh for that bramble fence our neighboring farmer had built! So much for our experiment. We had no way of knowing how much crop the cattle ate or from which quadrant of the field. We imagined the farmers chuckling amongst themselves over the ruins of our science experiment, thinking, "These Westerners aren't really as smart as they think they are."

HARVEST

The busiest time of Rich's work year was after harvest in October-November when he helped Abarshi oversee the peanut market organized by his employer, the cooperative, UNCC. Growers brought their peanuts from all the villages in the canton.

Farmers streamed into town leading camels or ox carts laden with sacks to sell to the cooperative. I could observe their arrival from the porch of the dispensary where I worked in the mornings. Sometimes I saw them stop to put on sandals. Their feet were heavily calloused from going barefoot all their lives. Shoes were only for wearing in town.

As thousands of bags of peanuts arrived at the market, they were weighed, purchased and stacked in tall pyramids, awaiting trucks to haul them to peanut oil factories. Niger's peanuts were too small to end up in a can of Planter's Peanuts.

There were eight or ten heavy-duty scales, which could weigh as many as three bags at a time. The weighers were relatively rich, powerful men from around the canton. They paid the farmers on the spot, but not always fairly. These middle men sold those same peanuts to the cooperative. Many days, Rich came home frustrated and furious that the weighers had resorted to tricks to cheat at the scales. He and Abarshi were rarely able to catch them at it.

For the eight to ten weeks of the peanut market, people came to town from all over the canton and a holiday feeling was in the air. The butchers were extra busy, and beef and occasionally even camel meat became available. I was never allowed to even taste camel, because it was said that if a woman ate camel, she wouldn't be able to conceive.

The assumption that I would want a baby was thought incontrovertible!

Aguie's peanut market

During the rest of the year there was no alcohol in our traditional Muslim town, but during the market weeks women brewed millet beer. Several households became makeshift bars, featuring live music that wafted through town in the evenings. Beer was one liquid I felt somewhat confident drinking, figuring the alcohol would kill any bad bugs, but we never went to the bars as it was considered unseemly for a respectable woman to frequent them.

My work was busier during the peanut market, too. Aguié had the only dispensary and nurse in the whole canton. Many villages were more than a day's walk from Aguié, so people delayed seeking

Western medical help in our dispensary until market days, which meant that we saw a virtual parade of suppurating sores, long-term gastrointestinal problems, horrible conjunctivitis, and other seriously neglected ailments. I was grateful that Mustafa was usually there to treat sores; I became nauseated at the sight of maggots in untreated wounds. Maimouna and I used the opportunity to teach mothers from other villages about preventing malnutrition, diarrhea and malaria.

On the periphery of the open-air market, the barbers, many of whom were traditional healers, would set up shop. Their traveling equipment was packed in a beautifully worked leather barber bag, no bigger than a woman's large purse. In it the barber carried everything he needed to cut hair, shave heads and faces, clean ears, and heal all manner of ailments. I was fascinated to see snake skin, bird heads, talons, dried herbs and roots drawn out from various small pockets in the bag. I admired these barber bags so much that I negotiated a trade with one of the barbers, my bag for his, sweetening the deal with some side-money.

Once, I was able to observe a blood-letting. The barber made short razor cuts in a person's back, then cupped the cuts with the large end of an animal's hollow horn and sucked on the small end to create a vacuum. When the horn was removed some minutes later, blood dripped from the slashes. Blood-letting was the remedy for many complaints.

Barbers also lanced boils, pulled Guinea worms out of people's bodies, twisting the worms around a sturdy twig, and prescribed various mysterious potions whose ingredients might include head of lizard or sinew of bird.

During the peanut market, Aguié seemed to expand into a bustling city. People were happy to have money in their pockets. The tailors were busy sewing, the butchers were butchering, and many goods and services exchanged hands. Since no one was exempt from work on the family farm, everyone was grateful to have completed the harvest. Until the next year's rains, there would be no more farm work.

JOURNEY TO CHRISTMAS

Thank God it wasn't hot! Rich and I had been sitting beside the road playing gin rummy with the raggedest deck of cards you ever saw, waiting for any kind of vehicle which might take pity on us and pick us up so that we could go to the volunteer Christmas party in Zinder, about ninety miles east.

News of the Christmas gathering for our region had traveled by word of mouth and by way of a small volunteer-produced newsletter named *"Sha."* (*Sha* had helpfully – in this case - ambiguous meanings, often translated drink, breath or smoke.) It was our first Christmas in Niger and we were, by now, very close with the six volunteers within a seventy-mile radius. At this gathering we anticipated seeing others who were stationed farther away. Our training group had bonded during our three months in the Virgin Islands, but opportunities for sharing our struggles and successes came very rarely, and we relished them. Additionally, a party like this gave us the chance to get to know members of the group who had been in Niger a year longer than we had.

Rich and I had made a point of getting up and out early in the morning, walking through the crooked streets of Aguié to the National Route. No cars had passed in the hour and a half Rich and I had been sitting beside the road. The sky was overcast with Harmattan dust off the Sahara. Our playing cards were ragged because the neighbor kids had been teaching us *Kwoss*, in which it's extremely important to slap the cards down as noisily as possible. That had made the cards easier to identify, and therefore to cheat with. We sat on our two loosely packed sacks, filled with our necessities for a few days away.

Hitchhiking beside National Route

Shy Nissa came by, a brightly colored enameled plate of *rogo* balanced on her head. She knew I loved a snack of *rogo* in the mornings at the dispensary, so she was hoping for a sale. Maybe two.

Nissa's mother had removed the tough skin of the manioc and cut it into short, cylindrical pieces, about three inches long. Then she'd boiled the pieces over a fire in a big round-bottomed clay cooking pot perched on a tripod of three rocks. When done, the *rogo*'s flesh loosened from its tough twine-like fiber wick and broke apart easily into wedges. She sautéed the wedges in peanut oil and cayenne and added a pinch of salt. They were best eaten warm and were as addictive as French fries, especially when we hadn't been near fast food or even a grocery store in six months. I guessed Nissa's mother, Lale, had seen us passing by on our way out of town and had sent Nissa to sell us some as soon as the day's batch became ready.

I paid Nissa with small coins, which she tied up safely in the corner of her *zani*, tucking the cache back into her waist. She watched us eat our snack, perhaps hoping we'd buy a second round; then lingered longer, watching our card game. After a while she placed her plate back on her head and meandered off to make the few more sales her mother would expect.

About two hours into our vigil, a heavily laden peanut truck came by and stopped. We counted as a stroke of luck that the first vehicle that came by actually stopped for us. The driver was not a Nigerien, but Hausa is the trading language for most of West Africa, so we completed a successful negotiation, probably paying twice what a native would pay. We pulled ourselves and our bags up, using the slats on the side of the flatbed as a ladder, onto what Rich knew to be a full load of gunny sacks full of peanuts. As an official of the national peanut cooperative, he knew peanuts!

There was one other rider aboard, his head so swathed in scarves that we couldn't detect his features. Rich and I settled in as best we could, wedging ourselves and our belongings into whatever gaps we could squirm into. The peanut sacks were hard, heavy and rough-textured; the road severely rutted, and the driver fast. It was a common notion that when a vehicle hit enough speed, it produced a smoother ride, but this ride didn't make me a believer. It seemed to me that a washboard road was more punishing the faster the driver took it.

The air was thick and the Harmattan dust made visibility almost zero. Our eyes stung and every breath brought more discomfort. It wasn't long before Rich and I swaddled our own heads to protect ourselves from the dust. Could our driver actually see the road? The only consolation to our suffering was that the dust screened out the sun and made the air cooler. The swirling wind in the back of the careening truck made it feel like we were being buffeted by a tremendous storm.

My whole body was in trauma and on alert, and I could sensed that Rich's was as well. I couldn't see where we were going, the speed seemed reckless, and the truck was piled so high with peanut sacks that I figured I would be the first item to bounce out of the load if we hit a particularly large pothole. We tried to talk, but the wind and grind of the motor made it too difficult. I turned inward and eventually began to relax. I spun the story I would tell my family when I next wrote home: "There we were perched precariously on the back of an overloaded peanut truck..." How exotic and adventurous! There was no way to control the situation, so I surrendered to it.

A new feeling began in my feet and traveled up my body. It felt like a sensation, an emotion and a thought all wrapped up into one. My precarious position on the truck threw me into sensory overload and momentarily into an altered state of consciousness. I was filled with the certainty that I was complete; that were my life to end at that moment, I would have no regrets. I had gotten from Africa what I had come for. I held contentment and satisfaction and completion in my body and soul.

The experience may only have lasted a minute or so, but now, fifty years later, it is still a vivid memory, a touchstone that has continued to nourish my spiritual life.

Arriving in Zinder at Mike's house, we jumped into the shower and soon felt less bedraggled. Friends began trickling in. Even our friend Major got off his horse, away from his solo trek teaching literacy in the hinterland, to come in to Zinder for Christmas. This amazing volunteer made rounds from village to village with a lantern, wicks and lamp oil, teaching phonetic Hausa and basic arithmetic to Hausa men at night.

We were giddy to be together, a bunch of American friends celebrating our "American" holiday together, enjoying the ease of communicating in our native tongue and letting our hair down. We danced to the Beatles, the Mamas and the Papas, and Bob Dylan. In St. Croix we had trained together, serious students during the week without a moment to relax. But on the weekends we had transformed into a bunch of wild banshees, haunting local bars and downing endless rum & cokes and pina coladas. So for us to be together again, we fell into a natural camaraderie.

The next morning we were all drinking eggnog and cooking up a feast when, according to a letter home Rich wrote on December 29, 1967:

"Ed, a Zinder-based vol, walks into the room and announces that the soccer game against a local Zinder high school team was about to begin and we had better go to the field. Stumbling, grumbling with fresh hangovers and wearing sandals about five of us guys and four girls walked into the stadium. A fairly good-sized crowd was sitting in the bleachers and on the field, practicing, were about 20, lean, hard-kicking soccer players taking turns ramming the ball into the goal, donning red shirts, white shorts and vicious-looking soccer shoes. Looking on the bright side, the situation appeared a little humorous if we did not stop to consider what could happen to us if we actually did step onto the field."

"Most of us didn't know the rules of the game. More of our players straggled in and so the game began with 4 Nigeriens playing on our side. Luckily, one was a goalie who made many saves that day. Three of us, including me, naturally, had to play in bare feet! Somehow, we lost 4 to 1, throwing in a completely illegal play, a flying wedge, from American football. We gave both fans and players a good laugh."

They limped back sweaty and filthy but feeling victorious merely for having survived.

In the kitchen, Gayle slathered some chicken in a sauce laden with cumin, a spice I hadn't yet learned to use. I soaked the fresh lettuce and tomatoes in an iodine solution and dried them, my mouth watering in anticipation of a fresh salad. Connie was making corn bread, which couldn't fit in the small oven until the chicken came out.

In sisterly fashion, we maneuvered around each other in the tiny, dark kitchen.

Before, during and after the festive meal we drank. There was Nigerian beer, which we referred to as camel-piss. Red wine, purchased in five-gallon glass *bon-bons*, flowed like water. It may have been French, but it was still rotgut and all we could afford. Some drank Hennessy Cognac, purchased in Zinder. Many of us smoked tobacco and there was marijuana to be had off in a corner of the compound.

We shared stories around the fire. Joel told how he and his site partner Sandy had set up housekeeping in Gesheme and had found a young villager, Ali, who knew French and could teach them Hausa. Every morning the boy would bring his grass mat, unroll it on the floor in the house, and with a French-Hausa dictionary they would sit down together and start studying. Joel applied himself seriously to learning Hausa.

One day when Ali unrolled his mat, out slithered a viper, a tiny but deadly snake. Sandy grabbed the shovel that stood against the wall, and smashed it until no part of the snake was still wiggling. The very next day, again Ali unrolled his mat, and again there was a viper hidden in it. Sandy crushed this one with even more vehemence, while Joel rocked with laughter.

Of course, the story of the snakes spread through the village and villagers dropped by to see the remains and to tell their own viper stories of an uncle's death-throes, a sister's legs turning purple, and snakes finding their way into bedding. The stories upset Sandy so much that he started barricading the doors at night. He strewed broken beer bottle glass across the threshold and locked the doors by roping them shut, all to Joel's amusement.

Then Joel fell sick with diarrhea. Suddenly Sandy's precautions created a new problem. The latrine was outside. Joel couldn't get out fast enough. Joel told us, "There was nothing for it but to bring out buckets and brooms the next morning."

After storytelling, the guys built a bonfire in the backyard. Mike, Dick, Jim and Tom played their guitars. We sat around drinking, smoking, talking and singing folk songs and blues. Rich was the star vocalist, as usual. The guitarists set the pace for a walking blues, and Rich started improvising as he went along, coming up with rhyming couplets about our lives in Niger and the things we missed. They were songs about hunger for ice cream and hamburgers, the weather, work, boredom, the drinking, the loneliness, all the themes of our collective lives. It was a ten-minute marathon, his voice raspy and expressive, some of his rhymes perfect, some less so, and some missing rhyme altogether. When he finally stopped, there was a burst of applause and laughter. I felt a glow of pride in Rich's unusual talent. In some ways he was larger than life, which gave me plenty of space to hide behind him.

These kinds of gatherings brought our Peace Corps group closer to one another and also allowed us to get to know volunteers from earlier and later training groups, providing the basis for life-long friendships.

At a city volunteer's house

A SPY IN OUR MIDSTS

Rich and I were the first Westerners ever to live in the village of Aguié. Millie and George, who ran the Sudan Interior Mission agricultural school outside of town, kept very separate except for occasional forays to town to proselytize -- a futile effort as far as we could see, as the Muslims weren't interested in Christianity. The only Nigeriens the mission school attracted were lepers. The lepers were outcasts, but at the mission they got treatment, safety, shelter, education and work.

So we were a novelty and the townspeople were naturally curious about us. Anything we did interested them. Sarki Brazaki, in particular, made it his duty to find out everything about our life in the village to make sure we were happy, safe and had no complaints about his domain. It was a big responsibility to have two young Americans living in his town, and he took it seriously.

Unbeknownst to me, he had commissioned my little friend Tal Hadji to be a spy in our house. He could observe from his sling-chair in the town's main square that she had free access to our compound and evidently, he milked her for information about our life. And he probably engineered the arrangement that Tal would spend the night with me on the frequent nights when Rich's work took him out of town. The Sarki let me believe that Tal's mother, Akwiya, and I had come up with the plan.

I wasn't aware of Tal Hadji's reconnaissance duties until one day when I was irritated with her and sent her home. Within hours, I was surprised by a rare visit from Sarki Brazaki. He wanted to make sure there was nothing seriously amiss between us.

The Sarki, draped in his light blue, grand boubou and embroidered *kufi*, was about my height and thin, but he held himself with the dignity of a respected chief. Usually our exchanges were light and humorous, but this day he questioned me quite sternly about what had passed between Tal and me. I felt intimidated by the interrogation. I was surprised that he didn't see that my irritation with her was understandable. It almost seemed that he thought I was in the wrong. I wondered why in the world the chief of the canton was mediating an argument between me and a nine-year-old girl? I began to suspect that Rich and I had less privacy than we had imagined. Yet we adored Sarki Brazaki and, as far as we know, he always looked out for our welfare for our sakes as well as his own. Talking it over, Rich and I concluded that good intelligence is necessary for good leadership.

Anyway, in a village everyone knows everyone else's business. It was no doubt said of us that we were too permissive with the town children. There was no school for most of the kids. No TV, no playground, no daycare center or toys, except the ones they made for themselves. The older kids watched the younger ones and they congregated at our house when we let them. Rich had a reel-to-reel tape recorder and I recorded the children singing songs. They listened to the playback, delighted to hear themselves. This often went on for hours. "Just one more, just one more," they'd beg, and I complied.

It seemed to me the girls had the advantage when it came to singing because they had circle songs with elaborate hand clapping routines. I loved one song in which a single girl broke from the circle and flung herself towards the opposite side of the circle. The girls there caught her flight before she reached the ground and bounced her back to the side of the circle she came from. This went on; round and round, until they tired.

Tal Hadji's siblings and cousins were frequent visitors. They hung around when we permitted, and taught us Hausa. Since I was home more than Rich, I benefited more than he did. They'd point to an object and tell me its name and I repeated after them, writing it down phonetically in my notebook.

One day Tal and I were joking around. She was looking at our French calendar hanging on the wall. Since her brother Muman went to school, she had learned from him the days of the week in French. She pointed at the calendar and chanted the days of the week: *Jeudi, Mardi, Macaroni...* When I howled with laughter at her delightful mispronunciation of *Mercredi,* she cracked up too and decided to repeat it that way whenever it occurred to her that we needed a laugh. It always worked.

Rich and I imagined that we were the sole inhabitants of our house, but we were mistaken. We found insects living in the mud and straw walls, and spiders in the stick-and-waddle ceilings. They were just the beginning. At night we were visited by *guhiyas*, small hedgehogs, who stole potatoes when we forgot to latch the metal armoire.

Another visitor was a very small but deadly viper Rich discovered under the kerosene fridge; it sent him in a panic onto the kitchen table, while I ran for help. A snake-savvy villager dislodged the viper with a stick and took it away for destruction. The snake drama took only minutes to play out, but long enough for quite a crowd to assemble in our yard.

We also had visits by winged creatures. Since the weather was uniformly warm, we left our windows open, and birds flew in and out at will. On rare occasions a sudden rainstorm would descend upon us with only a few minutes' notice, sending us scampering around closing the shutters on our six windows. These windows had no glass or screens and only two positions: open and shuttered. It was at these times that house-sharing became a problem for the birds, who found their nests inside our home suddenly unreachable. They perched on the roof, hopping about noisily and launching bewildered exploratory flights to the closed shutters. To our avian friends' relief, the storms passed almost as quickly as they had gathered, and the shutters flew open once again.

One memorable storm was accompanied by thunder and lightning, not something we got a lot of in the San Francisco Bay Area. So we took our chairs outside, turned on Beethoven's Ninth Symphony as loud as it would go on our tape recorder, and Rich waved his arms, conducting both Beethoven and the storm, drenched and delighted. He was sure the birds enjoyed the concert.

Because the sun beat down on our new patio, we needed to erect a shade structure, called a *runwha*. Our helpers constructed it with posts made from the trunks of small trees, with a criss-crossing and lashing of branches, covered by thickly woven grass mats tied down to protect them during Harmattan season, when the persistent winter wind blew in off the Sahara. Some days the wind looked like thick tule fog, carrying fine particles of dust that got in our mouths, eyes and ears.

It turned out that the dust also lodged in our shade structure. Frequently when we sat down under the *runwha* to eat a meal, Kitty would climb on top and stalk around up there, releasing a fine sprinkling of sand down into our food. Rich's psych degree came to the rescue. He used reverse psychology on poor Kitty. He'd toss him up onto the *runwha*, and when he climbed down, we'd throw him back up again and again, so that he ended up refusing to ever go up there again. No more sand in our food!

Tal Hadji's uncle Neino, had an entirely different sort of unwanted visitor. It happened soon after he married his second wife, Aisha. As soon as she moved into her new hut, she started having bad luck. She became ill, she twisted her ankle, she lost a chicken. Aisha was sure that Neino's first wife had paid a medicine man to put a curse on her and her dwelling.

One night we heard a loud commotion in their compound just on the other side of our bedroom window. Many high-pitched women's voices were shouting, while many beams of light from flashlights flickered onto, into and around the exterior of the new hut. All the while, the chaotic shouting continued. This went on for at least a quarter hour. Then silence.

The next day, Tal Hadji, who had seen the drama up close, reported, "Aisha invited all her friends to come last night to drive out the evil from Amina's spell. There must have been eight or nine of them. They woke up the babies and scared the little kids." She went on to say that her mother believed they did the exorcism correctly, so it probably worked. "I guess we'll see," Tal concluded.

FORAYS INTO FRIENDSHIP

I visited the women of the village sometimes as part of my job, but often just to spend time with them. I remember one time I decided to visit Hauwa, a woman of about thirty, though she seemed older than that to me—life was very hard and people aged rapidly. I arrived at her compound entry and clapped. She called for me to come in. When I did, she was surprised to see who was visiting. She grabbed her headscarf and quickly tied it onto her head, something she might not have done for another neighbor visitor. But she didn't bother putting on her blouse. Women's bare breasts were more acceptable at home than an uncovered head. A visit from me was considered something special.

Hauwa greeted me with a lilting welcome: *"Lale lale Laouré, lale lale Laouré,"* with small bows and touching of hands, and then many animated inquiries as to my health and the well-being of my husband and house, which I, in turn, asked her. When the formalities were over, Hauwa attended her fire and then ushered me through a very low doorway into the dark coolness of her mud hut with its conical grass roof, and offered me a grass mat to sit on. Then she took a small enameled Chinese tin bowl from the ground, uncovered it and sorted through the *goro* nuts, which she'd kept fresh with a lid of moist cloth. When she had separated out a few perfect nuts, she broke them in half along the seam, the two halves parting neatly, and offered me my pick. They were the size of chestnuts, bitter and crunchy. I chose a cream-colored one because I had found they were milder, and together we chewed our *goros*, which contain a lot of caffeine, and commenced our visit. A sister-in-law and a co-wife joined us, not to miss out on such a perfect excuse to rest from their work, take a drink of water and enjoy a *goro*. One of them slipped her baby off her back and nursed. Hauwa, not one to waste time, brought out a gourd full of dried beans and started sorting through them as we talked and laughed together.

We all joined in the bean-sorting, happily working together and resting out of the heat of the day. Laughter was a freely traded commodity in village life, and I provided amusement for reasons I often couldn't fathom.

Though I thoroughly enjoyed these visits, I had to be careful not to overstay my welcome, as the women had a lot of work to accomplish in any given day.

The Sarki was always curious about our comings and goings. If I saw him sitting alone under the big tree in the square, I would usually go exchange greetings with him. There were predictable themes to our conversation: how was my work? How was my health? And when would I come visit his wives. "They keep asking after you," he would cajole. I felt sorry for them because they were isolated in their compound; not allowed to come out like ordinary village women.

I did enjoy visiting them, partly because of the elaborate entry into their living area. Entering the owl's mouth of a doorway, it took my eyes a few seconds to adjust to the dark. A watchmen led me through a narrow mud-brick corridor, open to the sky. This ended in a small dark room after which we turned left into still another sky-lit corridor and into a larger (open) patio occupied by a tethered horse. After a final twist and turn I was ushered into the main compound. Traditionally this labyrinth would have made it difficult for enemies to enter the Sarki's domain, with it's honeycomb of wives' dwellings, cooking areas, a large tree, animal enclosure and a dovecote.

On one memorable visit through the labyrinth I brought popcorn, fresh and buttered. The wives had heard about popcorn through their children who, unlike them, were free to roam the village. Eating it delightedly, they wanted to know how my corn made such a transformation. I assured them that ordinary corn didn't behave this way. Another time I brought them a melon from the huge Maradi market. This too we enjoyed together, shooing flies away from the kids' juicy faces.

Sarki Nouhou Brazaki with his wives and children

Longing for the company of other women was a steady desire in my life in Aguié. I would return home from such forays satisfied with the friendship-deepening experience and proud of myself for overcoming my natural timidity. Though as part of our work,

Maimouna and I visited with women every day, and going to the market was another comfortable place to briefly chat with female villagers, actually visiting women in their homes informally took all the gumption I could summon.

SAI ALLAH

I awakened slowly. I had been having a happy dream of home. My eyes, glued shut from the dust of the Harmattan winds, opened a crack as I reluctantly left my dream in which I and everyone else I know were marching in a parade down the middle of Miller Avenue in Mill Valley. All of us were dressed in Halloween costumes, holding colorful balloons and twirling hula hoops, roller skating, or eating ice cream cones. The glorious reds, yellows, oranges, greens spiraled in a kaleidoscope of moving shapes.

My eyes pried themselves open a little more. Awake now that the reds and yellows and greens had departed, I saw only brown: the mud walls, the herringbone patterned branches holding up the roof. A dullness descended; a brown wash obliterated my festive parade. I groaned, rolled over, and pulled the sheet up over my head, willing myself back to sleep.

But it didn't work. I was awake and in a funk which I recognized as a state of mind familiar to me many days during the winter. The dust was as thick as San Francisco fog, but instead of moist air, it was so dry it oppressed my spirit.

And I felt lonely. Rich was an early riser. He was up and out before I awakened, off to his engrossing work at the peanut market for what seemed like months.

I slipped out of bed and peeked at the small square of mirror hanging askew in the bathroom. I saw gummy, brown eyes, brown hair, and I groaned again, longing for a day that was not like every other day. I wanted to be entertained, surprised, astonished or delighted. I wanted to dress up and go to a party. I wanted to dance wildly in stocking feet on a polished wooden floor. I wanted anything but the dun-colored day ahead of me.

Once Rich and I had set up our home, got to know our neighbors and settled into our work routines, there was a sameness to our lives that was challenging for me.

Our diet was simple. There was little variety in food available. People didn't have vegetable gardens, nor was there much choice at the market. During the best growing season of the year we could buy dried tomatoes, onions, limes, guavas, papayas, oranges and some wild-harvested leaves, but most of that produce was grown elsewhere, often brought up from Nigeria. Never did I see a head of lettuce or broccoli or an apple. And oh how I missed bacon, ice cream, celery and cottage cheese.

The flatness of the diet was matched by the topography and the endless mud walls in town. Outside of town there were only flat vistas, farms and semi-desert scrub lands dotted with scraggly, infrequent tamarind trees.

The temperature too had little variation. It was either hot or hotter, even in the rainy season. But at least then, when the millet and sorghum stalks shot up taller than a person, it was thrilling to walk the snaky paths between fields surrounded by tall, green growth. Though humid, it was shady and private there, the moist earth rich and fecund.

The discomforts of extreme heat, flies, mosquitoes, and dirt, plus the lack of running water and electricity, were constant challenges to my customary cheerfulness and optimism.

There was no nightlife in Aguié. When the sun went down, the people did too. Cookfire smoke and the smells of dinners wafting through the streets gradually dissipated as the night advanced. A gentle quiet accompanied the cooling of the air. Few families owned kerosene lanterns, which might have allowed them to play cards or do handwork. Their days were so full of tasks to keep themselves fed, clean and sheltered, by nightfall, they were grateful to rest work-weary bodies.

I was glad for Rich's company the evenings he was home. As dusk grew into darkness, we could hear the soft voices of Tal's extended family next door. Then quiet. Soon all we could hear were the occasional snorts and pawing of Doikie and Neino's horse, tethered outside our back window.

When Rich was in town, we had our evening routine. After dinner, he cleaned the glass chimney and lit the wick of our kerosene lantern. We sat outside playing gin rummy or canasta for a while before settling down to read. Bye and bye our eyes stung from reading by the lantern. The Petromax, our Coleman-type white gas lantern, would have provided better light, but would have attracted bugs in squadrons. Also, it would have drawn too many curious onlookers. Bright light at night in the village meant that there was something unusual afoot, perhaps a rare traveling entertainer in town.

The six shelves of our Peace Corps book locker were full of paperbacks. Fiction was all I was interested in, and the shelves were loaded with classics. I read Dickens, Melville, Dostoyevsky, Hawthorne, Vonnegut, Steinbeck, Nabokov, Chekhov, Stendhal and dozens of others. When I loved certain authors, I pleaded in my letters home, "Send me the longest books by any of these authors. I have lots of time on my hands and I hate for a book to end." One of many things I liked about visiting other volunteers was swapping books. Arriving with our own stack of reads, we'd dive into their lockers, sharing recommendations and seeing what trades we could make.

I remember being particularly entranced reading *Moby Dick*. There I was, at the edge of the Sahara, while my imagination was staggering across the deck of a wind-tossed whaling ship, pummeled by waves of salt water, suffering from bitter cold while pursuing an elusive white whale. Other nights I found myself traveling across the landscape of Tsarist Russia, suffering despair with Anna Karenina. Those books were my favorites because they provided me with the most dramatic escape from the hot, predictable conditions of my life in Africa.

Rich and I often read late into the night, trading books with each other and sharing our enjoyment of the writing, the story and the characters. I think my village friends, who had to wake up early in order to get strenuous work done before the heat of the day, would have been amazed to hear that I'd been on the high seas with Captain Ahab or in Tsarist Russia while they were sleeping.

We had no radio. The town had no phone or two-way radio communication, nor was there a car. With this degree of isolation, it was not a good idea to get an attack of appendicitis as did our friend, Fernand, the youngest of our group, who lived in an even more remote village. Luckily, he survived his appendectomy after being evacuated to an Army hospital in West Germany.

So I understood the Peace Corps firm rule about volunteers not getting pregnant. The Corps was loath to assume the liability of childbirth or child-rearing in a remote nation with facilities no Western doctor would consider adequate. Having no desire to be sent home, I reluctantly took the birth control pill as prescribed. But the longing for a baby was a constant, adding to my bouts of low spirits. In my thoughts sometimes I argued with the no pregnancy policy, reasoning that my advice to the mothers in Aguié would be so much more credible if I myself had a child. But mostly I just tried to make do by just enjoying all the adorable babies in my care.

Outside of my work six days a week, and our Sunday farming, there was little else to do. The three hour daily lunch break left me restless. I longed to go to a movie, go swimming, play tennis or throw a party. I missed simply going to a shopping center with my sister.

The lack of stimulation put our marriage to the test. We talked about our work and our reading, our reading and our work. Being newlyweds, we had our share of relationship challenges and no one to turn to for counseling. It wasn't a subject I felt comfortable writing home about. Being so isolated from our culture, our families and all that we were accustomed to, and having only one another for mutual aid, was not an ideal way to start a marriage. We were the only married couple from our group that remained for the full two years, and though being single had its huge drawbacks, it was a strenuous learning curve for young newlyweds.

Letters from the U.S. were on airmail paper, thin sheets in delicate envelopes. Every gram meant more postage. Some were air letters, one thin blue sheet comprising paper, envelope and stamp all in one, they purchased at the post office. The news was rarely exciting, but reading it made me homesick. The familiar people, places and activities of Mill Valley had little relationship to our lives in Aguié.

Our sources of U.S. and world news were old copies of *Time* and *Newsweek* magazines we read at the homes of our PCV friends. Since Rich and I had missed in-country orientation, we'd also missed the opportunity to subscribe on our own.

The news about the Vietnam War and the impending presidential election scared us. On March 1, 1968, Rich wrote home: "We enjoyed your letters immensely and in many ways they have kept us going here. Stay healthy, happy, vote for McCarthy, leave the U.S. if WWIII seems too imminent and all will be fine. I am certain we are much safer here than you are in the States."

Later that month he wrote, "If Nixon is elected, he could send his nuclear bombs, instigate his much-hoped-for war with China, accidentally find himself engaged with Russia as well....and then none of us would have anything to worry about."

My Grandma Laurie wrote about the robin she saw on her walk to the mailbox that morning in Enumclaw, Washington. She sent a well-meaning gift that revealed the depth of her misunderstanding of where we lived. It was a book called *Helpful Household Hints from Heloise*. It included suggestions about cleaning out dryer lint and making drawers smell sweet. Despite our descriptive letters home, it must have been too much of a stretch for my grandmother to imagine that we had no dryer and no drawers. Nor did the hints dealing with household dust seem entirely germane in a house of mud walls and ceilings, with no glass in windows through which dust storms blew dirt into every possible crack and cranny.

My sister Francie's rare letters described her first job out of art school, teaching at a private girl's high school in Marin County. Mom and Dad wrote about friends, improvements to the house and garden, and stopped just short of revealing how worried they probably were about us.

These envelopes arriving from home were exciting to anticipate, but somehow disappointing when we actually devoured their contents. What really made a splash were the care packages they sent us filled with dried soup packets, Kool Aid, pudding mixes, powdered eggs, Fizzies and toys for our young friends.

On March 20, 1968, I wrote to my parents: "About those kids toys you sent for Christmas: the kids love the balls, cars and dolls. We gave away very few, and lend the other toys when kids come to visit. They've constructed a banco (mud) garage for the little cars and have races with them. Now, when the kids visit, we get them busy playing with each other instead of bothering us. Plus – Rich got the long-awaited basketball and basket and gives impromptu coaching and finds the kids catching on fast."

Kids loved Rich

Since there was so much sameness in our daily lives, our letters back home, after the initial few months, were probably not very exciting either. What was there about our daily activities in the village that they would find fascinating? It became more and more difficult to know what would seem newsworthy. Our "exotic" life had become mundane to us.

Rich and I relished the rare entertainment that broke the monotony. One day near the end of an afternoon rest period, Tal Hadji and several of her girlfriends came to visit, giggly and animated. Tal, always a great source of village gossip, urged us: "You need to come out to the square tomorrow afternoon because there's going to be a *dambe* (fight). Everyone's going. You'll see. Come!"

Sure enough, the next day as I returned home from work, I heard drumming in the town square, a clear sign that something was about to happen. Lots of men and a few women were beginning to form a circle under Sarki Brazaki's shade tree. The Sarki signaled for us to sit with him, ringside, so to speak.

The fighters wore blousy short pants, their strong torsos already gleaming in the heat. The first two combatants circled one way and then the other, looking for openings, darting in for a jab when they found one. The noise from the crowd rose and fell with their strikes and falls. I couldn't fathom the rules, but eventually a winner was proclaimed, and there was a long wait until the next pair of fighters were decided upon.

From a March 25, 1968 letter home from Rich: "Tuesday was one of our big treat days in Niger as the *dambé* or Hausa boxing was going on. A typical Hausa affair, more talking and haggling than fighting but the whole ritual was about as exciting as anything I have ever seen.

The fighters ranged in age from about 8 to 20 and the procedure is for someone from the audience to place money on a particular fighter and challenge someone else to face him. If the challenge is taken the fighters are compared in size, relative age etc. to judge if the match is fair. If the match is approved the fighters fight using only one hand which is wrapped in cloth. The fight ends when one is hit down or when the fight is judged a draw. Some of the fights were vicious and quite bloody—almost all were exciting. Throughout there was drumming. There were two referees and even clowns in the afternoon. We sat close to Brazaki so we had a good view of it all—really a great time."

Young wrestlers

Another time our private informants announced a bicycle exhibition. That evening we joined with others who were strolling up to the area by the road near where the dispensary and school were perched near the National Route. We contributed our entrance fee of a few coins, and helped to form a big circle, children in front, tall people in the back, to watch a young man from out of town who made his living performing feats on an ordinary looking bicycle.

He lit a *Petromax* lantern, creating a circle of light around him. He rode a battered old, gearless bicycle in an ever-tightening spiral, then balanced himself, standing on the seat of his now stationary bike. When he raised one foot and leg in the air, still balancing, the crowd gasped. He rode sitting backwards, leaning way over first one side and then the other. He rode peddling with his hands, his legs suspended straight above him into the air. He slipped his lanky body this way and that, defying gravity. He performed deluxe wheelies and thoroughly entertained all of us for a half an hour or so. We all expected to witness a scene in which he wound up with multiple fractures, but, miraculously, he never faltered or fell.

We knew how unique an experience we were having and took advantage of participating as fully as possible in the life of the village...BUT...it was inescapable how different our lives were from the daily toil that consumed most villagers' lives. Even with the progress I had made in speaking and socializing, I sometimes dreaded going out into the village. I felt I would always be a curiosity. I would never really belong

Mirroring the villagers, I tried to learn acceptance. Every day I heard the phrase, *Sai Allah*, which meant, *It is Allah's will*. If the baby died, if the rains were late, if someone broke a bone, *Sai Allah*. It is not our place to question the will of Allah.

THE BIRTH OF TRUST

Rich and I had been living in Aguié just under a year when Akwiya invited me to attend the birth of her fourth baby. Tal Hadji, Muman and little Oumarou were soon to get a little sibling.

Since the only births I'd been called to help with were those of women I didn't know where I was a last desperate hope in emergency situations, I felt honored to be invited in advance by a friend who would simply appreciate my presence at the birth of her child.

It was an early evening when Tal showed up at our door to tell me it was finally time. I donned my headscarf and shawl, and followed her out our doorway and into theirs.

"She's in there," Tal indicated with a jut of her chin toward a round grass hut just inside the compound walls.

I stooped down to get through the low doorway and, by the light of a lantern, saw Akwiya sitting on a typical low wooden stool and straddled by her midwife and sister.

"*La lé, la lé, Laouré,*" Akwiya said warmly as she rested between contractions. "I'm so glad you've come."

"How's it going?" I asked.

"This one is in a hurry!" she answered, and we all laughed. Feeling more relaxed, I took a seat on a mat at her side. The hut smelled of incense, sweat and a sort an ammonia-like scent which I guessed was from the water sac, already broken.

Amina was sitting behind Akwiya, bracing her back. Aisha and I supported her on each side. Her *zani* was bunched up around her abdomen. We used cool rags to wipe her face, neck and arms. Akwiya was an old hand at this and seemed not to need help. She was confident that the baby would come when the time was right.

With each contraction, she gripped our arms and we held hers. She made guttural noises in her throat, which were forcefully restrained yells. We all cheered her on, telling her it wouldn't be long before she'd meet her new baby.

Akwiya continued squatting on her stool when, after about two hours, her pushing began. The midwife then positioned herself to catch the baby. The light was dim. For our small circle of women there was nothing else going on in the world. The village beyond the walls was quiet; not even the bleating of goats could be heard. The anticipation was electric.

Finally, I could see the top of the baby's head. Akwiya pushed with all her strength. The patch of dark scalp gradually became larger and finally, the whole head appeared. I was trembling, awestruck with the miracle of this one being having created another, ushering it into its new life. With a few more mighty pushes the shoulders, torso and legs slithered out.

"It's a girl!" reported the midwife, and Akwiya's sister relayed that information outside to Mazadou and the rest of the waiting family. I could hear their excited murmurings. Before long, the placenta followed.

I was handed a sharp knife that had been sterilized in the coals of the fire. The umbilical cord was held for me by the midwives so that there was no question where to cut. I sliced, wincing at the sensation of cutting into human flesh. Neither the mother nor the baby reacted in pain, so I relaxed, enjoying the feeling of being an important player in this human drama.

So this is what it's like to attend a normal birth, I said to myself, and my self-confidence ticked up a notch. I didn't need to be afraid to participate. Now I could get really excited about being a midwife, or at least assisting one.

A letter home a week after this experience:

"Rich and I were invited to a naming ceremony today. It was for our neighbors just over the wall. I got to help bring the kid into the world. That was 7 days ago. Namings take place 7 days after birth. During those 7 days the mother is secluded in her hut. The other women in their compound were up at the crack of dawn today to fix tons of food for all the guests. Her husband went out inviting last night, giving handfuls of goro nuts to those he invited.

"Early in the morning we went next door. I went into the compound to sit on mats with the other women and Rich stayed out in front with the men. We waited – then waited. Then a small group of criers sang out a sort of eerie mournful, slow chant-prayer in which we heard for the first time the name of the child. (A child's name is given by the mallams or priests.) Four times during this chant, we all cover our faces with our hands and draw them slowly down (like peek-a-boo only slowly.) When that's over we all eat tuwo and give gifts. Her name is Zeinabou by the way, but it seems her nickname is Ta Laouré (Laurie's). I gifted her with the only set of clothes, a little top and pants I'd had made—real cute.

"Feeding guests goes on all day—Oh, I forgot, during the chant a gorgeous white ram was killed. And then there was drumming this evening for dancing.

"On the seventh day a child's head is shaved and, if facial scarification is to be done, it would be done at this ceremony as well. The facial designs denote tribal affiliation. In our region it's a multi-veined leaf-like pattern on each cheek from the corner of the mouth up towards the ear. Again, I believe it's the mallam who makes shallow incisions on the cheeks and rubs goro nut juice into the cuts to darken the lines. (Male circumcision in Aguié takes place as a rite of passage when a boy reaches puberty.) [Gratefully, our region did not practice female circumcision. I didn't even know about this inhumane tradition.] Before the naming ceremony it is considered unlucky to give any gifts. As it was explained to me, it's because a baby isn't considered a "person" until he or she is seven days old. It would be too easy for Allah to take him/her away before he/she has full personhood."

A few weeks after Zeinabou's naming ceremony, I was at the market when Maimouna's visibly pregnant friend Shaibou came over to me with her normal warm greetings. We talked briefly about our finds in the market and then she shyly asked, "Laouré, will you come with Maimouna to assist at the birth of my baby?"

"Why, of course, I'd love to! How will I know when to come?"

"Well, I think it won't be for another month, but I'm sure Maimouna will come get you."

And so it was arranged. After almost a year in Aguié I was beginning to gain a reputation as a midwife, though in reality, I'd still done very little to deserve the title.

So, I was excited a few weeks later when Maimouna told me one afternoon, "Shaibou's contractions started this morning, so be ready for me to come get you sometime this evening."

It was almost bedtime when Maimouna arrived to collect me, saying, "Hurry, Shaibou's contractions are coming really close together now. We should rush."

I grabbed a scarf and a clean *zani* as a shawl or, if needed, to wrap the baby in, and trailed after Maimouna, the five dark, quiet blocks to Shaibou's compound door. Maimouna clapped and we entered.

Shaibou's hut was in the back of the compound. We passed shadowy figures sitting wrapped in blankets, and stepped through the low doorway. Shaibou's mother and midwife were there with her. Seated on her stool, Shaibou was so absorbed in her labor that she barely greeted us.

"Her contractions are really close together. She'll be pushing soon," said her mother.

Maimouna and I sat on mats and settled in for the long haul. The evening was cool but the circle of our bodies created a cozy warmth. The smell of my favorite incense, a dark knobby, black root, permeated the hut. Maimouna and I encouraged Shaibou with words and support during contractions. Her increasingly frequent groans became more like growls as she tried to hold them back.

I thought about how many of my ancestors must have delivered their babies in much this same way, at home with sisters and mothers helping. I tried not to think about the eventuality of going through the pain of childbirth myself.

In a couple of hours, after giving some mighty pushes, and a few more unexpurgated moans, Shaibou delivered a tiny girl baby who slithered out into the hands of the older midwife. The baby let out a lusty cry and was placed, skin to skin, on her mother's chest. When the placenta emerged, I was again honored to be asked to cut the cord.

On our way home Maimouna and I walked quietly, both in awe from the miracle we had witnessed together. She broke the silence, turning to me saying, "You'll be an expert by the time I give birth."

"Oh yeah? When's that?" I joked.

"In about six months."

"What!?"

"Yes, I'm expecting and I want you to be with me when the time comes."

I skipped ahead of her, turned and encircled her in my arms. "That's wonderful! How long have you known?"

"About a month. I was telling my sister how wretched I was feeling all the time and she guessed. I hadn't suspected, even though it's what I want more than anything else in the world. I've been waiting so long that I guess I got used to waiting."

"Well, now you have to wait some more. But a very happy waiting."

"Konko is sure it's a boy, but I'm not so sure. He's bragging to his brothers, but so far, our families and you are the only ones who know. We don't want to risk annoying Allah by talking about it too soon. When I start really showing, that will be soon enough. You can tell Ibrahim, though."

"I'm so excited it would be difficult to keep it from him," I answered as we rounded the corner to my house. "OK," I said. "Now, I'll walk you part-way home."

I loved this tradition: A friend walks you home, and then, because you are still deep in conversation, you turn around and walk her back halfway, before finally, often reluctantly, ending the conversation and returning home alone. Sometimes Maimouna and I changed directions several times before actually saying goodbye and parting ways, and that was true of that night's homeward walk as well.

CHRISTMAS COMES TO AGUIÉ

At Christmas-time Rich and I were in a world of our own. In our little Muslim community of course there was no corner tree lot, no carols on the radio or colorful lights on houses. Neighbors didn't wear red and green or bring over cookies. But we managed to celebrate in our own way. When I was home alone, I made Rich a booklet of stick-figure cartoons depicting small services he could redeem from me as Christmas gifts: a massage, a haircut, his favorite French toast with coffee in bed. I bound the booklet with needle and thread, and hid it away until Christmas Day.

Inspired by a slight cool edge in the air suggestive of winter, we made hot beverages like chocolate milk and mulled cider from tin-foil packages and hummed Christmas carols to ourselves to summon a yuletide spirit.

We received a package of gifts from home but had no tree to put them under. "This simply will not do," Rich declared. "Something must be done!"

Determined, we éd through the streets past the edge of town, between fields of millet stubble where a goat—forelegs tied together so he couldn't stray far afield—munched on the husks of last harvest's stalks.

Resolving our holiday dilemma wouldn't be easy. We didn't want to kill any of the sparse vegetation on the outskirts of town. Dead wood was almost as scarce, since it was sought as firewood far into the bush. In the cool of the morning the velvet spiders were awake, positioned next to their round holes. Their bright, Christmas-red velvet coats looked like incandescent buttons on the wind-swept sand. We trudged on several miles, past manioc enclosures, more fields of millet and sorghum stubble, beneath the occasional acacia tree, and came upon a young goatherd and his charges.

Then Rich spotted a gray and brittle dead branch. "Hey, what about this one?" he said. "It doesn't have leaves, but there are lots of smaller branches where we can hang ornaments." I immediately loved it, the same way I'd always loved whatever Christmas tree was chosen from the lot, once decided upon.

Rich carried it home carefully over his shoulder so as not to break off any of the precious branches. Back in town, curious stares followed our progress. As we passed Momadou's compound, our friend called out, "Greetings, Ibrahim and Laouré. Hey, whatcha got there?"

Rich retorted, "We're going to plant it. We want a tree in our compound but we don't want to have to water one." Momadou laughed, accustomed by now to my husband's quirky sense of humor.

Further on, we passed a Koranic school consisting of a couple of grass mats just outside a *mallam's* compound. On the mats sat white-clad, shaved-headed boys, each with a smooth wooden slate. In thin, droning voices they sang out the verses they were memorizing that day.

On the same street we passed Fati and Rabi, the two wives of Hussein the butcher. They were sitting outside their compound door selling *kwokwo*, ladling the smooth, greenish-gray millet dish into customers' containers. The steam rose up invitingly. I made a mental note to come back later with my bowl. *Kwokwo* was my favorite millet dish and only available sporadically during the cold season. Made with finely pounded millet and involving a fermentation process, it had a satiny texture and a lemony-creamy warmth I had come to crave.

Back home, Rich busied himself stabilizing the tree in the corner of our living room. He anchored the trunk in a bucket of sand and I swathed the ugly base with a bright cloth. Then we started in with the can opener, cutting the bottoms off discarded tin cans so we could shape the remaining cylinders into sliver-moons, stars and hearts. We folded the lids this way and that, punched holes in them, and strung them onto the branches as well.

With scissors, glue and wire, we made anything that might resemble an ornament. When we were done, we stood back, feeling the satisfying camaraderie of a shared project's completion. And, lo and behold, our Christmas tree looked far better than we could have imagined when we found it out in the bush.

Tal Hadji and Muman sensed there was something unusual going on next door and crept over to see what we were up to. They waited eagerly for some rational explanation. We tried our best to share our rather pagan take on Christmas and got them enthused about stringing popcorn with us.

As she knelt at her task I noticed that the soles of Tal's feet were still dark blue-black from a henna treatment, decoration for the celebration for the end of Ramadan. I imagined all the women in her family gathering to decorate each other, slathering paste made of dried green henna leaves, onto their feet and toenails, then wrapping them with rags. Hands were usually treated as well, but I imagined Tal being too impatient to allow for that. For the women sitting around waiting for the henna to set was a rare luxury of idleness, when they could talk and laugh and sing songs all afternoon. When they were done, their toe and fingernails would be brilliant red, while the calloused parts of their hands and feet turned purple-black.

When we had finished stringing the popcorn and draping it on the tree, Tal skipped along beside me to buy some *kwokwo* from Fati and Rabi. We brought two steaming bowls back to the house, and the four of us slurped joyously.

Two days before Christmas, Jim and Connie arrived from their respective towns. Connie had brought all the ingredients to make stollen, including a packet of yeast sent by her grandfather. I never would have attempted such an endeavor, but Connie loved the challenge. I watched and helped as she sifted, stirred, kneaded, put the aromatic dough in a bowl, covered it with a dampened dish towel, and set it out to rise in the sun. When it was time, we used a wine bottle for a rolling pin. Working in the kitchen with another woman made me homesick for such shared pleasure with my mom and sister, especially during the holidays.

We stuffed a chicken, cooked green beans Connie had brought from her larger market, and made mashed potatoes and gravy. We ate our little feast slowly to make it last, and we told each other about our families' Christmas rituals. Later we sang some Christmas carols, drank too much wine and played increasingly uproarious games of rummy.

We were able to accommodate our guests on traditional Hausa grass-stuffed beds made with log cabin-stacked palm ribs lashed together to give the bed height. We draped them with mosquito nets and put them out on the patio. We often slept out there ourselves so we knew they would be comfortable. We all slept contentedly, with visions of the morning's scrambled eggs and stollen dancing in our heads.

Typical transport problems. From left to right
Matt, Rich, Steve., Connie and Jim

VISITING THE LADIES DURING THE COLD SEASON

One cool day during the Harmattan I decided to visit Hadiza, who lived a couple of streets east. I had gotten to know her when she'd linger to joke around with Maimouna after the other mothers left the well-baby clinic. Her daughter, Bulki, was Tal Hadji's age, and visited our compound frequently.

Because of the Harmattan dust that lodged everywhere and impaired vision, few people were on the streets. But rounding a corner, I spied Hadiza and called out to her. She was bouncing a small object from one hand to the other. Coming closer I saw that it was a hot coal. Rarely would a woman let her cookfire burn down to nothing, because if it did, there wouldn't be coals to kindle a new one. She would then go next door to a friend's fire to borrow a coal, like my mother would borrow a cup of sugar.

"I was just coming to visit you, Hadiza. Is this a good time?"

"Welcome, welcome!" she answered, keeping the coal moving from hand to hand. "My fire went out. I was just at my sister's getting a coal." I marveled at the way she could juggle the piece of coal without burning herself. "Yes, yes, come with me and we'll have a visit." Hadiza was what I considered middle-aged, but was probably thirty-five at most. I liked the natural way she was with me. She didn't seem to change her demeanor when we met the way many women did, making me feel set apart. Her warmth and humor put me at ease.

I continued to find that creating friendships in Aguié wasn't easy. The women were so nice, but often formal with me. Attempts at finding common ground were fraught with language and cultural complexities. And visiting just for social contact was not part of the culture.

Women had times and places they met one another: at the well, at the market, out near the fields pounding the chaff off the millet, and when dancing on holidays. I'm sure wives found excuses for social contact, such as going to a neighbor to borrow something. But since I had few of those points of contact, I had to really assert myself to develop the friendships I sought.

It took great courage for me to overcome my shyness and go to visit one of these friends uninvited, for no purpose other than to just hang out. And because I was something of a "celebrity," just hanging out wasn't all that natural an experience for any of us. For these reasons I was grateful for a friendship that flowed naturally.

Hadiza took the coal to her rock fire tripod, placed it in a bed of grass and millet stalks she had already laid and, squatting, blew life into it. While she slowly added larger and larger fuel, she chatted with me about having completed her marketing but having lost her kids somewhere along the way. "They'll come home when they're hungry," she said, laughing.

When the fire was well established, she led me to her hut, we ducked our heads and entered. Her sister-in-law and a co-wife were both inside. I sat, like them, on a soft grass mat, and was passed a small metal bowl of *goro* nuts, both red and cream colored. I'd developed a taste for this stimulant that seemed to be intrinsic to any social gathering, the way my American cohorts and I lit up cigarettes. With the shape and skin type of a chestnut, the *goros* were hard like a carrot and more bitter than anything I would normally put in my mouth. I chose a smoothly separated half of one of the cream-colored nuts, and took small nibbles.

The women were shelling peanuts together, usually a job relegated to evenings, so I rarely saw this work in progress. I was handed a small calabash scoop on the mat in front of me and joined in gratefully. Silences were comfortable because conversation was our secondary activity. One of the women, responding to a signal from the infant on her back, unwound the wrappings, deftly hauled the little one under her arm and gave it her breast, barely interrupting her work. We spoke about the cold and about Maimouna's pregnancy and the last clinic day's activities. They had been at the dispensary when a particularly outraged baby ejected herself off of the scale, nearly landing on the floor, and we all laughed together, remembering.

Hadiza at her cook fire

They wanted to know if I had siblings and how long I'd been married, but their curiosity about where I had come from was strangely limited. They may have thought it was impolite to ask, or maybe they didn't want to seem uninformed, though it occurred to me that their world was so circumscribed, they may have imagined life wouldn't be much different in another place, even a place far away. Most villagers, especially the women, had never ventured farther than thirty miles in any direction. I had often been asked by children, "Where is your village, Amerique?"

The monotonous noise and action of cracking the small dry seed pods between our fingers and teeth lulled me into a comforting rhythm, while at the same time the caffeine in the *goro* sprinted into my brain and supplied a euphoric glow to this ever-so-ordinary gathering. The conversation among the three women sometimes left me behind. I had trouble catching the subtleties of meaning or not knowing the people they were speaking about. They would laugh, but never in a way that made me feel left out.

Because Hausa is a tonal language, it was easy to unintentionally say something hilarious. When I wanted to say, "I went to the market yesterday," it might come out sounding to them like, "I cleaned the tree".

One easily misunderstood concept was admiration. I might say, "I like your scarf." The problem being that *to like* and *to want* are the same verb, so you might inadvertently have hinted that you wanted their scarf. And if you did, they were very likely to offer it to you. But even simple admiration, correctly phrased, could evoke such generosity.

I was content to notice that I felt like an ordinary woman, joining in with the work at hand. It was rare, since there were many daily activities I couldn't share. I didn't gather firewood, carry water from the well, pound millet or cook over an open fire. I did farm, but not together with others. So, I relished joining in with this circle of friends, working side by side. I tried to follow their words and to keep up with their nimble fingers as they slipped the papery brown husk off each peanut before popping it into the calabash with a satisfying *plunk*.

Hadiza's hands were deeply calloused from pounding grains and farming. That is how she could juggle hot coals without hurting herself. At one point, she took my hand in hers and showed the other women my uncalloused palm and fingers. They all exclaimed at how soft my hands were. This was a dead giveaway that toil was not my usual habit.

My eagerness to seek friendships was not just a personal desire. Being liked and accepted was an important element of being successful in my work, building trust. But for my own sense of wellbeing, I needed this sense of easy friendship too.

From talking with other volunteers, I knew I was lucky to be part of a couple. Most didn't have someone they loved to come home to, who spoke English and understood the joys and frustrations they were encountering.

But Rich was often gone, and when he was there, his companionship could only go so far to assuage my feelings of loneliness. I was lonely for my family and friends, classes, teachers, movies, and all sorts of familiar activities with people who shared my language and heritage.

My afternoon with Hadiza and the other women was a heavenly respite. I took a second half of a *goro* and floated into the tingling happiness of belonging. I probably kept them at the peanut task longer than they would otherwise have stayed at it. Undoubtedly, they should have been attending to children and dinner, but I think none of us wanted to break the spell.

TABOO

Though Akwiya performed all the typical chores of other Aguié women and earned extra francs cooking the millet snacks, she also participated in Bori or animist rituals which were holdovers from before Islam took hold in western Africa.

I remember from time to time we'd hear strange noises from over the wall to Akwiya's compound. It sounded like a traumatized animal; it would go on and on for many minutes at a time. Then stop and commence again. I couldn't guess what it was! At first, when I asked Tal and Muman what was happening next door, they'd say, "Mom has a devil on her head." Eventually I learned that she would get terrific headaches and be possessed by spirits. While in the spirit trance, she spoke in tongues and had the power to see into the future. Women would come to consult her during those periods when the spirit was on her. They did so on the sly, sheepishly, and possibly without telling their husbands, especially if their husbands were devout Muslims.

No adult ever talked to me directly about Bori. I only knew what children told me, and it always seemed as though they were sharing a secret with me, something taboo. Bori was underground, offbeat, and not quite acceptable, even though it seemed to fascinate everyone. It was the town's delicious secret—weird, edgy and forbidden

On occasion, when Rich and I stayed up late reading or playing cribbage, we'd overhear late-night music in the street not far from our house. A time or two we went out to see what was going on. There were people in an alley behind the mosque making music whose melody came from a small stringed instrument, doing ritualized dancing and emitting strange utterances. I distinctly remember a man on the ground acting like a dog. The next morning, there was no mention of its having happened at all, and if we asked about it, we got embarrassed explanations and shoulder shrugs.

One day when we were hearing the guttural noises from over the wall, Tal Hadji came into the compound to tell me that Akwiya had messages for me. Wondering what that could mean, I followed her back to her compound, and ducked my head to enter Akwiya's hut. It took a moment for my eyes to become accustomed to the dark, and then I saw her, looking completely altered from the stately wife and mother I knew. Her hair was a mess. Sweat was pouring off her body, and her eyes were closed.

"I'm glad you've come, Laouré. I'm getting messages for you. Give me your hands." I reluctantly put my hands in hers. Then she closed her eyes and began to speak in tongues in a hoarse tone, much lower than her ordinary voice. The gibberish went on and on, rose and fell, loud and strong, strange utterances wrenched from her small body almost as if she were vomiting.

I watched, frightened but fascinated to see this transformation. Finally there was a lull and, switching back into Hausa, she said, "I have been given some information for you. The spirits tell me that you can't have any children." She hesitated. "But there is more. Something will prevent you from staying married to Ibrahim. I don't know why."

I didn't give her words much credence, and yet I hoped if her reading was accurate, it was only picking up on the fact that I was taking birth control pills, because I wanted to be able to have children eventually. As for staying married to Rich, well, only time would tell.

FORGIVENESS

One day we had an unannounced visit from some Peace Corps friends, a rare enough event for us to stop work early and call it a holiday. They arrived early in the day so I had time to "order out" two chickens from a woman down the street. They would be caught, killed, plucked and roasted and brought to us in time for dinner.

I cooked rice and onions to go with the chicken, and we poured rounds of red, rot-gut wine we had purchased in Maradi in five-gallon, rattan-encased jugs. One of those jugs usually lasted for months. This felt like a special occasion, being able to laugh and sing with friends, tell stories English, and complain about our lives and brag about our exploits. It was a welcome time-out of our routine, as Jim played the guitar and Rich made up hilarious blues lyrics. At a very late hour I dropped into bed and was instantly asleep.

Some time later, I heard clapping and calling at our compound door. It was still dark out. In a haze, I recognized Maimouna's voice and realized her calling had been going on for a while. "Laouré! Laouré! Wake up. Come quickly. My sister is worse. Please come."

Usually a woman full of vitality, Madai had lain in bed for several weeks with no energy, her oldest daughter preparing meals for the family.

I staggered out of bed and went to the doorway. "You must come," begged Maimouna. "Madai's fever is high and she's in a lot of pain."

I sent her back to her sister's, promising to follow. When I returned to the bedroom to dress, in my drunken state, despite my best intentions, I couldn't resist lying down on the bed, just for a minute. I fell asleep.

When morning came, I slept through the roosters but as the light filtered through the window, I slowly emerged from my sleeper's fog and hangover to the memory of Maimouna's nocturnal summons. Dread and disbelief gripped me between my ribs. I made a plea to a God I did not know, "Please let this be a dream. Please give me a chance to do this right. I'll never ask again. Ever. Please!" But no god or fairy godmother responded. I was on my own.

I flung off the covers and looked for Rich. He was already gone. I dressed, downed two aspirin for my headache, brushed my hair and slipped on a scarf, rushing to go to Madai's.

But before I could get out the door, there was Maimouna, still in yesterday's clothes, tears streaming down her cheeks. "Madai didn't make it through the night," she cried. "She's gone. My sister's gone. Why didn't you come?"

I embraced her as she wept. Then she stepped back, cocked her head and looked at me, as if reevaluating who I was. "She died. Why didn't you come?" She peered at me through her tears, waiting for an answer.

I tried to explain that I had had too much to drink, but there was no way to excuse my irresponsibility. I knew, and undoubtedly, she did too, that there was nothing I could have done to save her sister, but she had every reason to expect me to come and do whatever I could do, and to simply be there for her as a supportive friend. I realized this was a serious breach of the trust that had grown between us. I broke down, sobbing.

"Please forgive me." We wept together in each others' arms on the street before my doorway.

"*Sai, Allah.* It was Allah's will," Maimouna said softly. She turned and without the normal formalities, went home, leaving me standing alone in my misery.

The following day I awoke, fearing the worst. Maimouna had every right to be sullen or even to quit working with me. I knew she was hurt and probably angry, but at our usual hour there she was at my door, fresh and ready to go on home visits. No recriminations.

I relaxed, but still felt a knot of remorse in my chest. Neither of us spoke of it until weeks later. I was her teacher and employer. I paid her wages out of mine. I hoped those were not the only reasons she forgave me and continued to be my friend. In any case, I believe she forgave me before I was able to forgive myself, which only came years later.

FULANI INITIATION

Way off in the distance we heard the steady rhythm of drums. It was Saturday morning; Rich and I were eating breakfast on our patio. I cleaned up our dishes and went next door to ask Akwiya if it was time. She had offered to go with us to the Fulani celebration.

We had learned about the Fulani tribe's initiation rites in Peace Corps training and, while thinking the ritual beatings barbaric, it didn't keep us from wanting to see for ourselves.

Out on the sandy streets, villagers were striding toward the marketplace. As we approached, the drums beat louder and faster. A crowd of Fulani and Hausa men and women were beginning to form a large circle. We could easily distinguish the Fulanis by their lighter skin and longer, thinner faces with straighter, narrower noses. The men's hair was longer and braided, unlike Hausa men; and the women's hair, though covered in scarves and shawls, was braided and wound in ways very unlike the Hausas. Here and there we could distinguish a characteristic knob of hair just above the forehead. We were fascinated by the Fulanis' facial scarification, full of its angular and broken black lines and dots, completely different from the Hausas' more serpentine markings. The Fulani women were usually dressed in homespun, hand-dyed indigo blue skirts and wound tops, an indigo so dark that from a distance it appeared black.

But on this day, the indigo-blue skirts were festooned with blocks of colored embroidery in white, yellow, red and green patterns, and the blue head shawls sported red and white stripes. Multiple necklaces and leather amulets hung from necks, some of them with brass wire wrapped around them, others incorporating bullet casings, coins, buttons or tiny mirrors. Most also wore multiple silver hoops in pierced ears and many strands of colorful beads around wrists and just above the elbows.

Most of the men wore the same deep blue fabric, with many yards of it wound in turbans around their heads and necks. The unmarried men had bare torsos. Akwiya pointed to a group of them who stood off to the side. "They're chewing the crazy herb. It makes them crazy enough to not care if they get hurt. Maybe it helps them not feel the pain, too."

We peered over the shoulders of those in front. The drummers moved from the center of the circle off to one edge. Then one of the youngest men stepped into the center. He wore knee-length, baggy, indigo pants and a cloth hat with tiny mirrors and grigris sewn into it. His torso and arms were lean and tightly muscled. He flung his head and arms up into the air, signaling courage and readiness. Suddenly, I wasn't sure I wanted to watch this.

"That man is the *farawa*." Akwiya used the word that I guessed meant *initiate*. "Now look," she said, as another young man stepped into the circle. "This man is the *farawa*'s best friend." He carried a smooth four-foot-long branch stripped of its bark.

Women all around the circle began to ululate deep in their throats, an ethereal sound that intensified my anticipation and dread. The day was hot and the circle was cloudy with dust. The circle was at least four people deep. At the far rim Hausa men watched from horseback.

"I'm going over to join Neino and Mazadou," Rich said, pointing to a group of men standing in the shade of a tree. I considered going with him, but Akiwya grabbed my hand and held me to her.

The *farawa* paraded close to the side of the circle where all the unmarried Fulani girls were in a tight line, no space between them. They sang out at him to be brave. They reached their braceleted arms out to him playfully.

Suddenly there was a hush and the *farawa* again raised his arms. The drumming accelerated. His friend drew back the stick and whacked him across his back with all his might. The beaten man took the blow, staggering to regain his balance. Instantly a young woman ran up to him, showing him a mirror so he could see his own smile, proving his bravery.

The friend stepped back and again, swung his stick forward with a resounding crack. The *farawa* nearly fell this time, but again regained his equilibrium, undaunted. Once more the girl came, offering him the mirror. The drumming was steady, the circle attentive. I thought surely he'd had enough, but no, here they went again and again; and each time the girl ran up with the mirror. He may not have winced, but I know I did. I hoped that whatever the herb was, he had chewed lots of it, as the pain must have been almost unbearable. I could see welts forming.

After many minutes and five solid hits, his back was slashed with red, some of it flowing blood. The crowd opened to receive him and he disappeared in their midst, as the drumming once again got louder and the women's inner circle started dancing counterclockwise. Each woman turned to face the back of the woman in front of her and laid hands on each of her shoulders. Akwiya took my hand, drawing me with her toward the innermost circle. She broke into the linked dancers and guided me ahead of her into the line.

I was amazed and honored to be invited to participate. I had wondered if my just being there, a foreigner, would be too much of an intrusion, but now that I was there and felt completely accepted, I shed my misgivings and got hot and sweaty along with all the other women. We danced as I had learned to do, stepping, bouncing, swaying, stepping again, restrained but spirited. It wasn't strenuous dancing, more monotonous than anything, and I fell into a sort of trance, only aware of my feet moving in rhythm with many other feet. I felt grateful to be dancing, enthralled with being part of the society of women, celebrating a young man's passage into manhood.

The drumming climaxed and thumped to end the dance. The next initiate strutted into the circle, gesturing his readiness. The girls tittered at the attention he paid them, and then, as before, his chosen friend stepped into the ring with his stick and the second beating commenced. The ritual was repeated over and over most of the day. Some of the men who entered the circle had scars on their backs from previous years. Still unmarried, they invited a fresh beating, hoping that their show of courage would make them worthy of a good wife.

I entered so totally into the flow of the ritual's constant drumming, the dancing, the sun and dust, the smells of bodies, the heat and excitement and noise surrounding me, that I lost the sense that what I was seeing was inhumane and wrong. It was a little frightening how quickly I lost that perspective. Later Rich told me how amazed he was when he realized I was in the innermost circle, dancing. Having put my misgivings aside, I'd allowed myself to let go of right and wrong and just experience the rite with no judgments or labels.

However, during the following days and weeks, when those lashed young men came into the dispensary for treatment, I found some of my earlier thoughts returning, calling me to question the necessity of all that suffering. Was it wrong of me to have enjoyed something so barbaric? No firm answers emerged. But one thing was certain: it had been exciting and I knew I would participate again, given the chance.

FOREVER MAKING FAUX PAS

Along with my many faux pas from ignorance of Hausa customs, there were others that arose from difficulties in communication. These grew less frequent over time as my Hausa fluency increased. But my Hausa didn't help on the day I walked over to Maimouna's place to tell her something. I clapped at the doorway, as usual, but couldn't quite understand what her husband was saying. Assuming it was some unusual variation of the typical welcome, I entered. To my horror I came upon Konko in the washing area bathing, buck naked! Only then did I realize that the guttural sounds he had been making were, "Oh no! Don't come in yet." I quickly retreated to the street until I was formally invited in by Maimouna, who looked secretly delighted that both her husband and her teacher were embarrassed. She did have a wonderful sense of humor.

I was embarrassed again when on a chilly day when she and I had stopped by her compound to pick up an extra cover for her shoulders, I noticed a narrow millet-stalk teepee, no taller than a person, set up in the washing area. Since it was certainly too small for a person to stand or sit inside, I pointed to it and asked her what it was for. Without a shred of embarrassment, she showed me that inside hung the rags she used for her menstrual period, drying out of sight. I hadn't intended to ask such a personal question, and I quickly changed the subject.

There were also faux pas that I couldn't possibly anticipate, based as they were on such subtle cues of meaning. One day while walking along with Maimouna, my sandal strap broke. We stopped and examined the rubber flip-flop, tried a quick fix, but failed. I slipped it off and started limping along with one sandal, the sand being too hot to tolerate being completely barefoot. Maimouna giggled in a way I had come to know meant she was embarrassed. She put her hand on my shoulder to stop me, and said, "Laouré. You mustn't wear just one sandal. If a person wears just one shoe, it means that he or she is a bastard!" She left me in the road and quickly borrowed a right sandal for me to wear until we could get to my house, where I had a complete pair. I didn't share with her that this wasn't the first time I'd broken a sandal, and it made me appreciate the gallant gesture of the Emir of the Gobir nation in Tibiri all the more.

Wearing a ring on a middle finger was apparently another dead-giveaway of bastard-hood. And, by the way, never ever wave at someone with your left hand. Or eat with your left hand, of course. Since I am right handed, this was never an issue, but I imagine there were numerous instances of Rich and I embarrassing ourselves without anyone ever pointing it out to us.

Fortunately, we were not held to the same standards as the permanent population. The villagers seemed to make exceptions for us, probably because we were exotic, we were there to help, and the Sarki showed that he valued our presence. Rich's penchant for acting the buffoon probably helped to soften their judgments and give them permission to joke around with us. Surely, we must have provided many amusing stories around their evening fires!

BATTLING BUREAUCRACY

Dr. Fournier, the head of the hospital in Tessaoua, and the French *militaire* teachers at the secondary school had all discussed in great depth the idea of launching a training program for young local women to become health educators, who would work in clinics and dispensaries to follow up with women and children's health issues. But it was Connie's arrival in Tessaoua that boosted the idea into the realm of the possible. Aguié, got patched into the plans because it was close to Tessaoua, and because I already had Maimouna, with whom I was doing preliminary training. Connie drove the Peace Corps end of the endeavor.

Our vision was to make volunteers unnecessary, to train and empower Nigerienne women to do the very work we had come to do. Having been told during training about the vols who had cultivated counterparts in Niger, we took up the dream that we, too, would be able to replace ourselves after our two years. This had already been tried, but so far no lasting pilot program had emerged. The issue was, "How would they be paid?" Peace Corps volunteers had been successful in one town, but the funding for those counterpart trainees was local, tenuous and almost certainly temporary.

On our monthly overnight visits Connie and I had been brainstorming a way to up the ante by getting funding from Niger's federal government for a pilot project that could be replicated throughout the country. We envisioned a standard curriculum Peace Corps volunteers could teach, and standardized tests their trainees could pass to become certified Health Educators.

One month, when Rich and I came to Tessaoua to get our stipends, he went back to Aguié while I stayed on to work with Connie.

In the evening after taking turns in the shower, we sat, still wet, sipping iced tea, smoking and catching the feeble breeze in her patio. Since it took her little kerosene refrigerator an entire day to make ice, we parsed the cubes out carefully.

We knew our plan meant an uphill battle, with so many points against us: We were foreigners. We were young and inexperienced. And, worst of all, we were women. We'd need to convince the regional *sous-préfet* that he and his constituents would benefit from spearheading the program in his jurisdiction. We already had the players lined up and the plan fleshed out. The question, as always, was funding. After organizing our best arguments for the program including how we'd recruit trainees, Connie and I felt ready to make our pitch.

Donning long skirts and scarves, we walked out from Connie's narrow side street into the busy main streets of Tessaoua and the marketplace. Connie's passage through town was by now a familiar sight to the vendors. A few bowed their capped heads slightly, touching their chests in a silent greeting. Women and children greeted her with a singsong "Karima," her Hausa name. She was the only single white woman in town and her neighbors must have wondered about her. It would have been interesting to eavesdrop on their private thoughts and hear their curiosities and judgments: *How old was she? Had she ever been married or had children? How could she stand to live alone? How did she get along without a man or a family? Was she a prostitute?* Connie was only twenty-two. Most *Nigeriennes* had had at least three children by her age.

We passed stalls of oranges, onions, herbs, fabrics and meat, and turned into the long road leading to the government buildings. We were really doing this.

Tall trees lined the road. Looking up, I was startled to see them festooned with clusters of bats, hundreds of them hanging upside down. Because it was daytime, they moved very little, but their presence in those huge clusters was unsettling at a time I was trying to bolster my confidence.

We reached the office of the *sous-préfet,* the head honcho for the Tessaoua region. His secretary got up from her seat at a desk that had nothing on it except a typewriter and a short stack of files. Curtly she asked us to wait while she slipped behind a closed door. Shortly she came back to say without a hint of friendliness, "Sous-Préfect Hamidou will see you now."

After coming around his desk to greet us and shake our hands, he urged us to be seated. A small fan pushed air around in the otherwise stifling room. The only decoration was a large framed photograph of President Diori, dressed similarly to Mr. Hamidou in a light blue *grand boubou*, with elaborate, tan embroidery around the neck and down the front. Remembering how kind the President and his wife had been to Rich and me in our English tutoring visit our first month in Niger, I tried to calm my nerves.

After a few pleasantries Mr. Hamidou asked what he could do for us. Choosing her words in careful French, Connie proceeded to explain the educational work we were doing with women and children, and how sharing basic information prevents illness and saves money. "We would like nothing more than to work ourselves out of a job by replacing ourselves with Nigerienne women who would carry on the work with women and children in this prefecture when the Peace Corps leaves."

Mr. Hamidou's eyebrows rose and a map of lines appeared on his forehead. His chest seemed to cave slightly as he listened.

"Dr. Fournier has gotten the teachers at the *école secondaire* involved," I added, "and together we are developing a curriculum."

"Our hope is that the National Health Ministry would create a certification process," Connie said.

Mr. Hamidou squared his shoulders. With a condescending smile he said, "It sounds like a good idea in theory. I commend you two lovely ladies for your enthusiasm. You need to understand that this is a very small country with an even smaller budget. It's hard for us to pay enough school teachers and nurses. I hope you don't expect that I will be telling the people at the National Health Service how to spend their money."

"We know it's a long shot," answered Connie, nervously pushing her glasses further up the bridge of her nose. In a tone that didn't betray the frustration I knew we shared, she continued, "We plan to go into the capital ourselves to speak with the head of the National Health Service, but we'd like to do so with your blessing. We'd like you to talk with Dr. Fournier, and if he convinces you that our pilot project will work for this region, we'd like you to write a letter for us to carry to the capital, giving our plan your endorsement. Just think: Tessaoua could be the first prefecture to have such a program! It would be a model which other prefectures could copy."

"I agree to talk to Dr. Fournier," he said, frowning slightly. "That's as far as I'm prepared to proceed. I'll let you know after I've spoken to him. Don't count on it, though."

Meandering back to Connie's through the marketplace, we felt we'd done our best. At least the *sous-préfet* didn't say no. We looked forward to reporting our progress to Dr. Fournier that night at dinner in his home. We had certainly earned an evening of gastronomic indulgence. There would be wine, cheese, French bread and salad. Madame Fournier could make a cauliflower soup or leek casserole or a cold vegetable salad that rivaled a fine restaurant in Paris.

I knew I would have to endure the embarrassment of not always understanding the rapid French conversation that usually shot back and forth across the table. The dinner and the pleasure of spending time with their family were well worth the discomfort.

UNUSUAL FRIENDSHIPS

After Connie and I gave our pitch about our idea for Counterpart Training, there was nothing to do but wait. There were many hours in the day when I was not at the clinic and I yearned for companionship. During the rainy season, the village women were more likely to remain inside their huts, shucking peanuts or doing other inside tasks. I was welcome to join in, work beside them and chat. Otherwise, I knew I was interrupting their work and might get them in trouble with their husbands. I was in heaven if a baby was willing to sit in my lap. And though they knew they were welcome in my home, friends rarely visited. Once in a while several might show up, dressed formally, having convinced their husbands that they had a legitimate reason to come see me. I would offer them ice, ice water or popcorn, and they might liberate their warm, moist babies from off their backs and hand them over to me.

As much as I enjoyed their friendships, I often wished I could simply hang out with girlfriends with no chores to do, no children to tend—the kinds of friendships that were such a natural part of high school and college.

Well into the second year of our tour, I got my wish. And all because the road repair team reached Aguié.

The crew had been a year making its way west from Dosso, where the pavement stopped, along the National Route, passing Dogondoutchi, Madaoua and Maradi. They weren't paving the road, only widening it, smoothing out the ruts and laying a new top layer of gravel, using shovels, hoes and rakes.

With the road crew of twenty or so men came a makeshift saloon and a few prostitutes, both big-city attractions. And while these created major changes in the small world we inhabited, I would not have guessed how their arrival would affect my life. The prostitutes wore crisp new clothes and tied their head-scarves in rakish, non-traditional ways, city style. Their outfits had extra flounces, lower necklines and tightly fitted bodices with side zippers. Their necklaces and earrings were manufactured and sparkling. Their hair was neatly braided in sophisticated styles and their skin shone from care.

They strolled two-by-two through town, aimless and relaxed, in dramatic contrast to the village women who were only allowed out of their compounds for specific errands: to go to the well and the market, and to collect firewood. These city ladies were free to talk and laugh, stopping to chat and flirt with men as they went.

Most of them had been married and their husbands had divorced them. It was common for a woman to be divorced for the offence of not being able to produce children for her husband. A man only had to say, "I divorce you" three times in the presence of a *mallam*, and a woman was banished from his home. Women had no rights in the matter. If a divorced woman wanted to find a new husband, she needed to go back to her original family. If she didn't go back to her family, she was considered a prostitute. It became clear to me that prostitutes enjoyed a higher status in Niger than in the USA. They were an accepted, if separate, level of society.

These women gravitated towards me as the woman in town with the most in common with them. We knew more about the world, were more sophisticated. They apparently had no children. Nor did I. Although I was married, my husband didn't restrict my activities, and I had free time because I had household help. Two or three of the women became regular visitors during the afternoon rest period. I never would have guessed that this would happen, or that I would enjoy their company as much as I did. Two or three would come with their playing cards and teach me betting card games. I taught them Blackjack, War and Go Fish.

Zeinabou was my favorite new friend. She was plump, with many tiny braids tight to her head, a shiny, round face and saucy body language. Her shoulders talked, their movements highlighting her enthusiasm, distaste or curiosity; whatever it was she was saying or reacting to, her shoulders were there to express it. She taught me Mankala, a game of strategy and luck.

To create a makeshift playing board, she scooped out two parallel rows of shallow impressions in the sandy earth of our yard, six small pockets in each row and a larger receptacle at each end. Two players each start out with the same number of pebbles and by distributing them, following a few simple rules, the person who ends up with the most pebbles wins. We spent hours playing Mankala, often with the neighborhood children peeking over our shoulders.

One day Zeinabou came to the compound doorway and clapped. When I came out, she seized my wrist and earnestly invited me, imparting her excitement, as always, through her body language, to go with her the next day.

"Many people go out to the Sarki's fields. There is drumming. It will be fun. I'll come get you when the sun is here"—gesturing with her arm low toward the eastern horizon.

She and her friends arrived the next morning as promised, all in jovial spirits, and we took off. We walked south beyond the village edge on a single trail through the fallow fields, soon to be planted in millet or peanuts. Before long we heard distant drums. As we grew closer, we saw clouds of dust rising, and trail forks led us around the edges of fields, zig-zagging our way towards the commotion.

I'd seen many people working on their farms whenever Rich and I ventured out to our field, but never had I seen so many working together. I knew that the Sarki had large farms and that every family in the village was expected to help with his crops, but I hadn't seen them assembled in the fields.

The men bent at their work, using their *dabas* to break the crust, soften the soil, and create furrows. They were working to the rhythm of the non-stop drumming, sweat and dust layering their bare torsos. We fetched gourds of drinking water for them from a large jug someone had undoubtedly carried out there on her head. Close amongst the workers, we too became dusty, but I didn't care. There was an exciting energy coursing through my body, which I sensed everyone was feeling together. The drums, the heat, the dust, the unusual communal activity, all combined to thrust the group into a holiday spirit. I was sorry Rich hadn't come. I could imagine him jumping into the common activity. He was undoubtedly missing the team sports he loved back home, sweating together with teammates in a common effort. This would have thrilled him.

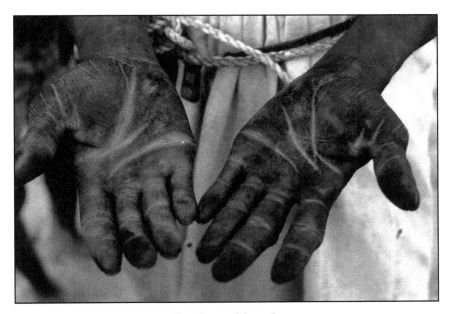

Hard-used hands

At the end, we women trooped home together, dusty and tired, but having had an unusually entertaining morning. We ended the day at my compound taking turns filling up the shower bucket and using our indoor shower, the only one in town, and then indulging in grooming ourselves. They had brought soap and scented oils for slathering on their dry limbs. They washed their still-braided hair, then oiled it up, tucking flyaway hairs into their braids. I learned from them the purpose of the mysterious balled-up dry grass I'd seen at the market; we used it like a loofa sponge. It was a leisurely, chatty time, making me nostalgic for my sister and the times back at home when we used to get ready for parties together.

THE JOY OF COOKING

The butcher wrapped my meat up in paper, and I plunged deeper into the marketplace to make other discoveries. With each purchase I continued to enjoy honing my skills of acting, arguing, flirting and on intuition to ultimately agree on a price far better than the one originally offered but still a good deal for the vendor.

Depending on the season, I might find papayas or small guavas whose smell set my salivary glands to dancing. Limes were often hard and brown but still contained some juice. On rare occasions I bought oranges with desiccated rinds, which looked as if they had been hauled over more than one national border. There were always onions, salt, heaps of small, dried hot-peppers, rice, brown sugar cones, dates, dried tomatoes, dried okra, peanuts and peanut oil.

On our monthly hitchhiking treks to Tessaoua, staying the night at Connie's house, we'd collect our Peace Corps stipends from the post office and then proceed to the market there to buy beef, lettuce, fresh tomatoes, potatoes, bread, oranges, bananas, carrots and other fruits and vegetables in season. Most of this produce was grown in Nigeria and hauled north in trucks, on camels and by horse.

In the market the hot red color of the meat-drying trays, covered with flayed beef were made even redder by the repeated application of hot chili sauce. Tessaoua was known for its hot beef jerky, called *kilishi*. It was too hot for most Westerners, including me, but Rich was a connoisseur. The vendors waved the flies off in a desultory fashion with bundles of twigs.

Vendors at the market

Connie was a good cook. She taught me how to make creamy potato soup with plenty of pepper, which became one of our staples. Our friendship grew on these monthly visits, smoking and drinking endless bowls of instant coffee, commiserating about bugs, heat and work frustrations; discussing favorite movies, our childhoods and food; and especially our shared hopes for funding to develop a program to train counterparts.

Rich and I carried huge baskets of our market treasures home to Aguié. If we planned to eat them raw, we soaked them for a long time in filtered water with dissolved iodine capsules to kill amoebas.

The local goat meat was tough, as was the infrequent beef and the ubiquitous chicken. The pressure cooker neutralized sinews, turning out delicious soups, stews and sauces, that I laid over rice or noodles.

There were occasions when I had to kill a chicken, not my favorite task, but at least I had my *Joy of Cooking* to guide me. Usually I just put out the word that I'd pay good money for a gutted, plucked chicken, and it would materialize. Our own chickens we kept for laying, since eggs were hard to come by in the market, as the villagers thought of them as a precious commodity, an investment in future chickens, so rarely sold them, even if offered a good price.

One Saturday morning Rich stormed in from the chicken yard, exclaiming, "Where in the hell are the eggs?"

It seemed our hens had turned barbaric. As soon as an egg appeared, the hens would peck it and eat it, shell and all. We needed eggs for baking and for French toast and pancakes, so we treasured them. We learned to pay attention when the chickens started making a lot of noise, and to take a broom and run out to the chicken coop to defend the egg from destruction. But we also learned to ask for our family care packages to include powdered eggs.

When volunteers got together, we often indulged in fantasy chatter about our favorite American foods: Pizza! Hamburgers! Milkshakes! Pastries! Ice cream!

We tried, with spotty success, to replicate certain familiar foods, using creative ingredients and utensils. Connie was my reliable accomplice in this endeavor. It began on a day she and I spent creating raviolis. We did, at least, have wheat flour, and we used an empty wine bottle to roll out the pasta dough. In lieu of a proper edge-cutter, we cut decorative edges with knives. I can't recall what we put in the stuffing, but amazingly, our ravioli turned out to be quite delicious.

Nothing gave Connie more pleasure than obtaining a Thanksgiving turkey. Somehow, she managed to get one brought up from Nigeria (she never said quite how she finagled it). We worked for several days at her place in Tessaoua, making creamed onions, mashed potatoes, stuffing, gravy, and even, thanks to a tip from Millie the missionary, ersatz cranberry sauce made from fresh hibiscus flowers she gave me. It was all delicious, and we were pretty pleased with ourselves.

Our Thanksgiving effort was somewhat deflated shortly after by an audiotape from my family, in which they joyfully recorded for us their own Thanksgiving dinner at home. Rich and I were drooling with all the, "Please pass the rolls and butter," and "Anybody want more pumpkin or apple pie? with ice cream?" That tape was definitely a mixed blessing.

The foods eaten by the villagers varied little from day to day. *Foura* for breakfast and lunch, *tuwo* for dinner. *Foura* had the consistency of a thin milk shake, but was made of finely ground millet flour, sour milk and hot pepper. *Tuwo* had a tasty hot sauce, flavored with dried tomatoes, onion, okra and a small handful of marrow bones, with a tiny bit of meat attached. When Rich and I ate with the villagers, we took what was offered and ate with our right hands. I developed a taste for their dishes, but never went so far as to try to replicate them at home. A few volunteers "went native," as we called it, and completely took on the lifestyle and diet of the people they lived amongst.

But even though Rich and I took advantage of the wider range of foods we could obtain, we still felt deprived. The austerity of our neighbors' diet should have made us feel grateful for the greater variety we could afford, but we were young and spoiled American kids, and couldn't help longing for the variety and abundance of home.

Charity is a highly valued virtue in the Muslim world and a part of everyday life. Each night after dinner at least one young Koranic scholar would come barefooted to our doorway asking for any leftover food, repeatedly singing: *"Ina tsa aka, ga ta nabe."* These were young boys who were studying the Koran instead of going to public school. They practiced writing Koranic scripture in Arabic on wooden slates, which they would then wash off and begin again. Maimouna explained that they would drink the wash water with the ink in it, ingesting the verses. I would pass clusters of these children chanting in unison, studying on grass mats at the doorstep of a teaching *mallam.* Whatever leftovers we had we'd give them. If they came from other villages and didn't have a family in Aguié, they depended on charity for their meals.

Slate with Koranic scripture

Some foods came right to our door from mysterious sources. Occasionally, we were brought duck eggs that we'd buy on the spot, nice large eggs. People also brought cheese, a strange yellowish, pancake-shaped, rubbery substance that tasted somewhat rancid to me. I never bought that. Butter arrived at our door on occasion with an "off" flavor I didn't care for; we managed fine with canned butter. Another unsought and unwanted food that was offered at our door was guinea fowl. I found it foul tasting!

On the other hand, we loved *kwokwo*, the dish that was only made in the cold season, with its nice balance of sweet and sour, like sweetened yogurt, and its pleasing texture akin to a milkshake or yogurt -- possibly a type of kefir.

Whatever leftovers we didn't want, and that weren't good enough to offer to the Koranic boys, were readily pounced on by the vultures that often assembled along the top of our compound walls.

IN SICKNESS & IN HEALTH

Rich had been out of town on a *tourné* for four days when my week-long bout of diarrhea turned into a fever and severe weakness. A young male friend with a bicycle offered to pedal me outside of town to the mission, where he handed me over to Millie and George, who put me to bed in their absent son's room. By sheer coincidence, the next day a Peace Corps vehicle with a Peace Corps doctor passed through Aguié. Guided to the mission by the townspeople, they plucked me up and took me with them to Zinder, where I could get serious medical care.

Here's a letter I sent home to my sister, Francie, from my sickbed in Zinder:

"God I'm tired! I've just woken up from a night's sleep and I'm still tired. I wish Rich was here. I feel so unmoored. Here I am in Zinder, not my home territory, and none of the vols here are special friends. I've got a place to sleep, but I need someone to bring me a hot drink or a good book. My connections here are weak. The vols who live in hub cities are called upon to be hosts a lot; they must learn to go on with their lives despite the invasion of their privacy.

"Yesterday was Hell! The Zinder hospital is medieval, and the unfriendly French doctor, a boor. I barely made it there. I felt so weak and he handed me a Petri dish and told me to produce some stool. My diarrhea has been going on for weeks. I figured it would be easy to produce something for examination.

"I found my way to an echoey tiled bathroom with two booths. The floor of the room was flooded. My sandals barely kept my feet dry. The place stunk of urine, hardly the antiseptic hospital bathroom of the USA! Each cubicle had one of those ceramic fixtures on the floor with places for two feet so that you squat over the hole. I was so weak I had to hold onto the walls when I squatted.

"Ironically, all I could finally produce for the brusque doctor was a tiny hard little turd that fell with a 'ping' into the Petri dish. Turning to go, the door of the booth wouldn't open. I fiddled with the latch, I put my weak-bodied weight against it and pushed as hard as I could. I could not have made myself crawl under the door in the sticky muck on the floor. I yelled and yelled, '*Au secours! Au secours!*' But no help came.

"Sick, my legs trembling from weakness, I finally was rescued by a nurse. Carrying my Petri dish with the tiny pellet in it, I returned to the doctor. I have to come back tomorrow for the results.

"The next day: Good news: It's just anemia. I've started taking iron pills. The doctor says I should eat more meat as well. I'll rest here for a couple of days before taking the bus back to Aguié. Hopefully my host will take this letter to the post office. City volunteers have motor scooters."

"Just anemia" was not the diagnosis on another occasion. As instructed in our Peace Corps training, every Sunday throughout our two-year stay in Niger, Rich and I took two chloroquine pills to prevent malaria. Maimouna and I administered bitter quinine to all the babies who came to the well-baby clinic. Malaria prevention was an important fact of life. Since I was religiously taking the prescribed dose of anti-malaria medication, when I started in with the fever and headache, I didn't immediately think of malaria. But the symptoms began to add up: fever, chills, weakness, headache .... then came vomiting and diarrhea...and finally, the wish to die.

I'd stagger out to the latrine and not know which end to apply to the hole. I've never been so sick and miserable. The Peace Corps had issued us a first aid kit complete with a Merck Manual for self-diagnosis. Especially in remote locations such as ours, there was no question of calling anyone for help; there was no phone or radio communication in town. One volunteer was medevacked to Germany for an attack of appendicitis, but short of that kind of life-threatening situation, we were on our own. Fortunately, Rich was not working out of town, and could help me. He delved into the Merck Manual and figured out what to give me. I can't remember what it was I took, but slowly, day by day, life became bearable again. I started keeping down chicken broth. Then rice. I lost weight and several weeks of work. It only happened once, but malaria can stay in one's system for many years.

Rich also became ill, but his illness was more insidious. He had off and on diarrhea, didn't we all? But his bouts continued, along with a slow loss of stamina. He lost so much weight that my big, athletic husband was scarily skinny. He finally got into a city for a meeting and got a battery of tests. His diagnosis was amoebic dysentery. Treatment was effective. Only his flood of new energy made him realize how drained he had been.

In Niger, I had a problem keeping my weight. When I left home, American girls were trying to emulate Twiggy, the super-thin British model. Slim was in. But standards of beauty were quite different in Niger. Plump Hausa women were considered the most beautiful. A heavy wife showed the world that her husband could provide well for her. If she had a gap in her front teeth as well, she was perfect. I, for one, could claim neither of these virtues. In Sarki Brazaki's eyes, I was skinny to the point of worry. He never failed to comment on my weight, peering at my collarbone to see if I had gained or lost weight.

Eventually, I gained some weight by developing a taste for fried *rogo* (manioc). I bought it from little Hadiza, who brought it on a tray on her head to the dispensary each morning. It was a starchy root rather like a potato, boiled, peeled and coated with peanut oil and hot pepper. Almost as addictive as French fries. Since the sarki worried so incessantly about my health, he took almost proprietary pleasure when he noticed my weight gain. Did he think my slenderness would reflect badly on his town? One time when I stopped to talk with him, he teased, "I can see you are content here! You're getting nice and plump. Maybe it's time for you and Ibrahim to start a family." He would not have understood that I took a little yellow pill every day to prevent just such an occurrence.

PERMISSION GRANTED

After almost a year of planning and politicking locally and in the capital, Connie and I, along with the doctor and the *militaire* teachers, succeeded in getting permission from the National Health Service to begin our counterpart training program. It was a strenuous course of physiology, history, math, French, geography and public health.

The French middle-school teachers volunteered their time after school to teach the six young women recruited in Tessaoua. There were no textbooks or handouts. Connie sat in on each training session and took complete notes that she would transcribe into detailed French. Then she handed off these transcriptions to the next bus driver going west, who then handed them out the bus window in Aguié to a child who brought them to me, so I had my next lessons to go over with Maimouna. This *advanced* communication system never failed!

So my work with Maimouna shifted to include lots of teaching and studying and less time at the dispensary. We still conducted well-baby clinics once a week, but our emphasis was on getting Maimouna to pass the test. Her pregnancy didn't slow her down a bit. She applied herself like a tiger.

As a side-benefit, I was able to watch on a daily basis as her belly got larger and tauter. I saw that her stamina lessened as the pregnancy progressed. I learned about back discomfort and was amazed at the growing size of her breasts. I took mental notes as I got my up-close, personal lesson in the realities of pregnancy, useful in my work and for my own mothering one day.

All our work proved successful. Maimouna was the only woman outside of Tessaoua to be included in the training. Come test time, her test scores were second best of the seven trainees. I was so proud of her!!!

MOTHERHOOD FOR MAIMOUNA

Rich and I had just returned from a few days away. Some other volunteers were visiting, and I was making them potato soup for dinner. Maimouna's friend Shaibou clapped at our doorway to let us know that Maimouna had had her baby that day.

"Oh no!" I cried. "I mean oh, yes! Take me to her." I threw on a scarf and we hurried towards Maimouna's parents' house. On our way through town Shaibou described a relatively quick, uncomplicated birth. Ducking into the warm hut, I saw Maimouna reclining on the bed, an adorable baby in her arms.

"Praise Allah," I said. "How are you? Is it a boy or a girl?"

"It's a boy," she said with a huge smile. "Konko is very happy!"

I didn't stay long, but promised to come back in the morning. When I returned to our house, I heard a lot of laughing and loud joking. I entered the house to see that the pressure cooker full of potato soup had erupted and spit soup all over the kitchen walls and ceiling. What a mess! I couldn't stop laughing. I was so happy and relieved that all had gone well with the birth.

RABIA AND THE DEADLY VIPER

One Sunday morning Rich had just won his second hand of cribbage on the patio and Issaka was finishing his chores when Talatu, a young girl I knew slightly, suddenly appeared, barely stopping to clap at the doorway of our compound. She was sweating, visibly distraught and out of breath. "Please, can you help? Rabia has been bitten by a viper. Come quickly! It's not far."

I grabbed the snakebite kit out of the fridge, tied on a headscarf, and followed her north through town and then out beyond the town limits. It was almost noon on a very hot day and the bush provided no shade. It was imperative to get to Rabia right away, since viper bites were often deadly. In my haste, all I wore were flip-flops, and trudging through sand was hard going. Since Talatu had said it wasn't far, I had assumed she meant in town, so I hadn't stopped to change into durable shoes or to bring a water bottle. Now that we were beyond town, I kept expecting that we'd come upon Rabia there in the bush. But not so!

As we walked, Talatu's yellow skirt and scarf bobbing along ahead of me, I thought about thirteen-year-old Rabia, who walked with a strange roll, and seemed extremely shy when she came into our compound. She was soon to be married to a much older man from another village. I knew such arrangements were common and went unquestioned. In some families, girl children were valued primarily for the dowry a groom's family gave to the bride's family on the wedding day. But I couldn't help thinking how Rabia's childhood was being cut off, and that she'd be going off to live apart from her family with people she didn't know, possibly as a second or third wife. Though I had learned to accept the culture as it was and tried not to compare it to home, it was impossible not to think back on my own long, leisurely childhood. When I was thirteen and in the eighth grade, my time was spent bike riding, having slumber parties, going to dance classes and looking forward to four years of high school and then college. I hadn't started menstruating, and my knowledge about sex was fragmented and confusing. It would have been unimaginable in my world to be thinking about marriage at that age! My heart ached for Rabia.

Soon both Talatu and I were winded. Sweat poured down our faces. I wondered where on earth we were going. As though she could read my thoughts, Talatu kept reassuring me, "Just a little bit farther. Just a little farther." It took about half an hour to reach a village of about forty huts. I was ushered into a small round hut, gratefully out of the glaring sun. There was Rabia, reclining on a grass mat, conscious, but looking ill and frightened. Next to her, on the ground, was the small, dead snake.

Tearfully she told me, "I was walking into the village and I didn't see the snake in time." There were two scarlet punctures just above her ankle. Someone had known enough to wrap a tourniquet just below her knee. As I murmured a few words of reassurance, a calabash of cloudy water was offered to me. Of course, I hadn't thought to bring quinine tablets with me. I thought to myself: "Die of thirst, or die of dysentery? Which will it be?" I chose to risk dysentery and drank gratefully.

Rabia's fiancée Mohammed had killed the snake. It was about ten inches long with a pear-shaped head and a zigzag pattern of black on brown down its back. The villagers knew snakes but I most definitely did not. Pawing through my Peace Corps snakebite kit, I read the instructions, then moved to assemble the syringe. But the needle pictured in the diagram was not in the kit!

The only solution I could think of was for one of us to rush back to town and get a needle from Somaila at the dispensary. Mohammed offered to give me a ride on his bicycle. I jumped on the seat, while he peddled standing up. I held tightly to his hips as we went slipping and sliding along the sandy track. I felt adrenaline pumping through my body as we flew through the bush, sure that Rabia's life was at stake, vitally aware of my responsibility. I cursed myself for not checking for the needle in the kit before leaving home.

"Thank God!" I said aloud, upon seeing that Somaila had not yet left for his afternoon break. He fitted the syringe with the proper needle and we were off again. The trip on the bike seemed to take forever.

Rabia was still conscious, though the wound looked more inflamed. Hands shaking, I was able to administer the shot. Then I rested with Rabia, soothing her, and myself, with reassurances. As she responded quickly to the treatment, I relaxed a little, relieved. I again drank cloudy water. When I sensed that she was stronger and decided that there was no more I could do, I directed her fiancée to let her rest, then ride her on his bike to the dispensary to see Somaila later in the day.

Crisis averted; I began to consider how to make my own way home. With so many tiny villages in the Canton of Aguié, all linked by a myriad of crisscrossing paths, it would be easy for me to get lost. Although I'd learned the landmarks on the route to our own farm, getting home from a village I'd never seen before was quite another matter. In the rush to help Rabia, I had paid little attention to our route, and the terrain was almost completely flat, with similar small scrub bushes, unfenced fields of millet or peanuts, and the occasional anthill rising like a miniature volcano. So when Talatu took my hand and said, "Miss Laouré, you should let me walk with you," I decided that I'd had enough excitement for one day. Getting lost in 105 degree heat was an adventure I could certainly forego. I only begged Aisha for a slower pace.

By now it was mid-afternoon and the heat pulsed in waves off the sand. My clothes clung and I was wildly thirsty, but grateful for the company. Aisha and I saw no birds, no lizards, no grasshoppers, and certainly no people. I thought, "Are we the only animals foolish enough to be out here in this heat?"

We passed a termite mound that was nearly a meter high. I'd come to think of these termites as industrious fungus farmers. Now I wondered what it would be like to be a termite with a predetermined role to enact. Wouldn't it be easier than having to decide what to be, whom to marry, whether to have chicken or bean soup for dinner or how to wear my hair? Wouldn't it be a relief to not have to make any decisions?

I realized at that moment how much pressure I put on myself to be "productive" here in Aguié. I expected to be doing meaningful work, but it wasn't always obvious what work would be of lasting value, or how to best use my time. I badgered myself about wasting time and being lazy. I vowed then and there, to try to trust myself and my choices more often. Maybe that would lift some of the heaviness I had been feeling about making our two years in Aguié truly count for something.

At last home, Talatu and I drank our fill of filtered water and I offered my thanks. Next, I stood under a shower bucket full of cold water. In the safety of home, under that cooling stream of soothing liquid, I put aside my brave adult act and wept. In the safety of Rich's arms, I shared my harrowing story. I wept for the danger Rabia had been in, and I wept with relief that she had lived. Then I collapsed and slept.

The next day before he swept the compound, Issaka told me that Rabia had survived and was doing well. And I was sure that the villagers had begun embellishing the story of Laouré, Rabia and the deadly viper, a legend in the making.

THE VILLAGE CHIEF'S WIVES

Though the *village* chief (not the sarki of the *canton* of Aguié) lived in
a different *quartier*, it was not unusual to run into him on the street. I knew he was grateful to me for helping his sister-in-law when she was in the middle of her difficult breech birth. With his high wide forehead, probing eyes and warm smile, he radiated friendliness, tempered by the slight hesitation born of the taboo against speaking with non-family women. He knew as an *anasara*, I could be considered an exception, but the habit of reserve was deep.

One day, he paused to speak to me. "Good morning," he said, touching first his forehead and then his heart. I did the same. "How is your house?" we asked one another, followed by the other traditional questions.

"And how is your husband, Ibrahim? Has he brought you home any rabbits for your cooking pot lately?" he added with a mischievous grin. I played along and agreed that Ibrahim was a good hunter.

He ended the conversation with a reminder that I hadn't been to visit his wives in some time. "They would like you to come see them again."

I knew this was true. Wives of wealthier men had a great deal less freedom than the wives of the majority of townsmen. Most husbands had to allow their women to go out to farm, the market and the well, among other chores that took them out in public. But wealthier men paid someone else to do these jobs so their wives had less strenuous but more isolated lives. So I assured the chief that I would visit them soon.

The following week I was in the Chief Aguié's neighborhood, giving the tailor the fabric I had chosen for my outfit for the upcoming Tabaski holiday. After discussing the style of bodice I had in mind and leaving the cloth with him, I continued on to the chief's house. Clap, clap, clap at their compound doorway. A guardian, a young man of the household, answered the door, greeted me and led me through a labyrinth much less elaborate than the entry into Sarki Brazaki's palace. We went through several dark anterooms and open-air horse enclosures to the open compound in which each of the wives had her own mud-brick hut, fire pit and millet-pounding area.

The head wife, Sa'a, came forward first chanting, *"La lé, la lé, Laouré."* Another wife, Halima, jumped up from the mat where she must have been having her hair braided. She was half-coiffed with braids along the crown, but still bushy from washing in the back. It pleased me that a braiding session was in progress. This would allow me to get in on normal living activities during my visit instead of just sitting and being treated as a special guest.

Amina, who had a sleeping child on her lap, greeted me without standing up. *"La lé, la lé, Laouré.* Welcome! Why haven't you visited us in so long? We're happy to see you again. Sit here next to me and have a *goro."* Because I had assisted at her baby's birth, she always greeted me with special warmth.

Sa'a settled back into the business of Halima's hairdo, while Amina stirred *foura* in a calabash, careful not to disturb the sleeping child in her lap. Halima was lying with her head on Sa'a's lap while Sa'a searched out lice nits and snapped them with her thumbnail. When that was done, she applied a small dab of sweetly-scented oil to the hank to be braided. Then she began braiding from the back of the neck up towards the crown, adding in tiny sections of hair along the path (a style the colonizing French adopted, thus we in the West call it a French-braid.) She attached each braid against the scalp all the way up, creating one tiny cornrow. Then she began the procedure again, forming a second braid, from the bottom, all the while chattering about her sister and brother-in-law's imminent arrival for the holiday.

The women were amused by the story of my trip to the market with Akwiya that morning. I couldn't tell if their amusement was in reaction to my imperfect Hausa, my almost child-like enthusiasm, or just the delight in having a new face in their midst to distract them from their ennui. I had found the pre-holiday market exciting, the buzz of energy as husbands purchased fabric for their wives' holiday outfits. Each length of cloth had to be long enough for a *zani*, blouse, head scarf and shawl/baby sling. I'd become accustomed to the bold patterns and color combinations on the cotton fabrics, but it still surprised me to see a portrait of President Hamani Diori printed on a woman's posterior as she walked down the street. In city markets I had even seen bolts of fabric patterned with the face of my beloved President Kennedy.

The men's grand boubous came in solid shades of pinks, pastel blues, light yellows and greens, and had massive swaths of embroidery in contrasting colors all around the neckline. The tailors made this embroidery by skillfully twisting and turning the fabric under the needle to form geometric designs.

Before a holiday, all the tailors set up shop in makeshift lean-tos on the streets next to their house walls, where they worked well into the nights, to get all the new clothing made in time for the festivities.

Akwiya offered to accompany me to the market to make sure I wasn't overcharged for the fabric for my holiday outfit. The selection of designs was much larger than at the regular Monday markets, and I had no trouble finding a print I loved. Akwiya did the negotiating and ended up settling on a price higher than what she would have paid, but less than I could have negotiated on my own. My fabric was more subdued than many— a batik design of light blue, dark blue and black. The ladies asked me which tailor I had taken my fabric to, and gave their stamp of approval since they used the same one.

As always, I was curious about how co-wives got along. I couldn't ask point blank, so I simply observed. I'm sure they had jealousies and complaints about one another, just as I had heard other village women mention on rare occasions, but these co-wives seemed very comfortable with one another, at least in my presence.

The conversation eventually touched on the day our friendships really began, some eleven months prior, back when I knew so little Hausa that I didn't understand that I was being summoned to help with Amina's difficult birth, right here in this very compound.

Since then a great deal of misplaced credit had been bestowed upon me for my minor role. The women still spoke of it with awe, as if my participation was something magical. I redirected the conversation to admiring Halima's braids, now finished. They joined in and then joked about braiding my very short, straight hair next!

When I sensed the women needed to get on with their daily routines, I got up and said my goodbyes, thanking them for their hospitality. Halima walked me out of the hut, where we encountered her husband entering the compound. He smiled broadly, and said, "Laouré, I see you did come visiting. Wonderful. I know my wives are happy today."

Halima complained to him, "Laouré didn't let us braid her hair. Maybe next visit." We all laughed. I walked back home with pleasant echoes of wifely chitchat still resounding in my ears.

TABASKI IN AGUIÉ

The next Tuesday I picked up my new outfit at the tailor's. Rich's preparations included buying fancy riding gear for Doikie—new saddle, blanket, reins and saddle cover. He would wear the light blue boubou he had bought from the chief.

We decided to stay in Aguié to participate in the Muslim High Holy Day of Tabaski instead of joining friends in Maradi again. By now we felt so much a part of the local community, and we wanted to fully participate in every way.

Also known as Eid al Adha, this "Feast of the Sacrifice" commemorates the Bible story in which God asked Isaac to sacrifice his son. Isaac, a man of faith, was willing to do so; and God, appreciating this, substituted a sheep instead. So, in Muslim Niger, every head-of-household kills a sheep on this day, and the family feasts.

Mazadou approved of our interest in honoring this tradition and agreed to guide us in the proper way to celebrate. Two days before the holiday he took us on horseback to a special livestock market in a nearby town, Gazawa, where the very best sheep could be bought. After Rich and I had picked out the fattest one we could find, the ceremonial price negotiation began. We sat on grass mats in a circle. I was the only woman. Most of the men had donned their market-day finery: their *grand-boubous* bunched up on the shoulders, over their pants and shirts.

The most richly dressed man in the circle poured millet beer from a clay jug into a small calabash bowl. He took a draught and passed the calabash to his left. Each man partook, and when the bowl came around to me, I dared not pass the milky liquid without taking a sip. Rich, giving me a tiny, reckless shrug, also drank. Again, the bowl was filled and around it went. As foreign as the experience was to me, these men had undoubtedly never shared a calabash of beer with a woman, at least not one who wasn't a prostitute.

After the calabash made numerous rounds, my bladder was nearly bursting. There were no latrines, so I did what had become normal. Just like any other local would do, I headed out to where the horses were tethered, and squatted behind a scraggly bush, my *zani* forming a natural privacy screen.

By the time I returned, the negotiation had been satisfactorily completed, so we thanked our hosts and led our excellent sheep back to Aguié behind our horses. I was in a beer haze, almost a doze, but it made no difference to my borrowed horse. Mazadou kept our nameless sheep for us with his own animals in the penned off area of their compound, where we could see it from our bedroom window.

On Tabaski eve, Rich and I accompanied Mazadou and the sheep through town once again, this time to the home of a *mallam* who was also a butcher.

Rich and I knew little more than our poor sheep did about what was about to happen. All animal killing was done by Muslim clerics in a ceremonial method facing Mecca. This one, dressed in traditional whites, sharpened his knife and began his prayers. Prayers and the bleating of the struggling sheep filled the air as its throat was slit and blood flowed out into the sand. I was squeamish until the animal stopped moving and was clearly dead. We stayed to watch the ritual blood-letting and gutting. Then the butcher cut another hole in the hide of the sheep and blew into it energetically. Repelled but fascinated, I watched the skin blow up like a balloon as it separated from the flesh, in preparation for flaying the animal. The skin was held in place by dry white membranes, and came off the carcass as easily as the peel off an orange, clean of any fluids.

When we left, having paid the prearranged price, we each carried a haunch of sheep, and I was busy distracting myself from recollecting our docile, excellent sheep who was no more.

Fortunately, Akwiya took charge of grilling our sheep along with theirs during the night. In the morning we all dressed in our elegant attire and took pieces of meat to the sarki's and other friends' homes as Tabaski gifts. In return, we received similar gifts, thus leaving everyone with more meat than would be healthy to eat. In the afternoon there was drumming and dancing, and a lovely hubbub of the voices of adults and children right in the square in front of our house.

Rich in his holiday finery

Rich looked regal in his beautiful new grand boubou and turban. He and our friend Jim Phillips joined the horse parade out to the parade grounds where the tribute was to be held.

Holiday horsemanship. Rich with friend
Jim Phillips on the way to parade grounds

Sarki and retinue on parade

The town emptied out and we formed a semi-circle around the field, accompanied by a group of drummers. There was much adjusting of horses to get them all in a line facing the Sarki. The drummers went silent and then signaled with one loud beat, the first five or six horses and riders urged their mounts forward as fast as they could go, pulling up, horses rearing, just short of the Sarki where they saluted him with a raised fist or sword. Again and again horsemen took their turns.

Rich and Doikie were lined up with the last group. At the drumbeat, Doikie made his way sideways to the right, instead of straight ahead. Rich pulled left on the reins at which point, Doikie thought he was meant to stop. Laughter broke out and crescendoed, accompanied by women's high-pitched ululations. So Rich was a lone horseman, eventually, saluting the Sarki who, with his henchmen, were duly impressed....after they finished laughing. Rich denied my accusation later, that he had done it on purpose to earn his growing reputation as *Sarkin Dariya*, King of Laughter.

Me in my holiday headdress

In the aftermath of the holiday, not surprisingly, many patients at the dispensary complained of *"chiwo 'n chicki,"* stomachache. Despite having no refrigeration, people had continued eating the meat for a couple of days, and some of the problems may have been from it having gone bad. But people might have had indigestion simply from eating so much meat, when their normal diet included only small amounts.

ESCAPADE ON HORSEBACK

Toward the end of our Peace Corps tour of duty our good friends, Jim and Dick moved to Aguié. They were in a PC well-digging program and we were excited about having some wells dug in Aguié Canton's villages.

Rich and I were also pleased to have comrades close at hand. Jim's girlfriend Jan, was a frequent visitor as well. On a hot Friday evening I made a big pot of goat stew. Jan brought French bread, a super treat since Aguié produced no bread of any kind. Jim and Dick brought beer and cognac. We were kicking off the weekend together. What a hoot!

After dinner we stayed up as long as the cognac lasted. When we ran out of our ice supply, we drank the liquor warm. We sat in a circle in the warmth of the moonless night, our fronts lit by the lantern glowing on the patio between us, Jim and Dick with their guitars hung from their necks. As we alternated between talking and music, the rest of the world disappeared in the black night. We shared our work frustrations, ate popcorn and listened to the fine finger-picking of Dick and Jim who were teaching each other various techniques. We sang a few old favorites like *Black is the Color of My True Love's Hair* and *The Long Black Veil*, the women an octave above the men, with me occasionally weaving in some harmonies. Rich improvised blues that further enumerated our complaints about in-country Peace Corps officers in his raspy tenor:

"We gotta shout. Shout so loud 'round here.

"We gotta shout. Shout so loud 'round here.

"They don't never hear us, and they never will, that's clear."

The next day the five of us planned to go horseback riding. Rich got up early to see if he could commandeer enough horses for all of us. Rich had asked Neino the day before whether it would be possible, and Neino had shrugged and said, "I'll see what I can do." I had watched his face as he said it, skeptical and amused. Going on a horseback ride just for the fun of it was a new concept to him, and for the whole town in fact, especially men and women riding together.

Morning was well on its way to becoming afternoon by the time five horses and saddles were assembled outside our compound door. It was hot, but not hot enough to dissuade us. I was curious what it had taken for Neino to get four horse owners to consent to this unusual request. The fifth horse was Doikie for me to ride. While I hadn't ridden him before, I did watch him sometimes out the bedroom window. To me he was majestic. He had a regal way of holding his head, as if to say, I am in charge here. His dappled grey and white flanks were full-muscled. I was happy to get the chance to ride him.

The horse owners, dressed in their long robes, were standing with their mounts, looking skeptical. Without a doubt these horses were their most valuable possessions. To loan them out to strangers must have taken some stiff persuasion on one side and courage on the other. My guess was that the Sarki got into the process at some point, twisting arms.

Pairing the riders and horses, checking and tightening the cinches, assisting us with mounting and adjusting the stirrups was a group effort, all the horse owners debating which rider should go on which horse. Many last-minute adjustments were made to our equipment. The horse Rich was assigned resisted the cinch tightening by pushing out his abdomen. The men agreed that that horse had *wayo*, a frequently used word meaning slyness or cunning.

Rich led the way at a slow pace through town, while villagers gawked, some bantering with Rich about his posse: "How many days do you plan to be gone?" and "Be sure to watch out for lions!"

Our horses' hooves kicked up a low-lying cloud of dust as we trotted north of town, passing our farm and then beyond where the village farms ended and the flat, sandy brush land began. Seeing the familiar terrain from a height was intriguing. I enjoyed the sense of being borne along, seeing but not touching the earth. The sounds of the horses clopping and saddles creaking, and the holiday feeling of our escapade, shifted me into a state of exhilaration. Even the horses seemed to relax and enjoy the outing.

As we rode, Rich regaled us with stories of his on-the-job misadventures riding Doikie. There was the time he had stayed up late into the night drinking millet beer with the village men at Dun Shiro, a town on his circuit. "I got up the next morning and was still so drunk I fell off Doikie as soon as I mounted him. But the worst time was on the way home from the town of Buba Ane. I was drunk when I left town and it was a long way home. That ride was the most agonizing ordeal I've ever been through. I got lost and rode way out of my way. It took hours and I got sores on my backside. At one juncture, I got down to rest and Doikie took off toward town without me, leaving me to walk the rest of the way. Doikie beat me back to the village by several hours. But I'm completely comfortable on Doikie nowadays. I sometimes ride fifteen kilometers to a village and then run a meeting."

Well, I couldn't imagine doing that, I thought, as I became aware of a growing ache in my nether region. The saddle was just leather stretched over wood. Not enough padding for me! Nor apparently for some of the others. Though we'd been out only a short time, we decided to turn back in the direction of town. Jim and Rich started trotting faster and then galloping. The horses were happy to oblige, home and food being in that direction. Just before they rode out of sight, I saw Rich begin slipping sideways off his horse, saddle and all. He was dragged, yelling obscenities, until he finally shook loose of the stirrups, leaving the horse to gallop off toward town. Rich was left, a crumpled heap, in the sand, fortunately unharmed.

Several minutes later we heard people laughing and calling out to one another. When the villagers saw the riderless horse, they instantly guessed the story and passed it along. No one would enjoy their reaction more than Rich, who relished his growing reputation for being the clown, their very own *Sarkin Dariya*. He walked with us the rest of the way back to the village, enjoying our own ribbing and anticipating the kidding he'd get from the villagers.

Entering town, a wise guy called out to Rich, "It was nice of you to let your horse go home ahead of you to get his lunch!"

Another said, "I see you prefer to travel on two legs instead of four." We enjoyed the international language of laughter, and happily relinquished the four borrowed horses to their relieved owners and took Doikie home.

THE LONG GOODBYE

A journal entry from April 9, 1969:

"The things I imagine I will miss the most when we leave Aguié will be the smells and sounds. The village literally pulses with rhythms from early morning's cock crows to the last of the five Muezzin's calls to prayer from the mosque tower kitty-corner from our house.

Cooking fires are being freshened; the comforting smell of burning wood, followed by the stomach-awakening scent of millet cakes being fried in peanut oil next door.

Our May termination date became more real to us when Rich went into the capital to take his GRE (Graduate Record Exam) and began mailing applications for graduate school. In the evenings we spread maps of Europe on the kitchen table as we began planning our route, deciding if and when to rent a car and wondering if we'd have enough money to do the traveling we were dreaming of. Letters flew back and forth to and from my parents, whom we happily anticipated meeting in Rome. It would be their first trip to Europe too.

As the day of our departure neared, it was clear that our villager friends didn't want us to leave. But since we were actually leaving, they wanted to be remembered when it came time to give away our belongings. The Peace Corps would come collect the stove, fridge, book-locker and any major furniture, but other items such as bed pillows, stuffed footstool poufs, buckets, kitchen utensils, bowls and blankets went to the giveaway pile, including clothes that we didn't want to lug through Europe on our way home. We did get to send a trunk home full of artifacts and Rich's *daba* which he treasured.

There was no delicacy in the matter of requests. Our neighbors suddenly resembled the vultures that habitually sat on our compound wall waiting for our scraps. Despite my having gotten used to Hausa ways, their bald, almost demanding, sense of entitlement felt impertinent. I had to set aside my hurt feelings and realize, once again, that cultural differences, not insensitivity or rudeness, were at play here. I reminded myself of our friends' countless acts of generosity towards us and their system of reciprocity, wherein we might well be considered in their debt.

I assured Issaka that he could have our big wash basin and shower bucket. I gave Maimouna my pretty watch, which I hadn't been wearing, as well as lots of clothes, toiletries and kitchen knives. We distributed the tiny cars and trucks and playing cards to the kids, who ran out of our compound in delight that they could at last take them home. The horse saddle went to Neino in thanks for keeping Doikie in his compound. Doikie himself was returned to the Sarki, who was pleased when I gave each of his wives a length of cloth for a new outfit. Tal Hadji and other favorite friends all got something of mine: scarves, earrings, sandals, bowls. And Akwiya agreed that Kitty could join their family.

We were notified by the Peace Corps the date we'd be picked up. As the countdown for our departure began, there was a palpable tension in our neighborhood. People stayed close to home, not wanting to miss our departure. Many visitors came and went, then checked in on us again the next day. The continual repetition of goodbyes was emotionally draining. With our home disassembled and our thoughts leaping ahead to our travels, our reunions with family and friends, and what the future would hold for us back in the U.S., much as we'd miss everyone here, we were more than ready to go.

So we were relieved to finally see the Land Rover pull up in front of Sarki Brazaki's palace, two days late. After so much waiting, suddenly everything was action. The Peace Corps chauffeur greeted the Sarki while the neighbor men helped Rich load our bags into the back of the vehicle. A crowd grew, as villagers came to see us off and wish us Allah's protection. Maimouna stayed close by my side as I hugged Tal Hadji, Muman, Oumarou and my little namesake Ta Laouré, as well as Tal's dear friend and Hadiza's daughter Bulki; then more hugs for Akwiya, Amina, Hadiza, Zeinabou, and Aisha. I shared intense handshakes with Issaka, Mazadou, Neino, Somaila, Abarshi, the village chief, and many more friends and neighbors who encircled the vehicle.

Sarki Brazaki and his entourage made their way to us slowly. I felt Maimouna's familiar hand now squeezing mine until it hurt. She knew that once we'd said goodbye to him, we'd really be done. Sarki Brazaki's wishes for us were brief but heartfelt. With promises to return someday, we climbed up and took our places in the back seat. Through the open window I held both of Maimouna's hands as the car started slowly to roll. She wouldn't let go. Tears streaming from her eyes, she grabbed the window frame, trying to ride along on the outside of the car, wailing.

I was desolate at the likelihood that I would never see her again. As her friends rushed to forcefully peel her off the car, she protested with a fury I wouldn't have imagined her capable of. My own pain was expressed in her flailing arms as she frantically struggled to be free so she could run after us. Then the dust rose up between us and we were gone.

All through town out to the National Route, whole families came out to wave us on our way. What a blessing to have been a part of this community for these two years. These dear villagers befriended us, protected us, educated us, laughed with us, cried with us, and forgave us again and again for our ignorance of their customs.

Rich held me as the tears I had been holding back overflowed.

ROUGH RE-ENTRY

After a whirlwind trip through eight European countries, Rich and I returned home to California just in time to watch the Apollo 11 astronauts walk on the moon. We felt we had landed on a different planet, so much had changed.

It became clear that we had changed as well. When some people heard we'd been living in a tribal village for two years, they couldn't imagine how we survived. Their only reference to anything African was shaped by Hollywood and cartoons' ridiculous misrepresentations.

While many admired what we'd done, none could actually imagine it anymore than we could when we first arrived in Niger. But the experience gave us a clarity of vision about what was important. Though by Western standards, most of the people we lived with were poor, with no refrigeration, electricity, running water, toilets or stores, they had a pretty good quality of life. Children were completely safe throughout the village. There appeared to be little mental illness, hunger, strife, homelessness or unemployment, and the villagers had a benevolent leader and systems in place to help in times of drought.

It would be myopic of me to ignore the harsh facts of village life. Drinking water was unsafe, health care was rudimentary, and people died from easily curable diseases. Drought came hard and long, women had few rights, and girls, even bright ones like Tal Hadji, were rarely allowed to attend school. Boys had more opportunities, but were still limited in many ways. But when I think of how extended families took care of one another and how the village was almost completely self-sustaining, their ways feel more life-affirming than our Western ideas focused on personal success. Living among them gave me a life-long perspective on the American dream, on our ethnocentric culture, what makes true community, and what is really necessary for a good quality of life. I felt that my two years spent in my adopted village taught me the most valuable components of happiness.

The summer following our return Rich and I were hired by the American Friends Service Committee to coordinate a project for Friends' teens, assisting farmworkers in building homes in a cooperative housing project in California's Central Valley. For two years we attended UC Davis, where I worked on my BA in English and Rich on a master's degree in African Studies/International Relations.

Every chance we had, we spent weekends in Berkeley with other returned Niger vols. We were all suffering the difficulties of reentry into a culture that had changed a great deal while we were gone. We had missed the Summer of Love, the assassinations of Robert Kennedy and Martin Luther King Jr., and hundreds of protests against the Vietnam War. People like us were burning draft cards and bras. Disillusioned youth haled the coming of the Age of Aquarius, forming communes and clothing themselves in Salvation Army cast-offs (when they clothed themselves at all), while the sexual, environmental, and life-style revolutions took off with new soundtracks to match.

We felt left behind. We circled the wagons, forming a small commune in Occidental, CA, a mecca for communes at the time. All of us but one wife, were ex-Niger vols.

After only one year, we began to produce families and peel off into discrete homes of our own, still coming together every Sunday for many years for volleyball and pot-luck.

Rich and I both worked and we produced two great kids, Zack and Reina. Gone were the days when I had to stay on the pill in Niger and make do with holding other women's babies. Now I was able to experience all the joys of motherhood myself.

We bought a home in Forestville, and I joined a women's group and did a lot of self-exploration. Rich and I had always had our separate interests but at some point we began to realize that we had drifted too far apart to sustain a healthy marriage. We sought counseling, and eventually divorced, making sure that our children had two safe and welcoming homes.

For the first few years after we returned home from Niger, I had corresponded with Maimouna, but in the early 1970's a severe drought in Niger disbursed the villagers and we lost touch. By then I had become engrossed in my life as a mother and a demanding career as a political aide. When I did think about writing letters again, I feared that many of my friends would no longer be in Aguié, or worse yet, had died. After becoming scattered by the drought, had they ever returned to the village? Even without drought, life in Niger was short—life expectancy was under forty years. I sadly gave up hope of ever hearing from Maimouna again.

Even with all that was on my plate, I managed to make the most of my single status in a period of greatly expanded freedom for women in the U.S., so different from the lives of my friends in Aguié. No one in my community thought of me as a prostitute because I didn't return to my parents after our divorce. I was free to date and have meaningful relationships outside of marriage. And I did.

About eight years later I reconnected with the son of old family friends, a talented musician and swing band leader, Bryan Gould. I confess I had a crush on him in my teens, but he was too old for me then. Now we were both adults and age no longer a barrier.

In 1989, I came down with Erythema Nodosum, an autoimmune illness, which had all kinds of painful symptoms and treatments off and on over twelve years. Bryan was supportive from the beginning to the end. We married in June of 1991, and I moved to his lovingly restored San Rafael Victorian

TO WHOM IT MAY CONCERN - 1994

In a dream so vivid it felt real, Maimouna came to our house in San Rafael. When I woke, I quickly jotted down my experience:

> *She bends again, now taking her colorful cotton scarves out of her suitcase on my bed, moves methodically to my drawer, and stacks them neatly beside my scarves. Her stack a swirl of primary colors, mine pastels, grays and browns. She's thicker, more confident, and gray around the temples, all things we have in common now. She says with irritation, "I've been buying grigri magic from every medicine man who comes through Aguié for many years now, and still you do not write or come back to us. So I decided to take matters into my own hands." The years dissolve as we hold each other's forearms and smile into each other's faces, transported.*

Fully awake, I quietly relished the miraculous presence of the woman I had known when she was a teenager. How did I recreate her twenty-five years older? So very realistic was the dream! Was it possible that she was transmitting herself to me somehow?

The realism of the dream dwelt in me for weeks. Her phantom visit made me believe that Maimouna might still be alive. I wondered how could I get a letter through to her? Where would I send it? Who would open such a letter if she no longer lived there? I decided to write a cover letter, "To Whom It May Concern," explaining who I was and that I had lived in Aguié for two years, twenty-seven years before. I addressed it to the Postmaster of Aguié, even though I wasn't sure if one existed. In the letter I included the names of my closest village friends from the late 60's. I made ten copies of a second letter, which I asked the postmaster to give to Maimouna and any or all of the friends I had listed. In that letter I described my life since I left in 1969. On the backs I copied photos of Rich and me then and now, and our respective families. Both letters were in French. Of the names on the list, only Maimouna would be able to read French, but others receiving a copy could easily get someone to translate for them.

Three weeks later, my husband was startled by my screams as I ran from the mailbox into the house. "Bryan, Bryan. I got a reply from Aguié! The postmaster wrote back and says that Maimouna is still alive and living there! I am so relieved and excited! He distributed the letters and, get this, he sent a photo of himself and proposed that I visit and bring my 'very pretty daughter' to marry!"

Laughing, Bryan said, "We'll have to give Reina a call and see what she says."

In a few more days another envelope arrived with Maimouna's name and address in the upper left-hand corner. She wrote, "I am so happy to get your letter. The postmaster gave it to me on September 16th at 4:20. I cried when I saw it was from you. I looked at the photographs and read it over and over again all night.

"You had that dream because I have been thinking about you. One night a couple of months ago, I sat looking into the embers of the fire thinking of you late into the night. I have no doubt that that was the night you had your dream."

She went on to share that she also had been divorced and remarried, and had ten children. Her parents had both passed away and she had grandchildren. I sat down on the spot and wrote her back in my less-than-perfect French.

After that we began a frequent correspondence. With one letter I sent a disposable camera. Soon it yielded a return letter, and when I developed the film, what a treat it was to see photos of her and her family, and of her work at the dispensary. I was gratified to learn that as a result of our training together, she had gained a paid position at the medical center, probably the only village woman with a monthly salary. My vision for her had come true!

The more we wrote, the more I remembered, and the more I yearned to see Maimouna and the village again. I began to realize how many things I'd loved about Niger. In my writing group, stories of life in Aguié began bubbling up more and more frequently.

Synchronistically, Maimouna's letters began to include invitations to come for a visit. What began as an improbable dream slowly began to take shape as a serious possibility. I took a deep breath and talked to Bryan about it. "Do you think I'm nuts to be risking my health on such an ambitious adventure?"

He surprised me by saying, "Nuts? I haven't seen you this excited about anything in a long time. This fits rather neatly with how healthy you've been for months now. Think of how much you've had to put on hold these twelve years. I'd go for it."

His encouragement pushed my dream toward reality. As Bryan pointed out, bad health could return again whether I went to Africa or not. Why not go ahead and hatch a plan? If my health took a turn for the worse, I could cancel. Had I only one last trip in my life, this was the one I would choose.

MY DREAM COME TRUE

My reverie ended when the plane started to descend into Niamey. Disembarking, I noticed that the small airport had not changed much, but the experience was different, mostly because I had no one from the Peace Corps to guide me through all the confusing lines, customs and baggage claim. Then there was the matter of getting into the capital. A taxi driver quoted a price in the thousands which sounded like a fortune. What a rip off! I turned him away. But the joke was on me; it turned out that the value was only about $4.00 USD.

It was nearly midnight and there were no taxis left. I began to panic, imagining having to sleep on the floor at the airport. Then, behind me, I heard a man speaking English with a southern drawl. I whirled around and practically grabbed him. Yes, he had space in his car, and yes, they'd be happy to take me into the city.

My savior, it turned out, was a geologist for a Texas prospecting company. He was quite familiar with Niamey and knew that Peace Corps headquarters was on the road from the airport. When we got there, against all odds, there was a Peace Corps vehicle about to take a volunteer over to the hostel. I switched cars, conveying my gratitude in both directions, and off we went. At that time of night the city was quiet. I recognized the entrance to the National Museum, though nothing else, but there were familiar things I was excited to see: street-corner vendors with small tables selling cigarettes and candy, mud-brick walls lining both sides of most of the residential streets, Neem trees here and there, and badly rutted unpaved streets as we drove farther from the center of town.

FINDING MY FOOTING

The young volunteer and I were let off on a corner in front of a wide, solid steel gate. A sleepy guardian let us in and we quietly found vacant mosquito-netted beds. Mine was a top bunk with no ladder up and an uncomfortably thin foam mattress.

When I woke up it was still dark. The shower had overflowed onto the tile floor and I had to remind myself that long ago, when I had served, we had only outdoor showers at the hostel, so this was at least an improvement. I went into the kitchen, heated some water, and sat until light, sipping tea and writing home to Bryan.

Gradually, volunteers emerged from their rooms. I met Jim, Sarah and Ted, more young volunteers. They were curious about who I was and why I was there.

"You were a volunteer in Aguié thirty years ago?" Sarah asked, sounding awed.

"Yes, do you know if there are any volunteers in Aguié now?"

"I don't think so, but my village is not that far east. I'm just north of Dogondoutchi."

Jim and Ted seemed equally impressed that I had come back, a fifty-two year old woman, alone, after thirty years. Jim asked if I'd kept in touch with friends in the village all this time, and I told them the story of my reconnection with Maimouna.

After learning where they were posted and why they were in town, I asked them my pressing questions: how to get to the *marché*, how much to pay for a taxi and how to change money. Taking note of their helpful answers in my notebook, I dressed, donned a headscarf, dark glasses and shoulder bag and crossed the spacious courtyard to the large metal gate. The guardian, whose quarters were just inside the hostel compound, appeared and opened the gate to let me out.

Another hostel worker sat outside the gate with his friends. His job was to screen people who wanted to come and go through the gate.

The mingled scents of decomposing fruits and vegetables, mixed with sewage and gas fumes -- a smell I vividly remembered -- made me giddy and a little dizzy. I stood on the corner with no map, only the vaguest notion of which direction to go to reach the center of town. I suddenly realized that the *marché* was where I wanted to go.

Standing there, feeling awkward and foolish, I felt stunned with jet lag, culture shock and brain fog left over from my long illness, all tossed together in my sleep-deprived body. I stayed rooted outside the gate, watching the parade of taxis and motorbikes magically avoiding potholes, people and animals. Women passed, some with burdens balanced on their heads, others on their way to market or work, walking their kids to school—all of them off to places I would never see, each of them carrying with her a story I wanted to know. Those who noticed me must have wondered, just as intently, who I was and why I was standing there, planted like a tree.

The gatekeeper, lank and slouched, took notice of me, got up, came over and introduced himself as Ali. He offered me a seat on the only chair, which I took, and then squatted beside me to sit on a mud-brick block. This was my opportunity to get my Hausa into action, and though he spoke French well, I kept bringing the conversation back to Hausa.

He obliged with, "*Ina wuri gidan ki?*" (Where are you from?) and other simple phrases I deciphered fairly well and was able to answer. I was grateful for my having taken the time before making this journey to brush up on my rusty Hausa with the help of a tutor, Nigerian born Yusuf Muhammad. I had been discouraged by how much I'd forgotten and how slowly I was relearning it. Now, I kept pausing in our conversation to jot down words and phrases that Ali spoke. He found this amusing.

I was just about to launch myself into the broader city when a lively young woman stopped by to flirt with him. She had adorable dimples that deepened when she smiled. Her flirting was tongue-in-cheek, her posture bold. When I learned her name was Zeinabou, like my favorite prostitute friend in Aguié, it seemed like a welcoming sign. We chatted in Hausa and before long, she had agreed to be my guide through the *marché*.

There in the open market, I came near tears at my first bite of *rogo*, still as delicious as I remembered, the boiled manioc perfectly coated with peanut oil and hot pepper. With the bustle of people around me, the vivid colors of the vendors, the smoke in my nostrils, and the taste and consistency of warm *rogo* in my mouth, I knew in every molecule of my body that I was finally here, in my beloved Niger. I shared the bounty with Zeinabou as laughter flowed over the tears that dropped freely.

I felt such relief that after all these years of memory keeping, and all this country had meant in my life, Niger was still the Niger I knew. Though the world had changed a lot in thirty years, the vital parts of Niger were still very much the same. I was reconnecting with an important chapter in my life, one so unlike the others: attending school, raising kids, being a single mom with a career, dating, courting anew and marrying. So dissimilar was it that Niger had become like a mirage, an insubstantial yet persistent dream world. Time collapsed for an instant, and I was suddenly the twenty-one-year-old Lauoré merging with the fifty-three-year-old Laurie, and I was thrilled with the sensation.

The huge market -- divided into sections for clothes, leather goods, produce, meat, tools, horse paraphernalia and so much more -- was now housed beneath a concrete structure resembling a city parking garage. I imagine the vendors paid more for a spot inside, but many of the booths, shaded by reed roofs, spilled out in every direction and continued on down adjacent streets, full to bursting with merchandise. Those selling cassettes had sample music blaring from boom boxes. I relished the more familiar sights and smells of the produce stalls, with their shallow baskets domed high with dried leaves, garlic cloves and dried tomatoes. The fabric stalls that still draped boldly designed prints of purple and orange; yellow, green and red, made me feel I was truly in-country. I wondered if I still had my negotiating skills, and tested them when I bought a scarf. It helped to have Zeinabou there. She didn't speak French, but was patient with my Hausa and was quick to laugh at almost anything, which fostered an easy intimacy. She didn't seem to mind stopping with me to try to identify spices or incense or taste some candy I'd forgotten about. She seemed amused by my excitement about what for her were mundane things. When the sun got too hot, we retreated to the cooler aisles under the concrete roof. With Zeinabou at the tiller, I could lose myself in the sensory feast and not worry about how to find my way back out and home again.

The incense vendor was burning a knobby black root producing a dark cavernous aroma I associated with winter days sitting with village women in their huts shelling peanuts together. When I asked the vendor about one particular aromatic plant, Zeinabou translated the answer into slow, simple Hausa: "This plant grows wild. I find it in the low-lying areas where water sits after the rains."

We encountered a woman selling squash stew, and the smell reminded me of dusk in Aguié. Next to her was what looked to me like a living pillow of scrawny brown chickens, feet trussed, piled together for sale, the birds motionless save for the quick shuttering of the cloudy membrane over their beady black eyes.

Zeinabou and I drank cool bottles of Fanta orange soda; the sticky, sweet stuff was just as awful as it had always been, but what a treat! We chewed on *kilishee*, a very spicy-hot beef jerky, and ate small green guavas with silky pink flesh, spitting the seeds onto the ground.

Eventually, we started the dusty trek home. I was impressed with how the cars and taxis, while staying roughly on two sides of the road, wove in and out of one another so closely that they appeared to touch in a carefully choreographed ballet.

Very near the hostel, Zeinabou pointed out a doorway and said, "This is my house. Would you like to come in?"

I thanked her, curious to see behind the mud walls. It was a compound very like those I'd known, with the living space outside and a three-stoned cook fire smoldering near a collection of pots and bowls. "This is my mother and my daughters," she said. The girls were identical twins! Round-eyed and shy, they stayed close to their grandmother, clearly not used to being so near to a white-skinned person. That too was a familiar experience I'd almost forgotten.

"They are darling," I said, shaking her mother's hand, using as many of the traditional greetings as I could remember.

Zeinabou's twins

We didn't stay long, but as we walked the short block between her house and the hostel, Zeinabou asked me if I'd take a picture of her girls, which I happily agreed to do the following morning. She tried to refuse the money I gave her for her services that day, but I closed her hand over the bills and wouldn't let her open it. She had done me an immeasurable service by accompanying me.

I had allowed for a few days in Niamey to recover from jetlag, put my Hausa into practice and get acclimated to being in Niger once again, but I'm not sure I anticipated the difficulties the trip would present. My laments found their way into my journal:

"I'm so unsure of myself in so many arenas at once: my Hausa is weak and so is my French. Slipping back and forth between them is a sloppy matter. My grasp on the monetary system is sketchy. My sense of direction is terrible under normal circumstances, but far worse here in this French-designed city, with roads radiating out like spokes from traffic circles. No easy squares or rectangles and to top it off, there are no street name signs. I'm discouraged time and again when I struggle for a Hausa word I used to know so well!"

While cars, bikes and occasionally camels shared the roads, the sidewalks were often filled with small tables of street vendors selling Chicklets, matches, cigarettes, dates or prepared foods. I wove through crowds, sometimes stepping into the street to allow passage for a woman with a wide load on her head, paying careful attention to the traffic, which flowed like a river. I noticed how few beggars there were now, and I hadn't seen any lepers.

At the hostel, the volunteers, hungry for home, sat around watching videos. There wasn't even a radio at the hostel to listen to what the BBC or Voice of America had to report about President Clinton's impeachment trial that had just begun. I had promised in an email to stop at the Peace Corps Office to meet the country director. It was a disappointment to find her too busy to sit down and talk with me, as I had imagined we'd do.

While in the capital, I took care of practical matters like money exchange and shopping for necessities. I was relieved to find a portable, single-burner propane camp stove with canisters. Although I didn't know what my accommodations might be in the village, I imagined I would appreciate being able to at least make my own tea.

I visited the National Museum and the zoo, all the while scouting out good places to eat. I especially liked one street vendor who put a scrambled egg into a light and tasty baguette. It reminded me of that first strange egg and baguette meal we had on arrival thirty years ago. But this one was even more delicious. Ah, simple pleasures!

A gift shop at the National Museum featured work by many artisans in silver, leather, wood, fabric, basketry and calabash. I was interested to learn that the country had an artisans' village somewhere north of the capital, where all the artisans were physically challenged. I imagined this was one of the reasons I had seen far fewer lepers and paraplegics in the streets.

On my first attempt to buy a bus ticket to Aguié, I made my way to the bus station by foot, enjoying the long walk within view of the Niger River. Men and women were bent at their work washing bright clothes in the river and draping them on bushes and boats to dry. Men fished from the riverbank and silent boats filled with cargo, their boatmen standing in the rear, plied the murky water.

I arrived at the bus station only to find it was closed on Sunday. So I went back again on Monday, but the electricity was down, and they couldn't issue tickets without it. On Tuesday morning, much less pleased with the walk, I was told, "Just wait. The man will be right back. Right back." He finally showed up an hour later, self-importantly unlocking the office and taking his time as he took my money and, at last, produced my ticket. He insisted that I needed to bring my bags to be loaded the night before leaving. I wouldn't agree to that. He then stressed that I would need to get there by 6:30 in the morning to load my baggage.

While planning my trip, I had been visiting my son, Zack, in New York, when I met one of his friends, Mike Tauber, a photographer. We met at a gallery show of his work, much of it from his travels. I told him I was returning to Niger and was hoping to write a memoir all about my experiences. He became enthused about my impending trip musing that it would be great to go too to chronicle my return to Aguié. This had all hatched and he now found his way to the PC hostel. The director wouldn't allow him to stay there; still, we enjoyed a leisurely meal together and compared our intended itineraries to make sure they would overlap some time in Aguié.

Falling asleep, I realized that even just four days in Niamey was too long when I yearned to be off to Aguié. My bus would leave in the morning.

JOURNEY BACK TO AGUIÉ

After the taxi left me at the Niamey bus station just before dawn, I sat down on a huge gunny sack of onions, reminded of all the times Rich and I had sat beside the road outside of Aguié, hoping for a ride.

Now I wondered why I had to rush to be here at 6:30. I was completely alone, and there was no bus in sight. Knowing that exasperation would do nothing to forward my wish to reach the village before dark, I thought ahead to the end of the day. I had written Maimouna to let her know I'd be arriving on the Wednesday bus. Now I imagined our imminent reunion. I pictured her at the road waiting for me, how we'd hug and cry, laughing through our tears. I wondered if some of her family members would be with her. Would we mix Hausa and French, confusing ourselves and each other? Whatever happened it would be joyful, and I couldn't wait!

I had also written that I would like to rent a place of my own during my stay. Would she have found a place, or would I have to stay in her compound? I didn't want to inconvenience Maimouna, but more than that, I knew I'd need more privacy and some degree of autonomy that would be hard to achieve in someone else's home.

I wondered if I would recognize the town or would the changes be too great? As I readjusted my perch on the lumpy sack, these questions repeated in an endless loop as my excitement grew in anticipation of seeing my friend.

Other passengers arrived, and when the sun was just high enough to begin to feel hot, the bus roared into the station. Workers started loading the top of the old Mercedes bus with our luggage, bundles and bags, including the onion sack, arranging them tightly from front to back. Like industrious spiders, they spun a net of ropes up and across, over and back, tying the whole load down, weaving luggage and produce together.

The passengers were of all ages, shapes and sizes; all black except one older white woman whose Western-style clothes were made out of African fabrics. Her head was respectfully covered and she used African baskets as her luggage. She was clearly a long-termer in Niger, for she bantered fluently with a few other passengers in African French.

As we all stood waiting to board, vendors with candy, fruit, bread and nuts went methodically up the line, quietly but insistently pressing for a sale from each passenger, then moving on to the next.

As I settled into a window seat close to the front of the bus, a woman with twin babies settled with an older woman in the seat behind mine. She was young, with a smooth complexion with almond-shaped black lines of her cicatrices that curved from her earlobe to the corner of her mouth, one on each cheek marking her as from the Maradi region. She was dressed in a crisp green and yellow top, *zani* and scarf. Her babies were warmly bundled in matching sweaters even though it was already getting hot on the bus. The driver and ticket taker left the motor running and disappeared into the office for a last cup of tea.

Finally, at about eight o'clock, the bus began its maze-like crawl through the narrow streets now bustling with walkers, bikers, taxis and school kids. A long-armed woman balanced a basket of small green mangoes on her head, her one raised elbow angled forward so as not to bump other pedestrians. High life blared from an immense boom box on the shoulder of a young man whose traditional white cap was cocked rakishly to one side. A shopkeeper swept the sidewalk in front of his store. A turbaned Tuareg man in dark indigo clothing, his head and face swathed except for his eyes, led a camel in the direction of the daily market.

At last we reached the open road. I'd been told that now the National Route was paved most of the way to the eastern border, instead of just the first hundred kilometers of road as it had in the 1960's. I was grateful not to have to ride the old washboard again.

I started conversing with the young mother and, much to my delight, she handed me one of her two-month-old twin girls to hold. The baby slept deeply in my arms for a long time. How odd to have met two sets of twin baby girls within a few days!

Through my window I was horrified to see that the countryside was scattered with little flappings of ugly plastic on the ground, stuck to grass, even hanging in trees. I hoped that as we got away from the capital the phenomenon would diminish. It didn't. In the 60's I had been fascinated by the way vendors used just the necessary size of paper to wrap, fold and twist up a measure of sugar, herb or meat. Now, as at home, unfortunately everything went into plastic sacks, but unlike home where there were at least trash cans, in Niger the plastic ended up all over the landscape, whisked here and there by the wind.

Despite that blight, this was still the Niger I remembered: flat and dusty, few trees and a glimpse now and then of a small village with its clusters of conical grass roofs. Out my window I saw men and women walking along the footpath that paralleled the road, carrying bundles or jugs or leading a scrawny goat; the long, hot trek ahead of them accepted without question. That was an assumption, I had to admit, but that was my sense of the hard-working, devout and good-natured people I lived amongst for two years. Their persistence and courage in the face of harsh weather, frequent drought, inadequate health care and a labor-intensive existence, taught me to admire them. And to be grateful for things in my upbringing that I had always taken for granted.

The monotony of the bus's movement, the wide empty spaces, the flat countryside, all conspired to lull me into an almost hypnotic trance, cradling me in the dark, warm interior of the bus.

Stopping in Dogondoutchi, the bus was surrounded by vendors of manioc snacks and roasted-salted peanuts, guavas, raising their trays up to the windows so we could see them. We were allowed to get out and stretch or pray. We'd been en route for about four hours and were about one third of the way to Aguié. At this rate it would be dark before we got there.

Back on board, I felt myself leaning toward the front of the bus, as one might lean on a bobsled, pushing the driver to go faster. Night fell quickly. We barreled through the darkness for many hours more before the bus driver stopped.

He called back to me that this was my stop. I said goodbye to the infant twins and their family and made my way down the aisle. A kindly male voice in excellent French, asked, "Are you sure this is where you want to get off?"

"Yes, I'm sure. I have friends here." I enjoyed imagining how this information might clash with his assumptions about me.

Stiff-legged, I stepped from the bus onto terra firma, Aguié. The driver and his helper liberated my suitcase from the roof, then boarded the bus and took off into the night.

And there I stood, alone in the utter darkness, feeling very small and foolish. Smugness vanished. Doubt crept in. This in no way resembled the entrance scene I had created in my head of Maimouna and me flying into an embrace the moment I stepped off the bus. There were no lights whatever and only a sliver of moon. Neither Maimouna nor anyone in her family had come to meet me. How would I find her?

A handful of boys in their early teens emerged from the darkness and I asked, "Do you know where Maimouna Liman lives? I want to go to her house." After talking among themselves, they answered in Hausa, "No, but we'll find someone who does." The largest of them impulsively hoisted my suitcase to his head and we made our way along the edge of the road. I had always felt safe in Aguié and I did now too, sensing in the boys a desire to help and also to be in on the action. A teenage girl materialized from the darkness and I asked her if she knew where Maimouna Liman lived.

"Yes. I can show you," she offered. I felt the tension in my body release a bit. "My name is Rakatou."

"Mine is Laurie...Laouré," I told her as I latched onto her arm, not wanting to stumble as our little troupe wound through the rutted, dark streets of Aguié, turning now left, now right. I could feel the leftover warmth of the day radiating up from the earth and off of the thick mud-brick walls on both sides of the narrow road. My eyes slowly adjusted to the dark and I could vaguely make out gateways and trees, the dark broken by an occasional glimmer of lamplight from inside a compound.

We stopped in front of a wood and millet-stalk gate. A boy of about seventeen responded to Rakatou 's loud clapping. "Yes, this is where Maimouna lives. Come in here and wait, please." He led us into a courtyard where, in the dim light of a kerosene lamp I saw a woman's profile in an inner courtyard, bowing in prayer. Not twelve feet away from us, she kneeled on a grass mat and faced a wall. The boy went over and said something to her, and she looked up briefly, and then went back to her bowing, her forehead lowered to the mat, then she stood. It was Maimouna, I was sure of it. I wanted to spring towards her. I thought she would come and greet me, but instead, she again went down on her knees in prayer.

Rakatou and the boys stood with me, watching and waiting quietly. I was stunned that Maimouna wasn't rushing to greet me after I'd come thousands of miles to visit her. She had never been this devout, and I was hurt and puzzled. Then I remembered she was married to a *mallam*, and no doubt being the wife of a religious leader was a role she took seriously. My rational mind glommed onto this excuse, but my emotions were in an uproar. Anger reared up in me and said: "Well, if this is how happy she is to see me, why did she urge me to come all this way? She even said she had stared into a fire and conjured me up! Now I'm finally here at her house and she can't even greet me?!"

The minutes ticked by. I couldn't help thinking about what I'd read about the oil rich Gulf Coast countries funding the spread of an anti-Christian form of Islam throughout this region of Africa. Was my dear friend being coerced by her husband? Was he standing off somewhere watching, making sure she finished her prayers before rushing to her old friend, an *anasara* who would fill her with crazy Western ideas?

These thoughts were just making me more upset. I took a different tack. Wasn't it possible that, like me, her spirituality had deepened over the years? At home I meditated every morning and attended a Buddhist insight meditation class once a week. My inner life had become rich. Could I allow for the possibility that hers had as well? That all she had gone through over the years, physically and emotionally, might have led her to a greater dependence on Allah?

Okay, maybe. But even so, if Bryan had come in while I was meditating and told me Maimouna had arrived, I would drop everything and rush to greet her. Why wouldn't she?

Finally she finished her prayers and came over to me, extending her arms, just as she had in my dream. A poised and stately woman, still slender and erect. Her broad smile reassured me. Yes. Here we were. The same two women. Time peeled back. I thanked Rakatou and tipped the boy who carried my suitcase.

"I thought you were going to be on yesterday's bus." Maimouna said. "I came out to the road with my son and waited. When you weren't on the bus, I began to worry that something had happened to you. I prayed you were safe and here you are. Praise Allah."

I couldn't quite understand how there had been this confusion. But what did that matter now? I was with Maimouna at last!

We went through some formal greetings and inquiries, and she introduced me to her husband, Mallam Hassan, and a mix of children and grandchildren. Since it was late, she suggested that we all go to bed and talk in the morning.

"Since I took the day off yesterday to meet you, I'll have to work tomorrow." I couldn't hide my disappointment, but remembered that there were plenty of places and people I wanted to see in Aguié, not just Maimouna.

I was relieved to hear that she had found two housing options for me. Tonight I would sleep here, and in the morning she would introduce me to the Sarki, the son of our beloved Sarki Brazaki, before she went to work. She said that he had offered a guest house not far from his palace. The other option was to stay with the missionary woman on the outskirts of town.

Maimouna at home

  She made up a floor-bed for me in one of their two indoor living spaces. I'm sure it was their own foam mattress she gave me. The whole family slept in the next room on grass mats, a beaded doorway between us. As I lay down to get some welcome sleep, she warned me that all of them would be getting up before light. "We're observing the fast of Ramadan, so we get up before daybreak to eat and pray. I hope we don't disturb you." I was surprised that even the children were participating in the daylight fast. I knew that men were not even supposed to swallow their saliva during that day.

Sure enough, I was awakened some hours later and became aware of shadowy movements and quiet preparations, sounds of the family rising before dawn to pray and eat. I drifted back to sleep, comforted by the lovely mixture of prayers and the sound of metal bowls, the sacred and the ordinary.

AT HOME IN AGUIÉ

The slanting sun made triangular shadows down the walls and across the floor covered with grass mats. A deep red Persian rug hung above the bed. Hearing sounds from outside, I rose, threw on some clothes and ducked through the low doorway. The children were polite, but were naturally curious about me, and surreptitiously watched me as I came out into the open area of the compound. Chickens scratched and pecked, gleaning bits of yesterday's food.

Maimouna greeted me with a huge smile and a bowl of water to wash my face and hands. She followed this with a bowl of warm yams with a flavorful, salty sauce on them. I ate them with my fingers, remembering how much I like the sensation of being more connected with food this way, instead of eating with a utensil.

She introduced me to a granddaughter and five boys ranging from five to about fourteen. In the confusion I was unsure which were her children and which were her grandchildren. As I ate, she took sorghum stalks out of the conical granary next to the compound wall and fed them to several penned goats. It all came back to me: these many chores, like feeding goats, that women were responsible for on a daily basis.

When Mallam Hassan departed after some cordial words of welcome, Maimouna and I relaxed a bit more. We brought out photos of our families to share. I handed out the gifts I had brought: reading glasses, scented bar soap, a large silky scarf for Maimouna; masks, bubbles and playing cards for the kids. It was a jolly little party until she reminded me, "I do have to work today, so we should go meet Sarki Brazaki and see about your lodgings."

Maimouna

The Sarki's guest house sounded ideal, but Maimouna, thinking I'd feel better elsewhere, said, "We'll go out to the mission after meeting the Sarki. I spoke to the English woman there, and she said you'd be welcome to stay with her." Though I agreed to her plan, I knew I did *not* want to stay out at the mission, which was a long way from town, and, more importantly to me, staying at the mission might identify me as someone who tells the villagers that their religion is wrong and that how they live is sinful. No matter how nice the missionary might be, I hadn't aligned myself with the kind missionaries thirty years ago, and I wasn't about to do so now.

As Maimouna and I walked out together, I felt a little shy and out of place. There she was, beautifully swathed in a bold yellow and purple print fabric, with her top shawl falling in full folds from her shoulders, squaring her into a formidable presence. Her matching cotton head wrap stood high, adding a crown-like dignity. And there I was, plain-Jane in my dull American pants and jersey.

Back when I was her elder, employer and teacher, she was also my language instructor and guide to the ways of life in the village, giving us a pretty even footing. But now there was no ambiguity about our roles. She led me confidently through the streets, answering my many questions about the big changes I saw. When I was curious about a wide, concrete street, she told me, "It's a flood control project." How strange, I thought. I'd never noticed any flooding in Aguié. Maybe it was a gift from a richer nation with good intentions? Or had climate change brought flooding since I lived here?

"See that spigot on the corner?" she asked, pointing at a man who was dispensing water into women's containers. "And that water tower? About fifteen years ago they came and put in two new wells and built the water tower. Now water is piped underground to thirty spigots all around town."

"What a change!" I exclaimed. "What about the livestock? Do they use the same well?"

"Oh no. The livestock well is on the other side of town. I knew you'd be happy to learn that we have much less dysentery since the water system was built."

"What a wonderful improvement! So there's a fellow at each spigot dispensing the water?"

"Yes, many of them used to be water carriers. It was a hard, hot job. Now they have an easier job. They collect a half-franc for each container they fill."

Maimouna's letters had caught me up regarding Tal Hadji, Issaka and Akwiya, and now I asked for more news.

"Only Issaka lives on this side of town," she said, as she gestured down a side street. "I'm sure you'll get to see them all while you're here, although Tal Hadji now lives in Maradi."

As vivid as my recollections were, no memory included all that bombarded my senses and stirred up my emotions now, simply walking through the streets of Aguié. During my four days in the capital, although there had been pleasant odors like coffee and baking bread, there was also a foul mixture of exhaust, sewage and cigarette smoke. Of course, I had quit smoking many years before. None of those scents were present here. Instead of city sewage, there were clean, farmy horse, goat and chicken smells; also millet cooking and heated peanut oil mingled with onion and the smoke from cook fires. All of these were yoked together with the basic scent of earth pulled up and out by the sun. It struck me once again how the entire town was built of the very earth beneath it: streets, walls, and buildings.

I told Maimouna, "I loved the roosters this morning. There aren't many people in San Rafael who keep chickens, but Bryan and I do. We only have hens though, because there's a law against having roosters inside the city limits. People object to the noise of roosters. It's hard to believe. It's wonderful to hear them here. They can crow all they want, day or night. I'll love it."

"But with no roosters, how does your flock grow?"

"It doesn't. We keep the hens for their eggs, but we never get to raise chicks unless we buy them." We laughed together, she in disbelief, and I from seeing the absurdity of my world through her eyes.

A boy of about four, naked except for a leather *grigri* amulet hanging around his neck, played in the doorway of a compound. Our approach suddenly broke his concentration, and he looked up at us with a little jump of surprise at seeing an *anasara* and scampered into his compound like a frightened gopher. I followed Maimouna through that same doorway, where she spoke briefly to another woman without introducing me, handed her something and turned back. I caught the boy sneaking a second look as we went on our way. With complete nonchalance Maimouna explained, "That is my husband's first wife. We have separate compounds." She had not shared in letters that she was a co-wife. I hid my surprise, not wanting to embarrass her by commenting. She was well aware that in my country, men and women have only one spouse at a time. Was being a *second* wife something she might have been loath to share with me?

Having arrived on an almost moonless night, and with my poor sense of direction, I had no idea which part of town I was in. But when Maimouna and I arrived in the big open area in front of the Sarki's palace, I looked around in amazement. Other than the addition of a circular concrete structure that could serve as a fountain if there were water in it, this spot looked exactly as it had when I lived right there, on the corner to our left. Peering in that direction I wondered who lived there now. Reading my thoughts, Maimouna said, "The Sarki's brother, Ibrahim, lives in your old compound with his wives and children. We'll visit them some day if you want." I realized that that would be the Ibrahim, the Sarki's son, whose small thatched hut had been in our compound when he had been a very young man.

Diagonally across from our old compound was the front wall of the palace. Obviously having been updated, it still held its Arabian Knights intrigue for me. It had been the only house in the village with decorations, a bas relief of sculpted plaster, colored with pastel pigments. As Islam forbids depiction of people and animals, decorations were always abstract, but to me, the design on the Sarki's house still looked like an owl. This was fitting, as I thought of him as a wise man.

Here also was the Neem tree with its dense green canopy, three times the size it had been when I left, where our Sarki, the present Sarki's predecessor, had spent part of the day sitting in his low sling chair with a child on his lap or in the company of a friend or two, holding court, resolving conflicts. I wondered if the current Sarki was as attentive, forthright, wise and well-loved as ours had been.

Standing there, it finally hit me that I had truly arrived. During all the months of planning this trip far away in California, this was the scene I'd pictured in my mind: this couple of square blocks where I had lived, known neighbors, danced in the square and heard the muezzin's call five times a day. I was happy to be here at all, but the extra thrill was discovering this part of the village, *my* home territory, had stayed nearly exactly as I remembered it. I took a deep breath, and felt comforted.

Maimouna, who stood quietly throughout my reverie, saw how very emotional this was for me. She seemed to know to let me take it all in without intrusion.

Though I knew my beloved Sarki had passed away, for a moment I fully expected to see him emerge from the doorway of his house. He would first have given me a warm and thorough welcome, then he would have scolded me roundly for taking so long to return. Who *did* emerge from the doorway was a slight, traditionally dressed young man, scooping up the side fabric of his robes, which he tucked up onto his shoulders. I abruptly halted, just for a moment, while I adjusted to the reality that this man, who looked so like our Sarki Nouhou Brazaki, was really his son, Sarki Abdul Brazaki. It was uncanny how much like his father he looked. He had the same protruding ears, penetrating eyes and the graceful, leaf-shaped scarifications stretching nearly from his temple, down across his cheeks to the corners of his mouth. We walked towards each other and after the traditional greetings in Hausa, we switched into French with Hausa interspersed.

Sarki Abdul Brazaki

"I remember you when you and Ibrahim lived here. I was just a little kid, but I remember you living right over there," he said, pointing to the corner opposite. "You probably don't remember me. I was very young."

"You must have been one of the little boys who sat on his lap under the tree."

"Yes, yes. I learned a great deal sitting on his lap there. We are so happy you have returned to visit your old friends in Aguié." He asked about the difficulty of traveling from the U.S. Then, as was the custom, we asked after each other's health, families, houses and so forth, and answered without much detail. That could wait.

After these formalities, I looked at his companion, a similarly dressed man in his mid-thirties. "Do you remember Muman?" the Sarki asked.

"Of course!" I exclaimed, suddenly recognizing the little boy I'd known so well radiating from this grown man's face. "Muman!!" I cried, "How wonderful to see you!" He grinned at me the way he used to when he and Tal Hadji would come next door to visit. I checked my urge to hug him. He wasn't five any more. Maimouna, breaking her silence, squealed with glee at the sight of Muman and me continuing to smile broadly, eyes locked in delight, as we exchanged formal greetings.

Sarki Abdul then explained, "I have a guest house across the way which you are welcome to use for as long as you like. You may be more comfortable at the mission, but you're welcome to stay here in town with us. Go to the mission first and when you return I'll show you the guest house."

"You see how welcome you are here?" said Maimouna. "I knew it would be like this." I floated in a daze, walking next to her through the same sandy streets we used to walk together to work at the dispensary or to go to the market. But instead of just one or two buildings on the opposite side of the highway, there was now a town that stretched as far as I could see in every direction. People greeted us as we walked past, clearly knowing who I was. Evidently, a white person visiting Aguié was still big news.

"See, here's where the dispensary used to be, where we held well-baby clinics." She swung her arm toward a block of dwellings where there had been just one small building. "The school was moved from this area to a new neighborhood on the other side of the Route. And way over there," she gestured to the left, "is the clinic where I now work. I'll take you there another day."

The open market was still next to the National Route, though now it had more permanent shade structures. There were only a few vendors selling piles of limes, salt, dried beans, brown cones of sugar, decorated calabashes and grass mats -- the bare essentials to hold people until market day.

I was astonished when we came upon a car park with at least ten vehicles in various stages of readiness to depart in different directions with people and goods. A flurry of men were making repairs, washing cars and vans, or securing goods onto roofs. There had been no vehicles in town at all when I lived here. A few blocks deeper into the "new town" as even they called it, I saw the impressive minarets of a very large mosque, surrounded by a tall wall. I guessed it was one of hundreds of mosques in the Sahel region I had read about that were funded by Saudi Arabian oil money.

We turned east along the highway and walked to the Mission School. By the time we got there, I was more than ready to get out of the hot sun and take a rest. Maimouna introduced me to Phyllis, the English missionary, who graciously invited us in for tea. She confessed she was not feeling well but said that I would be welcome to stay there in student housing and eat with the students.

I had the impression she would also welcome someone to talk to. I found myself telling her about my life in Aguié in the sixties, about my bus ride, about my excitement being here after planning for so many months. I even told her that I was shaken and off balance, also about the strange greeting I had received last night and my fears that I had bitten off more than I could chew, partly because my Hausa was not coming back as quickly as I'd hoped, and my French wasn't strong either. I was clearly enjoying the sudden novelty of being able to talk to someone in English!

I noticed that I was recovering some of my teetering self-esteem. Having to convey everything in one of two foreign languages with no fluency had made me feel downright stupid. Maimouna patiently waited, not understanding a word. I was very happy when she explained that she herself didn't have internet connection but that I could come, type up a letter, put it on a disc, and she would take it with her when she went to Maradi and see that my email to Bryan was sent. When we finished our tea she suggested that I could come back another time, and I agreed.

I hadn't seen the Sarki's accommodations yet, but I quietly resolved to stay in town, closer to Maimouna and the people I knew. That is what I had come all the way here for, not to stay with an English speaker, as nice as she was.

Maimouna and I returned to town, hand in hand. I had forgotten that lovely custom of walking out with a friend holding hands and appreciated the once familiar feeling of her hand in mine. Even men used to walk hand in hand through the village, and I wondered if that was still true. On our way, Maimouna and I conversed about many things we'd shared in letters. When I said that my long illness seemed to be gone, but that it was really draining, she said, "I'm glad it's over, Laouré. I've had some problems too. One prevented me from working for half a year and I also have problems with my eyes."

With health out of the way, we turned to other topics. What a pleasure to walk through these streets with my dear friend, smelling the smoke of cook fires, hearing soft cluckings of chickens from within compound walls and happy children's voices. When we arrived back at the Sarki's palace, Maimouna left me there while she went on to her work.

The Sarki was sitting outside in the shade with several of his retinue. Our conversation was predictable. I described my career, my town, my health and I filled him in on Rich and his second family. Then we moved on to the health of my parents and the age, location and professions of our children. The Sarki made a similar summation about his life since our departure in 1969. Parsing through our hodgepodge of Hausa and French to achieve near understanding with the help of Muman's more fluent dual-language ability, our meeting ended with him pressing me to come meet his wives and kids as soon as I got settled in.

Sarki Abdul then suggested that he, Muman and I walk the half block to the guest house he was offering. Curious onlookers stopped in the street to see what was happening. The small house was perfect. It had two rooms, a locking door, a foam mattress with a Hausa blanket, a terra cotta water container in the patio-courtyard, a kerosene lantern and a pit latrine. Pure luxury compared to what I had envisioned.

I gladly accepted the Sarki's offer. That settled, the three of us walked back through the square. When we reached the palace, Sarki Abdul said, "Why don't you and Muman go collect your luggage from Maimouna's house and when you get back I'll have my daughter bring you some dinner."

Sitting with Sarki Abdul Brazaki

There followed quite an installation ceremony, with a parade of family carrying my belongings through the streets from Maimouna's home to my new roost. Later, when the sun had gone down, Sarki Abdul's lovely teen-aged daughter, Zuli, came to the door carrying a covered enameled container full of delicious roasted chicken and a savory sweet potato dish over rice. "I can't stay now," she said, "but could I come back to visit?" I said she would always be welcome.

After her work, Maimouna had gone home and collected five sons and grandsons who had begged to be allowed to come too, and they now trooped in, carrying their grass mats and blankets. I invited them to help me eat the food, and they were delighted to dig in to the spontaneous feast.

The extra room in my guest accommodation soon came in handy. No one in Aguié lived alone. No one slept alone. A foreign guest, especially a woman, couldn't possibly be left alone without somebody watching over them. So I was told that these five boys would be sleeping in my second room. There was no room for arguing; it was a done deal. I gave the boys a deck of cards with which they entertained themselves while Maimouna and I sat on mats to talk. I shared more about my time in Niamey and the bus trip. She updated me about our mutual friends, Tal Hadji, Akwiya, Issaka and others. Most of this she had shared in letters, but it still surprised me how many of our close friends were still alive.

By the time she left, the boys already seemed right at home. I could tell that this "slumber party" was a welcome distraction from their usual routines, although there was some shyness at first. The eldest boy, Ishao, lit the lantern.

I asked them, "Do you know the game Kwoss?"

"Sure we do!" Because I hadn't played the card game in thirty years, they needed to refresh me on the rules. Off we went, into a mostly non-verbal yet quite noisy and high-spirited game. What I did remember about Kwoss was that the players slap cards down emphatically with a loud snap, and sure enough, that's what we did.

After a long and rambunctious series of games, with lots of laughter and disagreements, we all felt well acquainted by bedtime.

After I went to bed they continued to play cards on the patio with much soft laughter and squabbling, hunkering around the yellow lantern light. Though I didn't feel I needed to be chaperoned, I was really glad they were with me that night because a bat had taken up residence in the empty house, and it began swooping around the room almost as low as my pallet on the floor, scolding me for the invasion of its privacy. Hearing its squeaks and my yells, the boys jumped up, bringing the lantern inside. They whipped the air with their shirts and succeeded in stunning the poor animal. When they started flogging it I stepped in to keep them from killing it. We let it whisk out the propped-open shutter.

"LAOURÉ, GLACE"

The next morning, I sent the five sleepy boys on their way. They rolled up their grass sleeping mats, leaned them up against the wall, and slipped out the corrugated metal door, telling me they'd be back that night.

I washed my hands and face and ate leftovers from the meal the Sarki's wives had made for me the night before. Savoring the smell of my neighbors' wood fires, I saturated myself in the happiness of hearing Aguié's morning activities.

Maimouna had told me that she would have to work this day, too, so I figured I was on my own. I was still washing up my dishes and wondering what I would do with myself when there was a rapping on my door. Muman stood there in a white robe over white pants. His shy grin, the same as when he was a little boy, stole my heart all over again. He acted as if we'd made an appointment. What I learned, as the days went on, was that the Sarki had deputized him to watch over me, a job he took very seriously.

I thought about how the then little Muman was overshadowed by his boisterous older sister, Tal. Of course, I saw less of him because he attended school, but even so, over the two years I lived in Aguié, Muman and I developed a quiet appreciation for one another. He was always clad in shorts, his quarter-inch hair dusty black, sometimes sporting a sandy splotch on his forehead from touching the ground while attending prayers at the mosque with his father. He would slink into my courtyard, hoping no one would notice him. He'd often lean on the wooden pole that held up our shade structure, watching, alert and thinking. If our eyes met, he would immediately lower his. But just as quickly, he would burst into a deep-dimpled grin, revealing his new front teeth. It was as if he was in a boxing match with his emotions, and was embarrassed that laughter always won. On these occasions I'd have the urge to grab him and give him a squeeze. I did no such thing. We understood each other.

If he showed up alone, he made a timid series of three claps at the compound entrance. He wouldn't step through without being invited. Once inside, he'd consider it a lark just to sit on one of my kitchen chairs. He had no chairs at his house next door. He'd often not say a word; just smile and look around. I'd go about my cooking or my lesson plans with the pleasure of his gentle company.

His company was still gentle, and I was grateful for it. I surmised that Sarki Abdul must have immediately noticed my comfort with Muman the day before, and had asked him to come by that morning to see if there was anything I needed, and to take me wherever I wanted to go.

Sweet Muman

"Sarki Brazaki has invited you to come to his palace this morning to visit and meet his wives," Muman informed me. Although I had a list of things I wanted to do, I thought that was a good place to start. I grabbed my favorite scarf and Muman supervised locking the padlock on the outside of the door. "You must always do this when you leave, because here there are many robbers!" While I was skeptical about robbers, I said nothing. As we walked, I felt the magic of a sense of time travel. Here I was, walking the same streets in my long skirt and headscarf, just as I had done every day on my way to the dispensary, almost as if no time had elapsed.

A couple of dusty-legged boys with close-cropped hair lollygagged in the square as we passed, getting a good look at the stranger in town. They braved a few steps closer and I heard them chant: "Laouré—*glace!*" I stopped stock still. I was amazed and transported back thirty years to how tickled I was as a newcomer to the village becoming so popular thanks to my Peace Corps issue fridge and its miraculous ice making properties, greeted by children far and wide with, "Laouré *glace*".

I had to remind myself that these were not those same children. In fact, they were probably the grandchildren of those children. I could only conclude that those grandparents—when they heard about my return visit, had told the kids how they used to taunt me with their chant. This new generation even gave it the proper emphasis, pronouncing each letter of my name with a lilting upswing on the long *ah* sound before the "s" sound at the end of *glace*. They turned the one-syllable word *glace* into a two-syllable word by elongating the *g* at the beginning, just as their elders had done. Time stood still. I was thoroughly enchanted, and gave them a burst of astonished laughter as their reward.

When we reached the Sarki's palace, we entered the labyrinth of hallways and small open-air patios that eventually led into the main courtyard. Convoluted and twisting this way and that, we encountered a guardian in one, a tethered horse in another. Meant to thwart enemies from entering the Sarki's house, the maze design was a vestige from a distant past. Now it was more to impress visitors than to protect the Sarki from marauders.

In the Sarki's labyrinth

Finally, we were greeted by an attendant who notified the Sarki that he had visitors. Women and children peered at us from multiple doorways, greeting Muman informally, but staying back until the

Sarki emerged from a beaded doorway and walked swiftly toward us, a smile on his face and his hands outstretched for mine. At this, he beckoned his three wives forward and I met them and their children. My Hausa limped successfully through the greetings and my thanks to them for the wonderful dinner they had provided the previous night. I told the children that Rich and I had named our son, Zachary, after their grandfather, Nouhou Brazaki. And that we called him Zaki, for short. Muman stepped in to help them understand what I was trying to say. About this revelation there was much nodding and smiling.

After admiring the Sarki's dovecote, which was fashioned cleverly out of terracotta jugs stacked on their sides, we all took our seats on mats in the shade of the wall and *goros* were offered and chewed.

Muman proceeded to fill everyone in on what he knew of my travels so far. One of the wives loosened the shawl across her chest and adeptly leveraged first a leg, then the rest of a small, naked baby around from her back to her front, and commenced to nurse him. Having nursed my own children in the intervening years, I felt gratitude for the nursing know-how I'd absorbed from being around Hausa mothers.

I chimed in where I felt confident, answering their questions about my health and my family, and asked them about their readiness for the coming holiday. I shared what happened on our way to visit them, including the "Laouré *glace*" greeting I'd received from passing kids. Evidently, I expressed the whole long story well enough to be understood, because we all laughed together.

After a few more updates and pleasantries I took a jar of bubble soap out of my pocket, screwed off the top with the tiny wand attached and blew on it. Bubbles floated away. The children's mouths dropped open for a moment, but with a little encouragement, they all got up and started chasing, catching and popping the bubbles. We adults sat laughing delightedly together, a great way to finish up our visit on an informal and humorous note. As we took our leave, I promised to visit them again soon.

Sarki Abdul with his three wives and daughter, Zuli

As we walked together Muman said, "In one of your letters you asked about Bulki. She lives up this street and I know she wants to see you. Shall we see if she's home?" I was delighted with the idea. He knocked on the door. In the old days, doors were made of branches and millet stalks, so one always clapped. But now most doorways into compounds seemed to have corrugated metal doors, and clapping wasn't sufficiently loud to get the attention of the residents, but as Muman knocked, I felt sad at this "progress". A young woman with a baby on her back opened the door, immediately knew who I was, and turned swiftly, bellowing, "Bulki! Laouré is here!" A grown-up version of the little girl I had known so long ago emerged from behind a hut and hurried over to hug me, smiling the yard-wide smile I remembered well. "When did you get here? Where are you staying?" Her questions tumbled one after the other. But before she let me answer, she pulled out a grass mat and sat us down, passing around the *goro* nuts.

Bulki was short, which I would have predicted as she had been shorter than her pal Tal. She hadn't lost the low voice and impish face I adored. I explained I'd only just arrived two nights ago but that I planned to be here for the holiday and beyond. She expressed relief. "Good! Because I can't visit for long now. I was just about to take lunch to my sick aunt." She pressed me to agree to come back Sunday, when she and her daughters would be hennaing their hands, and it would be a fun afternoon to spend together. She quickly got the hang of speaking slowly and using hand gestures. Muman stepped in from time to time to help with translation, but Bulki and I did pretty well. With the promise of spending more time together, all the household's women and children saw me to the door. Muman guided me out to the street to continue our walk around town.

"It's not market day, but we can go see what's happening out there if you want." As we strolled through town, greeting people here and there, my stomach started to growl, and when we got to the market I spied what I was hoping for. A wrinkled old woman was sitting on a mat, legs straight out in front of her, with a calabash beside her full of cooked greens. They were coated with crushed peanuts, peanut oil and salt. These leaves, I knew, came from a tree out in the bush. I bought some, offering it to Muman, who graciously said no, since he was fasting for Ramadan. I knew there was also an Islamic stricture against a man eating with a non-related woman, so I doubt he would have taken it anyway. He seemed to enjoy how I indulged in the nostalgia of the aroma and flavor I'd once taken for granted. I had tried unsuccessfully to replicate this treat at home using chard and peanut butter, but it just wasn't the same. Knowing it couldn't be duplicated made it all the more delicious. Then I hunted down a vendor of *rogo*, and found the manioc snack still warm from the pot. With the majority of villagers fasting, the vendor was happy for my business.

I knew I was feeling at home again when it didn't seem odd that in the shade of a nearby tree, a barber was giving a man a shave. Any spot in the marketplace could turn into a barber shop. All the barber needed was a leather bag with the tools of his trade and a teakettle of water. Instinct told me to avert my gaze. Having a shave seemed to deserve privacy.

REUNION WITH NEINO

"Yes. Neino is still with us. I'll take you to see him tomorrow." Muman's assurance banished my fear that one of my favorite neighbors, Muman's uncle, may have passed away.

The next morning I was ready when Muman came to gather me. We walked through town towards the National Route that used to define the north edge of town but, because of Aguie's rampant growth, now bisected it. Along the way I relished the soft hubbub of millet-pounding, children's shouts, of chickens, the bleats of goats or sheep, all drifting up over the uniformly brown walls of compounds. Here, where there used to be two tiny shops, were dozens and dozens of small businesses.

Much of the growth was the result of a new formal road connecting Aguie with Northern Nigeria, approximately twenty kilometers to the south. Now trucks bearing Nigerian goods arrived daily in Aguie, often disgorging their goods, then returning to Nigeria with goods from Aguie's warehouses. Other trucks traveling the east-west route picked up many of those goods to distribute elsewhere.

A commercial strip had developed along the route. Small canteens, tea stalls and small warehouses strung themselves beside the road. Most of the structures were mud brick with woven grass roofs. I admired the industriousness of all this development, but missed the quiet little town whose streets I once knew by heart. Did all this "progress" give the people a happier life, I wondered? Children were much more likely to grow up, move away and start families far from home. Movies and other imported western culture created desires and dreams far exceeding the reach of local youth, creating dissatisfaction which in the past didn't exist.

Muman and I walking an Aguié street

Muman shepherded me into one of the warehouses. The entry consisted of grass mats tied onto upright poles crafted out of tree branches, affording the watchman a private patio area to sit. Inside the patio, to my surprise, was a horse and a very old man sitting in a low sling chair.

"Neino", called out Muman. "Here is Laouré come to see you."

Curved into his sling chair, the old man raised his face, his milky eyes straining to see me. Then a wide smile and eager hands reached up to me, bridging the thirty years between. It was he, the same sweet, ever-smiling Neino, his long body still slender but less upright. Unfolding slowly, he rose from his chair and, taking my hands in his, extolled over and over the goodness of Allah who brought me back to them.

His ardent words filled my eyes with tears, and welled up my feeling of love, not only for Neino but for myself, vividly recalling the young Laurie, who sought to establish herself in the village through good manners and thoughtful actions, never quite realizing that such gestures weren't necessary. With more courage and self-respect I might have discovered that those villagers liked and trusted me, not for my deeds but for who they could see I was.

In the two years that I lived in Niger, Neino and I rarely had more than superficial conversations. How could he and I have bonded in such an extraordinarily deep way? Our connection had grown rich through proximity, attitude, gestures, much less so with words.

Dear Neino

I felt a renewed compassion for the young woman I'd been, newly married, uprooted from family, isolated from all that was home and safety. Along with that came the recollection of the green-growing sprout of determination to grasp the wonder of her new life.

Neino and I stood, hands clasped, our faces both alive with the wide, silly grins of hearts-exposed. As we settled into chairs and

Muman took his leave, Neino and I traded explanations, me about Ibrahim (Rich), his health, his family, my second marriage and step-daughter, Neino about his work, his children, his health. Despite cataracts on both eyes, he was grateful to still be able to perform his watchman duties for this small warehouse. Neino introduced his horse which was tethered nearby. I remembered his natural comfort with horses. He was the neighbor who had so willingly boarded the horse Rich needed for work.

As always, the respectful distance in our sharing, shying away from difficulties such as my failed marriage. Preferable to both of us was revisiting the famous stories about Rich going off hunting with bow and arrow and his various misadventures with horses. Much to laugh about. We spoke affectionately of the original Sarki Brazaki. Neino seemed pleased that Rich and I had named our first born after the Sarki: Zachary, Zaki for short.

For the remainder of my stay I always stopped at his "patio" to spend a little time telling him about my day, admire his horse, and share with him newsworthy bits and pieces such as my delightful discovery of melon for sale in the market that day, or my purchase of a pair of Tuareg sandals to take home as a gift for my son. Our affinity graced every visit.

MAIMOUNA ALL TO MYSELF

I woke up excited. It was Saturday and Maimouna didn't have to work. I heard the boys rise and quietly slip out the door. I got up, stiff as always, performed a couple of quick yoga stretches and went out to the latrine. I uncovered the hole, and, glancing up to make sure the masons weren't at work on the neighbor's roof as they had been the day before, I squatted, grateful that I had been keeping my body limber with my yoga practice. Then I brushed my teeth exactly the way I had for two years in Aguié, spitting into a hole in the ground, one of many small enjoyments I had all but forgotten. I slipped the *whe whe* back over the opening in the concrete top of the latrine. The small, round, woven-grass disk, big enough to be the lid for a basket or bowl, was also used to winnow chaff from millet grains. When worn out, they could be used as a toilet hole cover.

I jotted down a few words in my journal, my mind galloping ahead to Maimouna's arrival. A whole day together! I heated tea water on my tiny one-burner back-packer's stove, and reheated the lamb and sweet potato stew from dinner the night before. The Sarki's wives sent me dinner every night, which I appreciated, but it was always more food than I could eat. The five young boys were happy to help me with that after the sun went down. They would have broken their fast at home before they arrived, but they were always happy to finish off anything I hadn't eaten. Returning the bowls to the sarki's wives with food still in them would be insulting. Where were the Koranic scholars when I needed them? Did they still beg for food in the evenings?

My bathroom

I filled my tea kettle with water from the huge cooling jug leaning in the corner and washed myself. It's amazing how clean and refreshed I felt using less than a quart of water. I washed up my bowls and shook out the grass sitting mats. Just as I was thinking I was ready to get out into the day, there was a clap at the door. Hooray!

And Maimouna didn't have any children with her. I had her all to myself.

My hostess instincts kicked in and, even knowing Maimouna was fasting, I couldn't resist offering her tea. She declined and I didn't feel the need for more. We sat facing one another on the mats which we laid out in the long shade of the morning. "So," I said, not knowing where to begin, "tell me about yourself since I left."

"Nine of my ten children are still alive." Her mouth pursed, and I knew we were both thinking about her first-born, Hamsa, whose delivery I missed because I was out of town visiting Peace Corps friends. I was so saddened to read in one of her letters that he had died at the age of three from pneumonia during an especially cold winter.

Now I could convey my condolences in person. I touched her hand and said, "I can't imagine how terrible losing Hamsa must have been for you."

"Yes. It broke my heart. But I had three more children with Konko before he divorced me. He was a terrible husband, so I'm glad he divorced me. He beat me."

A long-ago memory suddenly emerged: Maimouna had confided in me that she had had diarrhea in the night and had rushed out to the edge of town to do her business. He'd flown into a jealous rage, beating her, suspecting that she'd met a lover.

I shook my head, and said, "I'm so sorry he was that way. It was different for me: Rich was a good husband and father but we had grown apart. We were no longer happy together after thirteen years of marriage." I took her long silence to mean she couldn't really relate to that part of my world. I didn't expect her to, but because she had known Rich, it felt important to say.

In some ways it was just like two American woman friends, long apart, catching up with one another. It was a little awkward, since we were attempting all this in French, a second language for both of us, hers more accomplished than mine, with the added difference of our two cultures. On the subject of marriage and divorce, there was a gaping hole. How could I explain my divorce was initiated by me for reasons that probably would seem inconceivable to Maimouna. "Incompatibility?" "Sexual disharmony?" "Growing apart?" I imagine myself trying to explain these grounds and falling on my face in the attempt. Surely she would think these reasons trivial or unrealistic. So I didn't try, which made me sad.

Our talk then turned to easier subjects, full of information about children and grandchildren, both hers and mine, our parents, sisters, nieces and nephews.

In letters she told me she had remarried, but what she hadn't written was that she was a co-wife. I imagine being a co-wife and owning her own compound would have been a long and complicated explanation she might not have felt able to relate in writing. It seemed it would be hard even now, face to face, with our fractured languages and cultural divide. I was unaware that wives ever lived in separate compounds. Was this something new, or was Maimouna's situation unique?

I decided on another tack. "Ibrahim and I shared raising our kids and we stayed on friendly terms. He remarried fairly soon after our divorce and he now has a thirteen-year-old son with his second wife. I didn't remarry for twelve years. During those years, Ibrahim and I were equally involved in raising Zack and Reina."

Maimouna put her hand on my knee, and smiled, glad for me. In person, even without the words to share the details we wanted to share, I was grateful for all that was conveyed by our faces and our hands. This friendship was deeper than language. As we leaned into each other, and showed joy and sorrow in our eyes and expressions, we were saying without need of words, *You are a treasured friend...I have missed you...you are still the same to me.* Though I would have wished to know every detail and to be able to convey every thought I had, I was grateful for the unspoken but strong bond that clearly we were both feeling.

Reminiscing about Rich she asks, "Do you remember the time Ibrahim gave the griot his shirt?" Griots were traveling bards. They usually had a drum and often sang the news and gossip from town to town. "You and I were out making our rounds. There was a travelling griot in town who had attracted a big circle around him listening to his news from all over. He started teasing Ibrahim, telling him that he could make up a heroic story-song about him 'if only I had a shirt like yours.' Ibrahim accepted the challenge. He took off his shirt and gave it to the griot. Everyone laughed so much."

"I do remember that," I said, and we laughed together all over again, just the way we used to do. I was delighted to feel our formality, engendered by distance and years, begin to unravel. It felt like we were a team again.

She continued, "Then the griot turned it into a song, right then and there. Undoubtedly sang from town to town about being given the *anasara's* shirt in Aguié."

"Yeah, and that's why people called Ibrahim *Sarkin Dariya*. He was always joking around."

"Yes," Maimouna said, "that was something I had trouble getting used to. I couldn't always tell when he was serious or not. He would say things I doubted were true, but he kept a straight face, so I couldn't tell. Do you remember that you had to go into Naimey for training for a week, and Ibrahim took over teaching me that week: math, geography, history, biology...everything! He was a pretty good teacher!"

"No." I answer, puzzled by such a large hole in my memory. "I completely forgot about that! I'm surprised that Konko let you come by yourself."

"Maybe I forgot to tell him you were out of town." We laughed again, nothing held back.

"Mallam Hassan and I have been married for seventeen years now. He's very serious and kind. And he's a good father."

I smiled, so glad to hear it, hoping it was the truth and not just loyalty. She changed the subject by reminding me of how we found each other again after so many years. "I stayed up almost all night staring into the fire. I was thinking about you and wondering where you were and how you were. I'm certain that was the night you had your dream about me visiting your house in America."

"I'm just as certain. That was such a powerful dream that I felt I had to reach out and see if I could find you. I believed that you had moved away or possibly even perished during the drought. But after that dream, I had to try to write and find out."

Warming to her subject, she continued, "I couldn't understand why you weren't in contact for so many years. Every time a soothsayer came to town I would pay them to try to connect with you. I tried everything! I guess it finally worked!"

"It must have," I respond, "because here I am!"

Double enjoyment

We moved on to reminisce about our work. "You were such a good student. I was so proud of you when you passed the test in Tessaoua."

"I was so scared. I had never been to Tessaoua, and I had to go alone. I didn't know anyone except Karima," she said, using Connie's Hausa name. "Do you remember that I saw the French doctor using a telephone? They told me he was talking to someone in Niamey and I didn't believe them! I had never seen or heard of a telephone." We laughed yet again and I rose to prepare some tea.

"Have you had any other *anasaras* live here since us?" I inquired.

"There was a French woman who stayed a few months some years ago. She was teaching people how to make and use a type of stove that used less wood. The same American missionaries stayed for many years."

"I heard that there's an election coming up," I said.

"Yes, right after the Ramadan Festival. Issaka is running for council. I think he'd be good."

"I have plans to visit with him at his house tomorrow."

"Do you remember that awful guy, Sali, who worked at your house before Issaka?"

"I sure do." How could I forget that unfortunate experience?

"He stole from you and then the Sarki kicked him out of town. I never trusted that guy. He wasn't from here."

Perhaps the talk of the stolen money sparked a shift to a more personal topic. "Our country has had financial struggles, so now the primary teachers and the staff at the medical center, like me, aren't getting paid. We keep working anyway because we want the jobs when there *is* money to pay us. If we quit now, we'd lose our place."

I shared that I had worked for elected officials on the county and state levels during the many years I was single. "Eventually I married Bryan and worked for him, booking his band, Swing Fever. We dated for five years before we got married."

"Five years?!" The disbelief in her tone was clear. "You were lucky, finding two husbands who treated you well. I'm content now, but it took a long time." I sensed that she was fighting back tears. I took her hand in mine. "When Konko divorced me, I moved in with my sister's family. It was hard not having a home of my own. But because of my job, I was able to save and buy my house. I'm sure I wouldn't have had a salaried job if you hadn't trained me when you were here. I'm grateful to you every day!"

The Sarki's guest house-my home away from home

Our conversation was interrupted by a knock on the door. I frowned and explained that I'd been discovered by little boys who pounded on my door. I got up to chase the boys away, but opening up a crack, I found not a gang of mischievous kids but smiling Akwiya. I threw open the door and she walked into my arms. Then I held her out at arm's length so we could look at one another. Shorter than I remembered her, she stood erect and proud, though she had a large goiter in her neck. We grinned foolishly, happily staring. She explained to Maimouna and me that she had been away.

"I knew you were coming soon, Laouré, but didn't know when. The Sarki just told me that you were here with Maimouna." Then she gave me the traditional welcome: "*Lale! Barka da zuwa!*" She settled on a grass mat. I offered her a cup of tea, which she refused, just as Maimouna had done. "I've sent Tal Hadji news that you would be coming. She'll be sure to come while you're here." I was touched by her thoughtfulness; she knew how important Tal was to me.

Akwiya didn't seem that much older to me; she had almost no wrinkles. Because she was the mother of three in the 60's, I had assumed she was a lot older. I asked, "How many great-grandchildren do you have now?" Pausing for a minute and gazing into the distance she finally said, "Twenty-one, I think." I am impressed; I had no grandchildren yet.

Akwiya

"Your amazing son, Muman, has been my guardian angel ever since I got here," I told her, stumbling over that concept in Hausa. Maimouna stepped in to interpret, and that produced a guffaw from Akwiya.

"Yes. He was a rascal when he was growing up, but he's very responsible now. I'm proud of him." She described where all her other children were and how many children each of them had produced. I showed her pictures of my family, home and garden, and even a map of the USA, pointing out California and the Bay Area.

As she got up to leave, Akwiya invited me to come visit her that afternoon. Maimouna offered to walk me there when we were done visiting at her house. Akwiya departed and Maimouna and I realized we could be walking and talking, always our favorite thing. "Can I walk you home?" I asked her.

She laughed and took my arm. "But first why don't I walk you home?" Seeing my puzzled face, she laughed again. "I ran into Ibrahim who lives in your old house and he said to feel free to bring you by. So let's stop there on our way. If you want?" Suddenly her expression showed concern that maybe I didn't want to take a stroll down memory lane by revisiting the home I shared with my first husband. I quickly assured her I'd be happy to go. This whole neighborhood was a memory lane for me.

Ibrahim was gracious as he let us in the compound that was both familiar and not. As he introduced me to his family, I became aware of the changes: The shade structure over the patio that we had built was no longer there. A grass fence had been built close to the patio, screening the patio and doorways into the house. The doors we'd had cut between the rooms were still there, taller than the local average. I wasn't invited into the back rooms, so I didn't know if they kept our infamous window. Ibrahim seemed excited to have me visit and pointed to the small hut in the corner of the yard where he had used to spend time when he was a young man when we lived there. It all fell together at that instant. This was Sarki Brazaki's son who had shared our compound from time to time. I hadn't guessed that this Ibrahim was the selfsame person.

Visiting our old house

It all happened so quickly, and then we were out the door, and on our way with smiles all around, and a lingering sensation of familiarity and foreignness all in one. "Now it's time to walk you home!" I said, with enough cheer to reassure her I was fine. Then I took Maimouna's hand and we slipped back into our ongoing conversation.

"Laouré, did I ever write to you about the time..."

After lunch, Maimouna and I sat on mats on her patio. She brought out a ten kilo sack of sugar and proceeded to fill little blue, plastic bags with small quantities. This was her home industry, like those of many village women. Her granddaughter will carry these bags on a tray balanced on her head, selling to villagers who can't at the moment afford to buy sugar in large quantities. Maimouna explained that this made a very small profit, but since her paycheck had dried up, every little bit helped. I assisted her by tying the bags after she filled them; this entailed twisting the two top corners of the bag and tying the two together. As we worked she described her job in more detail and shared how much she liked the work and her co-workers. I gave her my impressions of how much Aguié had changed. When it was time for me to leave, she walked me across town to Akwiya's compound. We hugged each other, agreeing to see each other the next day at the dispensary.

AKWIYA THE PRIESTESS

Akwiya welcomed me into her compound with pride. Her square, brick hut was an indication of greater wealth than the typical round grass huts, like the one she used to have. The last time I had been inside her home was when she sent Tal to summon me to hear a spirit message she had for me. Thinking back to that odd encounter, I realized her prediction had been right about the end of Rich's and my marriage, but fortunately she'd been completely wrong about our not being able to have children (once I stopped taking birth control pills.)

Now she filled me in on her life. "My first husband, Mazadou, who you remember, died four years ago. We had been divorced for a long time." She showed me a picture of her current husband, a truck driver who was rarely home. I told her about Rich and his second family, and more about Zach and Reina, Bryan and my stepdaughter. "Bryan is a jazz musician. A band leader," I said, speaking in my plodding Hausa. I had hoped my fluency would somehow magically return when I arrived in town, but at least I was happy she seemed to understand and, in turn, slowed her speech for me.

I asked, "Do you remember inviting me to attend the birth of Zeinabou and that I cut the cord? It meant a lot that you invited me. A week later Rich and I attended her naming ceremony. These are very special memories."

"Yes, of course! And we always call her Ta Laouré."

Akwiya had just returned from doing Bori ceremonies in Gazaoua and Tessaoua. In response to my questions about her experience, she rose and invited me into her hut. I stooped low to enter. The rammed earth floor was swept clean and a brightly covered bed stood in one corner. It was clear from what hung on her walls that this was not a typical household. Food preparation items were scarce compared to the costume paraphernalia suspended from her rafters. Long strands of bright beads hung down, protected from insects in the mud walls by a layer of clear plastic sheeting. Noting my interest, she explained, "I wear these for the Bori gatherings. Would you like to see them on me?" I nodded.

First she donned a brightly embroidered blouse unlike any I'd seen before. Next came an elaborate headdress with dozens of Rasta-like tiny braids hanging all the way around her head and down to her chest, with just enough of an opening in front for her to see out. Then another crown of cowry shells with strands of the heavy shells falling below her knees. The main necklace was a choker festooned with many strands, yellow beads predominant, which descended to her waist. As if this adornment weren't enough, she donned a second headdress of cowry shells sewn onto a cushioned crown-like piece, the sort that village women use to balance loads on their heads. I gazed at my friend transformed. She looked like a priestess.

That's when I began to understand that in my absence, she had been elevated to a new status of respect in the community. Her pride in sharing this part of her life shone in her face.

"Would you like to take a photograph?" I had been hoping this would be okay with her, but for Akwiya to be the one to offer was unexpected. I took several photos and then she said, "Would you like to come to one of the rituals while you're here in Aguié?"

"Yes!"

"There's one planned after the end of Ramadan. I'll let you know when it will be. Muman can accompany you to the location."

Akwiya donning her regalia

MAKING THE ROUNDS

Early afternoon on my fourth day Muman escorted me to Issaka's, leaving me there after receiving strong assurance that Issaka would walk me back home. Issaka had come to greet me on my first day, and had invited me to come to his compound to have a real visit and meet his family. I thought how far he'd come from being our houseboy -- more correctly called steward now -- to running for the town council. I was proud of him and looked forward to spending some time with him and his family. But as we approached I couldn't help thinking back to the cold night in 1968 when he showed up at our compound, begging me to hurry and come help his wife, Aisha, who was in labor with their first child. As I rushed through town behind him, he explained with short, panting breaths that Aisha's labor had been long and hard. When we arrived, the baby, wet and quite pale, had emerged and was struggling to breathe. I urgently wrapped him tightly against the cold, flicked the soles of his feet, lay him face down across my knees and patted and stroked his back. Aisha, her mother and Issaka formed a tense circle around me, watching these unusual methods. When we heard the infant's in-breath, we too breathed "Ah!"

"*Akwai mutani,*" Issaka said excitedly, "There is a person." It was a long wait before another breath came, and with it we heard an ominous rattling in his lungs. "*Akwai mutani,*" Issaka repeated, but with less conviction. Seconds passed while the baby struggled to breathe. I passed the little one to his grandmother. Two more strained breaths and then, finally, Aisha whispered, her eyes tearing, "*Babu mutani.*" It was no good. After more suspended moments of silence and prayer, Issaka uttered my least favorite words, "*Sai Allah.*" It was *their* tradition to accept Allah's will, not mine. I wept with the women as we wrapped the child, heartsick. I hated that there was nothing in my power to change the outcome. I cursed the cold and the lack of medical care. I cursed my inability to save Issaka and Aisha's precious first child.

After the night of their child's death, a stronger bond developed between Issaka and me, beyond that of employer and helper. We had been together at a sacred moment, when his child teetered between life and death; when all our hopes and prayers were fused together, willing the small being to take hold, to live. One moment we had experienced a moment of pure joy, and in the next, pure grief.

Now, all these years later, Issaka had two more wives and many children and grandchildren. At Issaka's home, Muman left me and I was serenaded with a chorus of *Lale Laouré* from the semi-circle of women standing around the doorway.

Issaka with the women and children of his compound

Names flew by: those of his wives, his parents, his children and theirs. It took a while for everyone to settle down on mats to share *goros*, the children on laps or standing around the edges. It was a large household, and everyone was present, dressed in finery. We sat together, sharing the bitter nuts and memories. We reminisced about Kitty and Rich's antics. We had a good laugh when he reminded me about the time we found a baby viper beneath our refrigerator and Rich climbed up on the kitchen table. "And how about the *guhilas*?" he added. Those small hedgehogs lived in our latrine and raided our stored potatoes at night if we left the doors open.

And he was clearly still enjoying a good laugh at Rich's and my beleaguered attempt to create a demonstration peanut farm that couldn't demonstrate anything except the hunger of the trampling cattle.

I reminded him that, without our knowledge, whenever we left town overnight he had slept on our patio to guard our house, and told him how much we appreciated that when we eventually found out. He smiled, eyes downcast.

We happily shared various milestones in our lives, but when I tried to explain why Rich and I divorced, Issaka's face darkened. He made a so-characteristic facial and body response summarily repudiating the whole idea. Time to change the subject.

I figured since I'd heard he was involved in local politics, he would be a good person to ask why the village had grown into such a large town. He explained that a road had been punched through to Katsina, Nigeria, just thirty miles to the south. So trucks now came up loaded with Nigerian goods, which were then warehoused in Aguié before being trucked east-west on Niger's National Route. And Niger-produced products and wares, as he explained, could be shipped more easily to Nigeria.

He beamed. "I'm on next week's election ballot to become this town sector's council representative. I'm pretty sure I'll win." I beamed back at him with pride. He was now a respected elder of the community. Then I told him a little about my career in politics as a legislative aide. His look of surprise probably came from the fact that I had had a career that in Niger was only open to men.

Enjoying Issaka's company

Having depleted our memories for the time being, I rose for picture taking. I observed his leadership skills in action as he organized everyone for the shoot, never a simple matter.

Before accompanying me home, Issaka disappeared for a minute, returning with two live pigeons hanging from their legs. "These are for you, Laouré," he said. I was dumbfounded for a moment and then graciously thanked him, promising to ask the Sarki's wives to cook them for my dinner. When we arrived at my house, he unceremoniously tore the major flight-feathers off their wings so they couldn't fly away, and was amused when I winced. The squab I had that night was delicious.

The next day, as I walked to visit Bulki, something felt different in the village. More people were in the market, some from smaller villages nearby. I could hear the tailors' pedal sewing machines, busy in their makeshift kiosks in front of their compounds. The Sarki seemed to be in his sling-chair more of the day, talking with visitors. The children ran around excitedly. The town was preparing for the end of Ramadan. "The Celebration of the Breaking of the Fast" includes feasting, music and dance. I had coordinated my trip dates to be here for it.

"La lé Laouré," Bulki cried when she saw me at her doorway. "We were hoping you'd come to do henna together! We've already started. Come sit down and have a *goro*." She and her daughter had their left arms stuck into long, narrow calabash gourds, looking as if their arms were broken. Inside the calabash their arms were wrapped in plastic to keep the wet henna leaf mash in contact with their skin for several hours while the color penetrated not only their skin, especially under their fingernails. The aim was to turn the skin under the nails red. Obviously, women getting together and "doing their nails" is a universal phenomenon.

After initial greetings, concentrating hard to get the names of the women of the household straight, I watched Bulki duck into her hut and emerge carrying a small tin bowl half-full of dry, green leaves that looked like oregano. "I hope you want to do your hands too, Laouré," she said, as she threw the leaves into a pot of water boiling on the fire and stirred them up with her one free hand. The leaves disintegrated and turned into a dark green paste, like pesto. Then she commandeered my left arm. "Oh, look at these hands," she exclaimed to the others. "They're so soft!" She placed my hand in her own while the women tentatively touched my palm and fingers. All the women they had ever known had strongly calloused hands from the hard work of farming and pounding millet. Their reaction didn't surprise me because I remembered this type of response in the past to the softness of my hands. When the examination and exclamations were over, Bulki began to slather the paste onto my arms and hands, especially thickly on my fingernails. When I wiggled, she cried, "Hey, lady! Can't you sit still?" We laughed together at her feigned bossiness. She directed her eleven-year-old daughter to wrap up my right hand and lower arm with more stripped rags, kept and reused for this purpose. My curiosity and newness to this whole process kept them all amused throughout. "Now you'll see how impossible it is to get anything done with one of these contraptions on your arm," Bulki said as she slipped a long skinny gourd onto my arm.

Bulki with her wonderful smile

"How *do* you manage to get things done?" I asked her. I knew from before that only the coming of a special holiday allowed women to take time from their work to fuss over themselves.

"We co-wives, sisters and sisters-in-law help each other with our chores, alternating days when we henna our hands," she replied. Some of her Hausa escaped me, but I got a gist of her explanations through her body language.

"How is your mother?" I asked her. I hoped Hadiza was alive and well. She had been such a fun and easy friend, but I hadn't heard anything about her and was almost afraid to ask.

"She's fine!" Bulki answered. "She remarried and lives in Gazawa now. I know she'd love to see you but her husband is sick and she can't travel right now."

I breathed a sigh of relief. "Be sure to let me know if she gets a chance to visit Aguié before I leave."

While my henna set, the women of Bulki's extended family hung around to participate in the novelty of Laouré getting hennaed. Her sister was married to Bulki's husband's brother, and they lived next door to one another. Several co-wives and other family women and girls joined the grooming party, scattered about on grass mats in the long shade of the late afternoon. The younger women had more elaborate equipment and made beautiful designs on each other with a finely ground henna extruded from a gizmo resembling a cake-decorating piping bag. Daughters laid their heads on their mothers' laps while moms hunted lice, cornrow by cornrow, killing them one at a time with a satisfying little thumbnail jab.

The intimacy of grooming together allowed me to put aside my timidity and ask how long it took them to re-braid their hair. They all wanted to answer me at once. "We take turns with a sister or friend. It takes at least four hours and more for long hair. She'll do me this month and I'll do her next month, so it's two months in between." They hastened to clarify that they washed their hair every week. "The braids do start to loosen but we keep the wild hair down with clarified butter."

Finally, my arms were free of the gourds and plastic wrap. We all admired the henna decorations. And then I heard the rapping on the metal door as Muman came to fetch me. I bristled a little at his insistence on being my escort, and dictating when I should come and go. But it did feel like time to take my leave, so I thanked Bulki and said my goodbyes.

Friend Bulki, all grown up

I knew Muman had some sort of government job, but was surprised when he asked if I wanted to see his office. He explained that it was west of town where the Aguié Canton administrative offices were, and promised we could visit Maimouna at the clinic on our way.

Passing a doorway with several fellows sitting around it, Muman explained that the owner of that house had a VCR and TV and that he charged people to come and watch movies. Aguié's first movie theater! He went on, "We haven't had electricity very long. The biggest change has been that women can get their millet and peanuts ground by machine. Another is that one entrepreneur bought a freezer and charges for ice and for storing meat. Just a few days ago, the chief installed an electric light over his doorway."

Walking through a part of town I hadn't seen before, I observed, "There are more and bigger mosques here now."

"Yes," he said. "Some of the money for mosques comes from Saudi Arabia." I glimpsed the top of a slender minaret above a tall wall, knowing that inside that wall, being a woman, I wouldn't be welcome to visit.

We stopped at the post office to greet Amadou, the postmaster, since he had been instrumental in my reconnection with Maimouna. Amadou seemed very pleased to meet me. He was young and handsome. "So, you're here now. Excellent! I hope you've been having a good visit."

"Yes! Sorry that I couldn't bring my daughter. It's because she got married last year." We laughed.

"How long will you be staying?"

"Oh at least through the holiday. I'm looking forward to it."

"Then you'll probably still be here for the national election."

I mentioned that my friend Issaka was running for a seat on the town council. After a while, Muman and I proceeded on to the clinic a few blocks away.

Maimouna greeted us dressed in a white medical coat. "I hoped you would come today. There's not much happening, so I can introduce you to my co-workers." This she did right away as the staff gathered. None of them was Somaila, and when we were alone again I asked after him.

"Oh, he moved to Niamey! He has a job with the National Health Service. He's a big shot!"

It seems that his movie star's smile took him far! She nodded knowingly.

Maimouna showed me around the small concrete structure. Each examination room had two tables, one for exams and another for supplies. It was probably cleaner than it looked, and it's hard to beautify a concrete structure, but it was a huge improvement on the dark, one-room dispensary where we'd held our well-baby clinics. There was one unfortunate change, she told me: "People have to pay for treatment. Not like when you were here."

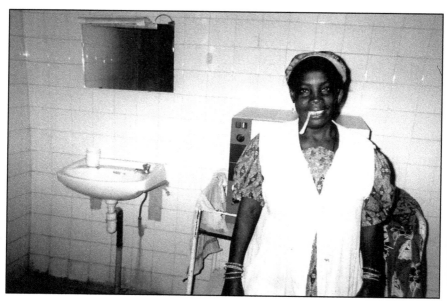

Maimouna at the clinic. Note the use of a
neem twig for tooth cleaning

She went on, "Next, they're going to build a maternity wing right next door. I hope to be able to work there. Now I do wound care, sterilize equipment and give shots and a few other things."

I asked, "Do you have an opportunity to teach women about diet and cleanliness like we used to do?"

"Not much. That's not part of my job."

I was disappointed to hear this but said nothing. Maybe if she got to work in the maternity wing, she'd be able to impart some of her knowledge to expectant mothers.

Noticing that there were patients lining up to be seen, Muman and I said goodbye and continued on to the Canton's administrative center. I thought how in the 60's the Sarki was the entire government, most run from one sling chair under a tree.

Approaching a cluster of buildings, Muman ushered me into his office, which to my surprise had computers and copy machines. I met Muman's colleague, Isa, who invited us to go with him to see a project he'd been working on. Following this tall man, we crossed a courtyard and entered an empty house, spacious and beautiful.

"This is a demonstration house for *sans bois* (without wood) construction," Isa explained. "We're offering training in building these houses, because wood is scarce, you know, needed for cooking and valuable for the environment. This house is made entirely of mud bricks." Looking up, I saw four arched domes forming the roof. It was magnificent, with four windows that let in lots of light. What an exciting innovation, I thought. "The problem is that builders are skeptical. They're used to traditional building methods with wooden roof supports. This *sans bois* technique is difficult to learn, and they're afraid that if they put in the training time, there won't be a demand for it because people are fearful that the structure will fall on them. We've trained a few builders but no buildings have yet been built in town." I said that I imagined it would eventually take hold.

On our way back into town we saw Ibrahim's son carrying a boombox, still inside its box, blaring music. I had seen his father with the same package the day before and assumed he'd just purchased it. Now, however, with the boombox still in its packaging, I wondered if this was a way of announcing to the world that it was new. Would he keep it in the box for weeks? I wondered.

When Zuli brought my dinner that evening she stayed to visit. She was happy to teach me a couple of new, stylish ways to tie my headscarf. Laughter at my clumsiness lent an informality to our visit and she began to open up to me about her impending engagement to someone from a nearby village. She was clearly unhappy. "I'm sixteen, but I don't feel ready to marry. I don't have anyone else in mind, but I want to marry someone I know and love." As unhappy as she was, she didn't think she could go against her father's wishes, and seemed resigned to it. I told her how sorry I was. We formed a sweet bond; I invited her to come talk any time she wanted to. How I wished there were some way I could help.

The Sarki's beautiful daughter, Zuli

REFLECTIONS AT THE POND

After almost a week, my system began to harmonize with the pace and schedule of the village. I woke early in the morning, thanked Maimouna's boys and sent them on their way. Then I splashed water on my face and dressed, enjoying the quiet morning sounds of the households surrounding mine. A woman nearby was pounding her grain in a wooden mortar, and goats bleated in the road outside my compound door. The occasional human voice filtered through the mud walls. A tingle of anticipation zinged through my body when I remembered that this evening the end-of-Ramadan festivities were to begin.

As much as I wanted to reconnect with old friends, I also wanted to experience, with all my senses, early mornings in Aguié. They were unlike anything else in my life, and I'd never let go of the thread of them. I wanted to wander aimlessly, exploring old memories and new areas of town, all senses on alert, out to the edges and beyond into the bush. I wanted to be alone, unescorted by Muman.

After making oatmeal with raisins on my camp stove, I slipped out my door, padlocking it behind me. Muman will know I'm outside, I reasoned, and not just sleeping late. If he wants to find me all he'll have to do is go up the street asking people which way I've gone.

I walked to the edge of town, towards the brick pond, where a natural declivity gathered water during the rains. I'd always found it remarkable that while the Aguié earth was mostly sand, in this one area there was heavy clay. Men made bricks here to build their huts, houses and walls. The small pond used to dry up in the hottest months, but decades of use as a clay quarry had now produced a small year-round lake, its surface covered with green flowering water plants. Orderly rows of bricks were laid out baking in the sun around three sides of the pond, like loaves of bread fresh out of the oven. Several scenic peninsulas reached into the lake, leading to large trees, which the brick-makers protected, taking care not to undermine their roots. These trees had once been at the edge of the lake but, as the lake grew around them, they found themselves rooted on narrow promontory of land, presiding picturesquely above a green plain.

Making mud bricks

Several areas were still reserved for brick-making, but in some other spots there were small vegetable garden plots down to the water's edge. I realized that as the dry season progressed, the pond water evaporates, leaving moist edges perfect for planting. The gardens grew with the shift of seasons, the diminutive plots protected from livestock damage by dense but delicate fences of thorn bushes held in place with anchored vertical sticks. Small boys seemed to be guarding the plants from goats and sheep.

Brick-making ponds

Cabbage, lettuce, tomatoes, zucchini, carrots, onions and even eggplant were thriving in great abundance. I wondered whether a government program had taught the villagers to value these foods and how to grow them. I thought about my little vegetable garden in our old compound, the only one in Aguié. Because all water had to be hand carried back then, my friends considered it extravagant of me to spill water onto the ground during the dry season just to grow a couple of tomato plants and some lettuce. But now there was a way for them to enjoy fresh produce, not trucked in from Nigeria. That's the kind of progress I liked to see!

I perched on the stump of a tree looking over the lake, watching ducks forage under the surface. Up and down they bobbed, gobbling their finds between dives. The tranquil beauty was balm for my overstimulated mind. It looked like a page out of a picture book of lush land in the West Indies or Cambodia. This was a thrilling new development in arid Aguié.

I caught myself romanticizing the way of life here: the closeness to nature, family farmers growing most of what they consume; a small community where everyone knows everyone else, where most people have extended families to rely upon during times of need; and where they have a beloved and reliable leader and a universal religion. Here breast-fed babies were strapped right up against the skin of a family member until they could walk; and grandparents were taken care of at home until they died. I treasured so many wonderful aspects of life here, especially compared to the complexities and difficulties of life in the U.S. where "rugged individualism" was the ideal of many, leaving so many others in the dust.

On the other hand, I reminded myself of the extreme drawbacks of life in Niger: torrid heat, mosquitoes, poor health care and frequent droughts. And it was impossible for me as an American, not to be disturbed by the lack of personal freedom and opportunity, especially for young women married off to older men with no say in the matter. Even as I visited my friends who were co-wives, and saw how they got along and appreciated the division of labor and mutual support in many cases, I couldn't see it as they did. For me it underlined the dramatic inequality between the sexes that continued. Maimouna was still unusual for having a modest education and a government paid job. I learned that even now, in 1999, only 30% of boys attended school at all, and their education was rudimentary at best.

Still gazing at the gardens, I found some peace, not quite to the point of accepting the will of Allah, but my own version of recognizing the hardships along with beauty and simplicity, and finding a way to be with them both. Above all that, I felt an abiding appreciation for this village and the people who had treated me like family during my two years so far from home. I relished the wisdom that comes with living in deep connection to the earth: food grown and raised by hand, water drawn from deep wells right under the town, reliance on seasonal rain to nurture crops. I remembered vividly how much their lives depended on cycles of nature, how when rain failed, crops failed too, putting life itself in danger. Yes, there was the extra grain the Sarki traditionally put aside for emergencies, but that could only go so far, as could help from the federal government and foreign aid. There are no insurance policies against drought, and I was saddened to learn that drought had been occurring with greater frequency than in past decades. I thought about the severe drought in the 1970's that had dispersed them to the south into neighboring Nigeria's more tropical and forgiving landscape. But they returned! Why? Because it was their ancestral home, of course. But there was something special about this place, something that had brought me back as well.

I left the pond, striking out on a path leading away from town. Doing so, I became aware of a steady stream of foot traffic in the opposite direction, flowing into Aguié from villages in the bush, no doubt coming in to spend the end of Ramadan holiday with family, purchase ingredients for their holiday meal, or pick up new clothes at the tailor. I tried to imagine how I would feel if I fasted during daylight hours for a full month. The evening meals I'd been experiencing would certainly make up for any sense of deprivation, but still.

Two boys passed me on bicycles. The bikes looked like they had been skillfully patched together over years of use and home-repair. Soon a cluster of children approached, driving an ox before them. The ox must have weighed more than ten times the combined weight of the boys. In all likelihood they had grown up with the animal, but what a big responsibility for such young children!

The land was more curved than I remembered. Gradual, extremely shallow hills undulated into the distance. Taggle ends of millet stalks poked up here and there, but most had been trampled in the three months since the last year's harvest. Even the stalks were cut and stored for kindling, animal food, ass-wipes and other uses.

A grand old tree, one of few which had survived being trampled, eaten, or cut down for lumber or firewood, dominated the horizon. Songbirds played musical chairs in its branches. I wandered off the path to sit in its shade.

A lilting human song caught my ear and I noticed a Fulani woman in a field nearby. She was willowy and dressed completely in dark blue. As it was very unusual to see an unaccompanied woman, I watched and listened from a distance. She walked slowly along the empty furrows, occasionally stooping, taking a handful of dirt and sifting it through her fingers, gleaning the beans which had fallen during harvest. As she worked, she sang a dolorous lament with which she seemed to be consoling herself. The melody rose and fell. She didn't seem to have seen me. I breathed in deeply and planted the lilting strains of her song into my heart's memory.

Strange sign location

Even this far away from the village I could still hear the rhythmic thumping of pounded millet. The air bore the scent of cook-fires. With over a hundred villages scattered around Aguié district, I wondered if there was anywhere one could walk and not detect smoke from village cook-fires. I settled in to really meditate; I was grateful for having learned this skill that could give me peace wherever I went.

Circling back toward town, my path paralleled a red clay road that was new to me. I noticed a road sign, and as I approached, I saw that it said AGUIÉ. It struck me as preposterous. This *was* a road, but there were no cars on it. Thirty years back there were no roads at all out into the bush. The idea that anyone needed road signs or maps would have been laughable to the walkers, horsemen or even the occasional government service Land Rover that passed through Aguié on the way to smaller villages off the National Route back when I lived there. In those days, officials would have followed the footpaths to remote villages, picking up a local guide from Aguié on their way through.

Four women carrying bundles on their heads passed on their way out of town. They called out to me, "Hadiza! Hadiza!"

Being confused with someone else was new to me here. I quickly corrected them. *"Ba Hadiza ba ne. Laouré che."* But they weren't buying my denial and introduction. One of them insisted, "I remember you. Ten years ago when my nephew was very sick we brought him into the dispensary. You gave him medicine and he got better right away." Obviously she was confusing me with the French volunteer who lived in Aguié then and took the name Hadiza.

'You are too young to remember me," I insisted. "I lived and worked here before you were born, thirty years ago."

Their hands went up to cover their mouths in astonishment. Speaking among themselves they repeated to each other what I'd just said, embellishing it with comments I didn't understand.

Then they started joking. "Won't you come home with us to our village? It's not far." Calling their bluff, I answered, "Sure. Lead the way," and I rose as if to follow them. They all laughed and slapped each other's shoulders as they turned about and continued along their path, their laughter and chatter fading.

Resuming my walk back toward Aguié, I sensed my growing anticipation about the holiday which was about to begin. There was some mystery about the exact start date. I knew that the head religious official for the area must wait until sundown to see if the crescent moon and Mars can be seen low in the west before announcing the official end of fasting. Whenever it began, it would be four days and nights of drumming and dancing in the streets. I was looking forward to it all. I'd bought a double *zani*, one to wear as a skirt and one as a shawl. The fabric was full of bright greens and yellows, with dark-colored shoes pictured all over it—very whimsical and very African. I'd also outfitted myself with a new scarf: a filmy green one with gold threads running through it.

My thoughts about the festivities, past and future, lasted all the way back to town. In front of a house wall near the outskirts sat an enterprising girl of about eleven. She was heating a cast iron skillet over a fire. The skillet had small pancake-sized depressions, into which she poured a few drops of peanut oil before spooning millet batter into them. The smell suddenly made me ravenous. The girl had several customers already waiting. I put in my order and sat on a wooden cart to wait.

Before long, a man came out of the compound doorway and gesticulated wildly to get my attention. It was a moment before I recognized Kurama One, the leader of the team of three deaf-mute masons, our first close contacts when Rich and I arrived in Aguié, whom I'd known quite well when we were renovating our compound. He seemed as pleased to see me as I was to see him; his welcome and his guttural vocalizations brought back all the fondness I felt for him. Meeting him again made me want to pinch myself to see if this was real or a dream. As we beamed at one another, somehow with his gestures he got across to me that he had known I was planning to visit Aguié but that he had been out of town on a job. He pointed at the girl and then at himself and at the house, nodding. Then he pointed to the girl and with skillful gestures sculpted imaginary breasts on his chest.

Then he made sucking noises, pointing to the girl once again. "Ah!" I said to myself. He ushered me into his compound and introduced me to his wives, his other kids and proudly showed me his horse. I was amazed that he was youthful and strong enough to still be doing masonry. He had seemed to me a mature man when I first knew him, putting him well into his sixties.

I chatted easily with Kurama, re-experiencing the relief Rich and I felt finding someone with whom we could converse without having to negotiate the language. I did my best answering the inevitable question: "Where is Ibrahim?"

"We are no longer married," I mimed, bringing the pointer fingers of both hands together, touching and parallel, then moving them wide apart followed with a shrug and wistful smile as if to say, "I know it's a shame but it can't be helped." His daughter began eagerly translating with hand gestures.

"We have two grown children, a boy and a girl who are twenty-five and twenty-seven. We named our son Zachary after Sarki Brazaki. Ibrahim remarried, and has a fine teen-age son. I have photos back at the Sarki's guest house, where I'm staying. Come visit me and I'll show you." This agreed, he left me with his daughter to eat my millet cakes, since it wouldn't be right for a woman to eat in the presence of a man.

I was filled with wild happiness at the exuberant, wholehearted welcome I had just received, and felt a joy almost as if I'd seen a dead friend rise from the grave, since I hadn't imagined he would still be living. This trip had already fulfilled my hopes many times over.

Back home I washed and rested, thrilled with my morning adventures. I was glad that Muman hadn't followed me. Late in the afternoon I went out to the market at the highway to buy a few provisions. On my walk back, just as I was passing in front of the Sarki's palace, appreciating the cool peacefulness of an ordinary evening, I was startled by an extremely loud, deep, drumming from inside the palace walls. Then, all at once, small boys were running from every street and every doorway, yelling as they ran, heading right into the center of the square. I had to back up against a wall to get out of their way. It was the beginning of the holiday.

They circled like swarming bees around the waterless fountain in front of the palace, excited and free. The group grew larger as more and more boys converged on the square. As in a frenzy, their bare feet kicked up a cloud of dust. Jubilant and proud of their important role helping to kick off the *fête*, they circled again and again.

When their energy ran down, they stopped to watch as the Sarki and his men appeared in the palace doorway and from the streets leading into the square. They strode forth in their finest robes, matching turbans, and sunglasses. Despite their almost total coverage, I recognized most of them as the "regulars" who sat with the Sarki each morning in the shade of the palace wall. I knew that their robes, with fancily embroidered necklines, spotless and ironed, were among their most prized possessions. Long ceremonial swords, jammed into red leather scabbards, flapped amid the tails of their flowing finery.

Each man led a horse, equally decked out in lavish dress. The holiday saddle blankets, deep red cloth embroidered with many colored threads and appliquéd with bright geometric patterns, stretched down below the stirrups. Red leather fringe and tassels hung from the saddle blankets to the horses' knees. Fabric saddle covers form-fitted the high-backed Hausa saddles and were studded with grommets and tiny mirrors. Decorative bridles, brushed manes and tails made the horses look proud and regal. Even the arch of their necks and the prancing of their hooves created a fine display.

At a signal from the Sarki, the retinue mounted their steeds and followed him through the streets, drummers following along behind. Fasting for Ramadan was over. Feasting, music and dance were soon to begin.

Horseman in front of Sarki's palace

END OF RAMADAN, END OF A DREAM

I hurried back home to eat something and dress, eager to go back out and take part in the festivities. As darkness fell, I could hear the drumming of three or four drummers. It started with a half dozen strong drum beats in unison, then a pause, followed by the drummers diverging into separate parts, the beats flowing in and around one another. One drummer held the beat steady with a regular, deep *ta da tum, ta da tum*, from which others took their cue to improvise. I felt giddy. I would soon be out on the square watching and listening. Maybe I would join in the dancing.

I changed into my new *zani*, tucking it snugly at the waist, worrying if I danced too energetically, my inexpertly tucked skirt would come loose and fall off. I experimented with how I might be able to carry my small tape recorder in my purse, with a tiny clandestine microphone sticking out the top. I decided to turn it on before leaving so I wouldn't bring attention to it. I knew the children would act differently if they knew I was recording. I also packed a handful of coins to give the kids and the drummers, as someone had advised me to do.

By the time I walked into the area there were two groups of drummers, both surrounded by children. Two or three youngsters were dancing in the middle while the others watched. When the music slowed, the dancers slipped back into the circle. Then one, two or three more dropped coins at the feet of the musicians and commenced their own turns. I joined the circle closest to my street. As I did so, the kids turned away from the drummers and dancers and greeted me excitedly. I had the first inkling that my presence might prove a distraction.

I gave a coin to Muman's son Ali, and immediately, all the kids were clamoring for coins. I tried to turn the situation around by firmly saying "no" and ignoring their pleas. I told the boys to be quiet and listen to the drumming. Nothing worked. The dancing circle was now a Laouré circle, with very little attention to the music or the dancing. I tried moving away to watch from a distance, but they followed. I tried to shoo them away. It was hopeless. I gave it up and walked back to my house, disheartened.

Later I tried again, thinking a bigger crowd would dilute the impact of my presence, hoping that more adults would be out by then and they would discipline the children. But that wasn't the case. Again, it was impossible for me to even watch the festivities without creating a huge disruption.

Bitterly disappointed, I went back to my lodgings, followed by kids begging for coins and jockeying with each other for my attention. I closed the door on them and shut off the tape recorder. Relieved to get away from their attention, but totally frustrated, I threw myself onto my bed and wept.

Before I realized what I was doing, I began a somatic process I'd learned back home in a practice called BodyTales. I began spontaneously moving in accordance with my emotions. I wrung my arms, kicked my mattress, writhed and emitted guttural sounds. I embodied my disappointment, crying loudly. I overcame my anger and confusion, slowly graduating to smaller but intense movements expressing my sadness, despair, frustration and anger. Thus released, I was able to see that although this turn of events was not my plan, not my desire, not my dream, I would have to accept that my presence at the festival had created the opposite of what I'd hoped. It became clear to me that I wouldn't be able to participate in Ramadan here in Aguié.

ESCAPE TO ZINDER

Drying my tears, I examined my options. I could go west to Maradi to visit Tal Hadji, but I would need Akwiya to go with me to guide me to her daughter's house and I couldn't ask Akwiya to do that on a big holiday.

Or I could go east to Zinder where I had planned to go after I left Aguié. I could stay at the Peace Corps hostel and join in festivities in the larger city, where the presence of a lone white woman wouldn't be such a novelty. Would my friends in Aguié understand? Would they be hurt or inconvenienced? Would it be okay with the Sarki if I changed my length of stay in his guest house? Would it be possible to get a ride to Zinder tomorrow morning?

With all these options and questions racing through my mind, I decided to sleep on it. I woke early and, still feeling compelled to leave, sent Maimouna's boys home with a message, letting her know I would be away for a while; that I was going to try to get a ride to Zinder. Then I sent a message to Issaka asking for his help getting a ride. Half an hour later, after I had packed what I needed for a few days, there was a tap on my door. Resisting the strong urge to throw myself into Issaka's arms sobbing, I blurted out what had happened. "The children wouldn't stop mobbing me. The dancing stopped. I couldn't be in the square without disrupting everything!" I told him I wanted to leave quickly and quietly and I would come back after the holiday.

Issaka, showing regional scarification

"I understand," he said. "You might be right. Going to a bigger town for the holiday would be better. Getting a ride might be difficult, though."

He hoisted my pack up onto his shoulder and walked with me to the car park. Thankfully, he was able to negotiate a ride and he helped me find food to take along. It was an eight-person van, but I agreed to pay extra so as not to have to wait until it filled. I knew on this day that most folks were already with family and not traveling. Issaka, my dear, understanding and helpful friend, stayed until the van pulled out onto the highway, waving me out of sight.

Upon arriving in Zinder, I wrote in my journal:
"Even in the middle of the 'cold season' it's still %#!*# hot! It's 90 degrees according to the thermometer here. I'm sitting on a clean tile veranda at a restaurant with relatively few flies and pretty tables. Well, Paradise popped: they've run out of food, but very gracefully. I'm famished, but compared to the fasting every day that has been going on around me, it's nothing to complain about. Zang! OK! I DO get to eat here after all. Omelet with bread and a Coke. Yum. The charming waiter is flirting with me. It's rare that I get flirted with by such a younger man. I'll bet it gets him places."

I asked the charmer if he knew where the Peace Corps hostel was. He disappeared for a few minutes and came back with a threadbare boy to take me there on foot. I went, having become re-accustomed to putting myself into the hands of strangers. It was no more than four blocks. I thanked my guide and gave him a coin. The hostel was comfortable, with a small room to call my own.

Much to my surprise and delight, I hadn't missed the beginning of Ramadan festivities in Zinder. For some reason I didn't understand, half of Niger ended the Ramadan month on one day, and half on the next day. This was decided by the higher-ups in the Muslim officialdom. Who was I to argue? It gave me the opportunity to begin again, but this time as a little-noticed observer, not disruptive at all. I could enjoy the drumming and dancing all night. The insistent and repetitive drumming had the same mesmerizing effect on me it always had. It was wonderful, even if not as personal as experiencing it in Aguié. But it was enough.

I woke up early the next morning and discovered that a newcomer had arrived in the night and simply crashed on the living room sofa. I had almost taken off in search of an omelet, when the figure on the couch stretched and sat up. Much to our mutual surprise, it was Mike, Zack's photographer friend. I had been counting on meeting him in Aguié and in my hasty departure had not considered how to let him know my change of plans. Neither one of us had planned to be in Zinder on that date, so it was a fortunate coincidence. We ate breakfast together and tried to synchronize our arrival back in Aguié as best we could.

Getting directions and advice from folks at the hostel, I spent a day exploring the market and the byways of the ancient walled city. Several warnings sounded very serious. I shouldn't take photos of the old fortress on the hill or I might get arrested for violating national security. Stay out of the ancient walled city part of town after dark, or risk being violated. Apparently, one of the female volunteers had been raped.

One of my ideas for passing time before returning to Aguié, was to take the bus to Agadez, a city at an oasis in the Sahara about seven hours drive north of Zinder. An ancient seat of learning, it was still an important trading hub. Photos of Agadez looked exotic and enticing. But the volunteers at the hostel informed me that the bus to Agadez only departed once a week. It took two days to get there and these days was always accompanied by a military convoy, apparently because bands of Tuaregs on camels, protecting their territory from uranium exploitation, have held up buses and kidnapped travelers. I crossed an Agadez side-trip off my list.

The guardians at the hostel, a Fulani couple, Yero and Jollah, lived in small quarters around the back with their young child. Recent drought had turned some nomadic cattle herders into city dwellers, and this family was a casualty of this development. They had the classic Fulani features of paler skin than the Hausa and more angular noses and jaw lines. They wore their traditional all-indigo garments. No wonder they have been referred to as *the blue people*. I assumed the indigo dye of their clothing tinted their skin as well, but I had no way of knowing, since only their faces were uncovered. Until meeting Yero and Jollah, who were now learning both Hausa and French, I had only seen nomadic Fulani from a distance at larger city markets.

Always, they held a mystique for me as beautiful, highly decorated and suggestive of the desert life I had read about. I wondered how many years Yero would continue to wear his mostly symbolic sword.

They were making part of their living as hostel guardians and part by embroidering clothing and making jewelry. I bought an embroidered blouse and pants and some jewelry made with leather, cowry shells, brass bullet casings and beads. The leather scabbard of Yero's sword was covered in green, red and brown geometric designs, seeming to be fresh off a Saharan trek. He noticed the man's high-tech watch I was wearing. It had been given to me by the wife of a good friend in the States who had recently passed away. I had no idea how to use all its features. Yero asked to see it and to my amazement, set the correct time, showed me how to set the alarm feature and revealed several other tricks I never guessed it could perform. I think flabbergasted is not too extreme a word to use to describe my response to his degree of tech know-how.

Jen, one of the Zinder PC Volunteers from the hostel, invited me to visit her at her place. As she and I walked in the heat of the late afternoon sun I complimented her on her attractive slacks, which were baggy-comfortable, made of some of the ubiquitous bright cotton-print cloth found at nearly every market in Africa. She encouraged me to go to her tailor, Ringo, to get some made while I was there, and described how to find him.

Her compound was modest but homey. The rough mud walls of the living room were hung with traditional Hausa blankets. Over a much-appreciated glass of ice tea, she told me about her recent adventure to N'Gigmi. She described taking the bus east of east, way over to where the edge of Lake Chad was before droughts, one after the other, dried its edges and shrank the huge, shallow lake. The city of N'Gigmi, once at the lake's edge, was now many miles away. Ninety percent of the lake, according to Jen, had evaporated.

"Out East, I had the most fantastic night out on the dunes. There are these two wonderful international aid guys, a German and a Swiss, who let me stay with them and arranged for me to get out to the dunes and even to spend the night out there. I know they'd be happy to do the same thing for you. You've got to go! It's a chance of a lifetime! I'm telling you, you've never experienced such peace in your life. It's practically the end of the world out there, thousands of miles from civilization."

As I considered what Jen was telling me, I could feel tension vibrating in my ribcage. I recognized the dynamic of strong indecision—wanting to do as she was urging me but knowing how unlikely, and even dangerous it could be.

She told me there were no Americans, no hostels, and no hotels. "That's all very well for you to say!" I said at last. "I'm more than twice your age and I certainly don't speak German." Despite my protests, I was flattered and pleased that she thought I could go on such an adventure, and, the idea of the vast quiet dunes *was* intriguing. One moment I could project myself into her picture, and in the next, I was drowning in a dozen logical and reasonable objections. I was just recovering from twelve years of illness! I had already done so much more than I would have imagined I could do.

I reflected that each stage of this trip— starting with the decision to come to Niger, my introduction to Mike Tauber, the cumbersome process of getting my visa, then the Niamey hostel—had been a further spinning out from my comfort zone, allowing wildness into my otherwise conventional life. I felt like the yoyo at the end of the string doing "around the world," describing a larger and larger circle around a center to which there might be no way to return. I'd let out a little more string and experience the exhilaration and the doubt simultaneously. I'd look back to see the increased distance from my starting point, take a deep breath, and let out just a little more string.

"Yes," I heard myself saying to Jen. "I'll go on the next bus." *Oh my God*, I thought, *I must be crazy!*

My new plan gave me just one day to visit the market and Ringo the tailor. On my first sortée alone on foot, I walked for several kilometers without seeing a taxi. Then I wondered if maybe some of the motorbikes *were* taxis. I flagged several and one stopped and confirmed he could take me to the market. I hung on tight. The auto traffic in Zinder was much lighter than in the capital, and we arrived without incident.

I bought Muman a grand boubou and, for myself, some Tuareg sandals, beautifully wrought in multicolored leathers. I could leave a bag of things at the hostel to collect on my way back through. For my pants I decided on a brown, black, gold and yellow fabric. I took another motorbike to the tailor, who assured me he would have my pants ready when I came back through Zinder on my return to Aguié.

I suddenly realized that no one I knew before yesterday had the slightest idea where I was, nor would they have any reason to suspect my whereabouts. Should I spin out too far and disappear, it would take a pack of bloodhounds to track me. Such was my trust of Niger and its people, and my instinct to follow the urgings of perfect strangers!

Before departing, I sent a letter to Sarki Brazaki in Aguié so he wouldn't worry. In it I tried to explain my abrupt departure and let him know my plans to be gone another five days or so, and I asked him to tell Maimouna and Muman. I hurried to give the note to the bus driver going west that day.

N'GUIGMI

The bus heading east hummed along smoothly, as I took note of my surroundings and let my mind wander. I marvel that the toddler across the aisle from me already knows how to say whatever she wants in what's considered a difficult, tonal language.

What is that smell? Does that man's satchel contain a chicken, terrified into stillness?

Why do we Westerners feel it necessary to stop, screen, buffer and overpower every natural, human scent of sweat, blood, urine, and bodily oils? I'd missed this cocktail of smells I lived among for two years so long ago.

I admired the efficiency with which African travelers tied up their possessions in a square of fabric, in baskets, large pockets, or just in tight corners in the folds of their clothing, parsing water out of small metal or plastic kettles.

The road disappeared into sand drifts, stakes sticking up to mark its boundaries, like snow depth markers alongside roads in the Sierra. Several times tires stuck in deep drifts up past the hubcaps. Everyone out of the bus while the men shouldered and rocked the bus up and out.

The passengers rummaged in their baskets; aromas of prepared foods wafted my way. Babies cried and were suckled. I napped, awakening once to see a woman with two children, laden with many baskets, exiting the bus where there was no sign of a village, only one flimsy branch-and-grass shade roof designating a bus stop.

Later during the changing of a tire, the men moved into the shade of the bus and squatted to enact their ritual pre-prayer wash with tiny amounts of water from their tea kettles, then prostrated themselves towards Mecca. We women wandered off away from the prayer side of the bus, also to squat, each of us creating a small tent around our bodies with our *zanis,* to empty our bladders.

Evening arrived; the air cooled slightly. The bus traveled on. Foreheads glistened, voices lowered, heads nodded. A snore from close behind me. Stiff and sore, I wondered at having made this rash decision to stretch my already ambitious trip. The six-hour trip took nine hours.

Finally, we entered a dark village. We descended from the stuffy bus into fresh, moon-shadowy, dirt streets. As I waited for my dusty bag to be lowered from the roof, I asked the driver if he knew the house of the *anusaras. Anusaras* like me.

My luggage coming down off the bus

A young man materialized out of the shadows. He said he knew and would show me the way. I wondered whatever would they think, being awakened in the middle of the night by a disheveled American lady?

A block and a half from the bus stop my guide knocked on a heavy metal car gate. No response. Again, this time with a coin; loud metal on metal...*rap, rap, rap.* Lantern light danced into the tree boughs above. Some questioning through the gate in a language I didn't understand.

A burly young African man holding a kerosene lantern opened the gate and picked up my bag, motioning me towards the house. By now the inhabitants were roused and came, flashlights in hand, rubbing their eyes as I babbled in French that I knew their friend, Jen, who had told me I could probably stay with them. With little more explanation than that, the two men conferred, then welcomed me, leading me into what was certainly one of their own bedrooms. They showed me a bathroom, rebuffing my apologies, and shuffled off to another part of the house to go back to sleep. Feeling like the worst house guest ever, I climbed into a still-warm bed, and fell directly into a deep and dreamless sleep.

Next morning, I awoke to the aroma of coffee brewing and gentle kitchen sounds. I showered, dressed and presented myself to my two young hosts, who were now wide awake, groomed and in good spirits. They offered me bread with butter, and a cup of coffee. We immediately hit upon a combination of French and English. I shared the broad outlines of my story and they gave me theirs: both of them worked for NGOs. Gunther was involved with economic development, seeking a foreign market for local basketry. Félix worked at improving agricultural techniques.

They were quick to laugh and joke with one another, making me feel quite at home, and I could sense that I was a welcome diversion for them. They remembered Jen's visit, and when I told them I hoped to go out for a night on the dunes as she had, they said they could easily help me arrange it.

After breakfast they left for work, generously offering me the contents of their small fridge and drawing me a map of town, showing the market, the civic center and their workplaces. I snooped around the whitewashed rooms a bit, discovering that the two of them had probably shared a bed after my arrival. It was unmade, clothing draped around it on the floor. There were a few minimal attempts at decorating the house. A red, yellow and white striped blanket adorned one wall, tacked up with nails to the wooden beams which supported the stick-and-waddle roof. A collection of small baskets caught my attention. Some had tight fitting lids; the work was tight and appealing.

I washed the dishes, postponing the moment I would have to go out and see where last night's bus had brought me. I amused myself with the absurdity of my plight. I was both the adventurer and the fearful one. I was curious to go out, but felt ropes of uncertainty holding me back. Yes, I reasoned with myself, there is always discomfort in stepping out alone into the unknown, but the unexpected is where you find what you love best.

Procrastinating almost as much as my dignity could bear, I finally donned my headscarf and left the house. The early morning sun was stinging hot. The few people in the streets scrutinized me. I greeted those I passed with *Sannu,* knowing that even if they didn't know Hausa, they'd know *Sannu.*

I was fascinated to follow a young goatherd who stopped at a doorway here and a doorway there, exchanging a few words and collecting one or two goats, which he added to his small herd, prodding them with a thin stick. This was goat day-care, I realized. How enterprising! I followed him to the edge of town. His charges needed no urging to plunge into the parched grass fields. They quickened their trot and spread out to enjoy the freedom to forage. It was a good livelihood for a youngster, since he probably didn't get to go to school.

Streets were lined with familiar looking mud walls, indistinguishable from a Hausa town. Following my hosts' map, I arrived at the marketplace, where most of the stalls were empty. Kanuri is the main language in this region but, Hausa, being a wide-ranging trading language, I did fine, buying a couple of small baskets and a pyramid of four guavas, enjoying the requisite haggle, always an excuse for human contact.

Two craftsmen were in the process of weaving grass mats. One wound rope, stringing it tightly around pairs of opposite stakes in the ground, forming a rectangle of tight ropes for the warp. The second man sat on the ground weaving strong grasses into a lengthy, continuous rope. I could see that the next step would be to weave the long rope over and under the tightened warp. The grasses they were using were longer and heavier than I was accustomed to. Since N'Guigmi was established on the shore of Lake Chad, I supposed these were water reeds rather than savannah grasses. My presence didn't seem to faze the mat makers as they continued bending over the work, their strong hands like cured leather. Escaping the intensifying heat, I returned to the house to rest.

Later Gunther and Félix, at home for lunch and a siesta, reported that they had been able to make arrangements with their chauffeur/steward, to take me that evening to the dunes in their Land Rover, and he would be my cook out there. Félix added, "Just take warm clothes, water and a flashlight."

"Wow! What service!" I exclaimed. Everything was falling into place effortlessly. My misgivings vanished and I was now unequivocally grateful that Jen had convinced me to come.

No cars and very few people were out on the streets that afternoon, though I could hear the pounding of millet and children's voices behind thick walls. Walking straight in the direction of the lake, according to my map, I came to the edge of town in seven blocks or so. There was no water, but I could see where the edge of the lake had once been. I then circled back toward the town center using a different route.

A couple of dusty-legged boys started to tag along after me, a few yards behind. They were joined by another and another. I stopped and turned to connect with them. They seemed curious about me. I had always loved to interact with kids wherever I traveled. I had always found the Nigerien kids to be open, fearless, and fun to be with, but when I turned and spoke, these boys formed a clump and pretended not to notice me, turning away as if disinterested. I could see that befriending them would be a tricky business. I walked on, wondering how I could reel them in. I wished I had brought a ball. Then I felt something sting my back. What in the world? I walked on, ignoring them. This time something thudded on my back and a rock whizzed by my ear, landing in front of me.

Incensed, I turned to confront the little devils. "Hey!" I said in a loud voice, "Stop that right now!" They did their clumping thing, pretending they didn't hear me. I turned and walked on, but this time many pebbles and small clumps of clay-earth found their mark, stinging me where they hit. Any timidity now disappeared and they hurled their voices at me, jeering, taunting.

I thought, *Oh my God! I'm being stoned!* By this time they were making enough noise in the street that adults stood in doorways observing us, doing nothing to intervene. I ducked into the nearest doorway, clapped for permission to enter, and in an agitated, halting Hausa told a woman that I needed help, that the kids were hurting me. She looked out at the kids, looked at me and shrugged. Even if she didn't understand my words, she could certainly understand the situation. Of course, the minute her door opened, the stoning stopped. To her it could have looked like I was needlessly afraid of a few little boys. Silly anasara. She closed her door. The pebbles started to fly again. I scurried to the next house, where a tall man with a long scar across his forehead came out to the road with me and scared the boys away. I was trembling with fear and indignation—fear at the experience of being attacked, and indignation at having found it hard to get adult cooperation.

That evening when I described the event to Félix and Gunther, they expressed some surprise but explained that in the east there was still a bitter memory of the colonial era. In the early part of the twentieth century, the native population had been enslaved to carry heavy burdens of timber all the way up from the forests of Nigeria, hundreds of kilometers away, to build fancy government buildings and homes. Not surprisingly the people of the eastern region felt residual anger knowing the brutality their ancestors had endured. I realized that this anger must percolate through the kids at times like this, and maybe in the woman who closed her door on me. I asked my hosts if they had ever had such an experience. They said they hadn't. I wondered if the boys were just bored boys seeing someone out of the ordinary and wanting to provoke, as they might poke at a mouse or lizard. Did my being a lone woman, behaving independently outside of the Muslim norm, give them male prerogative to abuse me? In retrospect, I realized that the adults I had tried to enlist for help might well have been Kanuri-speakers, who didn't understand my plea in Hausa.

The physical pain faded quickly, but the emotional turmoil of having been bombarded with negativity stung more than the stones. I felt somehow guilty too. Was I just an innocent bystander? Maybe they saw it through a different lens: I was a middle-aged woman, alone and dressed differently from everyone else, wandering around in their streets, sightseeing their extremely humble lives. Might that have been insensitive of me? Or at least ignorant of, or worse, flaunting those customs? But would that excuse stoning? No, I told myself, and tried to set the awful experience behind me and focus on my upcoming adventure.

I had heard about the very special dunes out east, but had never seen them or any other dunes in Niger. I thought back to my view of the Sahara out the plane window on my way from Paris. But the habitable southern one-fifth of Niger was all I had ever experienced.

A Land Rover roared through the compound gate, and I recognized the driver as the young man who had let me in the previous night. His name was Issoufou. He spoke to me in French. I had supposed Hausa was the common language in all Niger, but now I was in Kanuri tribal lands. I knew not a word of Kanuri, so French it was!

The roof of the vehicle was laden with rolled up rugs, which Issoufou explained would be our sleeping rolls. I grabbed extra water, a sweater and *zani* and we were off, but almost immediately we made a mystery stop. Issoufou jumped out and returned a few minutes later with a beautiful young woman, who climbed into the back seat as he introduced her to me as his friend, Haisa. As I learned later, Issoufou had one wife, but was courting Haisa as a possible second wife. I guessed that she had been married before, or she wouldn't otherwise have the freedom to spend the night with a beau. They might speak a different language, but they were still Muslim.

Issoufou loading the vehicle

Soon we were out of town on a faint track, and I felt as if I had truly reached the end of the Earth and was going beyond it. It was thrilling! We drove toward the sun, which nudged the horizon. Issoufou veered off the track into the bush, dodging shrubs that were growing in small clumps. All the gray-green bushes looked alike to me, small-leaved, spindly and tough, none high enough to be considered trees. But I trusted that he knew where he was going. I'd put myself in the hands of strangers yet again.

The flat, sandy terrain radiated heat. The land undulated with small mounds of sand, like gentle waves on a peaceful ocean.

Many kilometers out from town a man appeared, barefoot and dressed in a hide breechcloth. He carried a bow and arrows and a water gourd. Issoufou drove right up to him and stopped. They spoke for a short while before he turned to me and said, "This is Hamsa, my cousin. He's hunting gazelle. He's a really excellent hunter."

My mind whirled with questions and impressions: Has this man walked all the way from town? Does he stay out here overnight? Is this how he survives, hunting his own food, or is this an occasional pastime? Are there really gazelles out here? Is he a member of a tribe out here that subsists on hunting and foraging? I had never met or seen an African living so completely in the pre-colonial, pre-agricultural way. I felt as though I'd entered a time warp, meeting a man whose family's lifestyle may not have changed since...ever! His existence in 1999 seemed extremely improbable—an apparition.

I didn't get to ask my questions because Issoufou soon revved up the motor and off we went on our trackless way. Fifteen minutes farther along we slowed down to see and pass by a camel train consisting of at least twenty camels, some with riders, some bare, and several laden with large lashed bundles of household goods on both sides and litters on top, enclosed on front and back with red fabric, but open at the sides. Issoufou explained that it was an Arabic wedding party ferrying the bride to her new husband's dwelling. "It's forbidden for anyone to see the bride before she gets there. Judging by the number of camels which will be given to the groom, the bride's family is very rich."

Arab wedding party

THE DUNES

Dunes out to the horizon

I was enjoying being in the circle of firelight, watching how the firelight danced on their faces and accentuated the young couple's curves and shadows. But Issoufou's radio felt invasive. I had imagined a night of serenity in the moonlit dunes. I yearned to immerse myself in the total silence and vastness of the desert. To be alone, not with the courting couple.

I announced my intention to move away from the fire and the radio. Issoufou looked around uneasily and asked me where I would be. "Just right over there," I said. "And I think I'll stay over there to sleep." He evidently didn't think it was his place to offer an objection.

"Not too far," he said, his expression of concern reminding me of Muman. What was it with these Nigerien men?

I agreed, then gathered up my rug, water, flashlight and camera and made my way down the slope of our home-dune and through several troughs to the larger dune I had pointed out to him.

The sand was so bright in the moonlight it looked more like snow-covered hills. It was surprisingly cool after the heat of the day, and my sandaled feet sank into each powdery drift. Raising one foot and then the other took a lot of energy, especially while carrying the awkward roll of carpet.

I had promised to stay within view, so I put my rug down at the top of the first dune I climbed. On my back, quieting, I gazed up at the sky. Despite the moonlight, thousands of stars were visible. I could still hear the damn radio, but it was very faint.

I took a quick bearing. There was the fire; over there was the truck. I found a line of three bright stars, maybe Orion's Belt? Great. I could navigate my way if need be, like sailors do.

Satisfied that I knew where I was, I abandoned my doing-mind to just being. I wedged myself into the welcoming sand at the top of my chosen dune and became attentive. My heart and breathing slowed down. My imagination probed the miles of dunes beyond. I didn't feel small, as I had expected. I felt large—felt my breathing fill the space around me. I surrendered to a full and deeply satisfying aloneness.

Then I heard a strange sound, like panting. A night bird I couldn't see, its wings pumping. It sounded like a large bird, perhaps a raptor seeking prey. Then silence.

The moon moved slowly towards the horizon. A chill crawled under my clothes. I rolled myself up in the rug like a jelly roll. It was wide enough to cover my length, shoulders to ankles.

My body and mind slowed as my senses awakened. I felt I was probing the edges of space—or were there any edges? All inner chatter stopped. A small breeze fluttered over the skin of my face and lifted strands of hair. Curved shadows of dunes stretched out below me in the cool light of the wedge of moon, distinct but pale.

Orion's Belt was now much higher in the sky. It gradually dawned upon me that there was more to celestial navigation than just identifying a constellation and expecting it to stay put. How silly of me to have thought otherwise. I smiled at the thought that Bryan would be under this same moon in a few hours when it was night on his side of Earth. I snuggled closer into my rug roll attempting to pull my chilly feet in.

The moon had reached the horizon and would soon disappear. And then what? But I had my flashlight, and anyway, I'd be sleeping.

The wind increased, blowing sand into my face. I closed my eyes. My feet were cold. I was grateful for the thick rug but wished for a real sleeping bag.

After a while, I watched the moon vanish. Total darkness now, except for the undependable pinpricks above. The radio was off, or maybe I just couldn't hear it over the wind. A tinge of fear entered my mind. Wasn't there a movie where a character was buried alive in a sand storm? "This is not child's play," whispered my inner parent. "Sand can move around, or did you forget?" Why hadn't I considered this before?

The wind whipped at me. When I tried to open my eyes, sand lashed into them. Frantic now, I wondered what I should do.

Even if I wasn't in danger of being buried in sand, I wasn't comfortable enough to sleep. I needed to find somewhere more protected. Maybe I could get to the truck.

I unrolled myself, grabbed my rug, canteen and flashlight and began the trek down my dune in the direction I had come from. My flashlight dimmed, then went out. I shook it, but no luck. Stars above and blackness below. Moon gone. Orion's belt no help. I talked myself out of total panic, barely.

I trudged through the sand. The wind was somewhat weaker down in the troughs, but my stamina dwindled and my breath became labored. I had absolutely no idea where I was or what I should do. I thought I'd been walking more or less in the direction of our camp, but I didn't arrive. By moving had I made things worse?

I called out to as loudly as I could. My voice was swallowed by the wind. Again and again I called out, but there was no answer.

I labored on through the dark, hoping for a safe haven, hoping to stumble upon the sleeping bodies of Issoufou and his girlfriend. Anything that would give me reason to stop.

I stayed low, following the curve of an incline, and there, standing firm in the sand, was a small shrub. For some reason that seemed hopeful. The shrub had lived this long without being smothered by sand, so it might be a place of safety for me as well. I kneeled next to it, and yes, the wind did seem less ferocious. Exhausted, I rolled myself up again to wait out the windstorm.

I must have fallen asleep because when I next opened my eyes the day was dawning. The wind was gone; the sand was beautiful and harmless-looking. I left my stuff below and hiked to the top of the nearest dune to see where my meanderings had led me. It took a lot of effort as I kept slipping back. One step up, two steps back.

Issoufou in the dunes

From the top I immediately saw Issoufou and a clear trail of his footprints between immense dunes. I faintly heard his voice calling "Laouré, Laouré!" I called out to him and he whirled around, saw me and raised his arms in triumph. It took little effort to guess what must have gone through his head, conjuring the picture of the return to his employers without the nice American lady.

Soon our paths joined, and we shared breathlessly the stories of our night. "I was so worried about you," he exclaimed. "I trekked the dunes calling for you, but I couldn't find you."

"I'm so sorry to scare you, Issoufou. I got turned around."

He told me that he and Haisa had finally gone to the truck to sleep, but he had been very worried. He was jubilant with relief to find me safe and sound. We walked back to camp together, joining Haisa who had been tending the fire and brewing tea, thick with sugar. Issoufou poured it in the traditional way, trembling a little, holding the teapot way above the small glasses. We relaxed and smiling together, we drank the warm sweetness, and it felt to me that we were sharing a sacrament.

Tea ceremony

While he packed our rugs back onto the roof of the truck I wandered the dunes, grateful for the sunny calm. I took lots of photos and found some animal tracks. After the wind had stopped a small four-footed animal, a gazelle perhaps, had made its way from where to where, I could barely imagine. Either earlier or later, an even smaller four-footed animal, a mouse maybe, crossed from a different direction, creating and "X" of a crossroad in the whiteness. Except for our own footprints and the graceful snakelike patterns left by the wind, these were the only marks in the sand for as far as I could see.

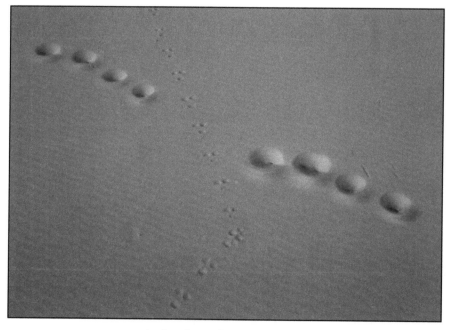

Animal tracks crossroads

HONORED GUESTS HOST A PARTY

On my return trip to Aguié, I wondered what I could do to show my appreciation for the warm welcome I had received there. I decided that a party would do the trick. I conferred with both Maimouna and Akwiya, and they endorsed the idea. On market day they arrived at my house from their opposite sides of town to accompany me to buy provisions. I was excited to be planning a thank-you party for all my Aguié friends. I wanted a *mishwi,* a sheep cooked whole over the fire. Maimouna and Akwiya thought a rice and sauce dish, and macaroni and sauce would round out the food pretty well.

After the plans were well underway, I realized that the very friends I most wanted to thank would have to be in charge of the large task of planning and preparation. What kind of thank you was this? And yet they were enthusiastic.

As we wove our way through the market, checking out the wares, many displayed in baskets and calabashes on grass mats, it was a delight to listen to my friends negotiate each purchase with consummate skill. We stopped to have conversations with curious friends, who were excited to hear of the party. We bought onions and garlic, tomato sauce, herbs, Maggi bouillon cubes, macaroni and rice. Finally, in the meat area, after scrutinizing our bleating choices, we came away leading a plump sheep on a short leash.

Even with three of us, it wasn't easy to carry the supply baskets and pull a very stubborn sheep across town. Nearing the ends of *our* ropes, we lucked upon a friend of Maimouna going our way with an empty donkey-drawn cart. She persuaded him to cart our sheep the rest of the way to her house, so we heaved the belligerent ram onto the cart bed and concluded the rest of our trip without incident.

The belligerent ram

Maimouna took my hand as I turned to go, saying, "I'll walk you as far as town center." As we left, hand in hand, I was reminded of the many times, thirty years before, we had walked each other partway home after work. We'd get to my house first. I would then turn around and accompany her halfway to her house. On other occasions, we'd arrive at her house from some mission of ours, the market or a home visit, and she would turn towards my house and join me halfway before we said our final goodbyes. It was a lovely Hausa tradition which I was delighted to be reenacting: walking a friend partway home before parting.

Maimouna now turned back at the opening into the main square, saying, "Tomorrow's the big day. I have lots to do to get ready. See you tomorrow, Laouré."

As I passed the Sarki's palace, nodding respectfully at the Sarki's retinue, then did a double take, for there among them was Mike Tauber. It was good to see him yet again, and I was especially pleased at the prospect of getting good photos of the party. I knew he appreciated the opportunity to have access to photograph traditional villagers, who would accept him as a friend of mine.

I joined the group, sitting on a mat, and was immediately pressed into service as a translator. Before long, Mike was taking pictures of the Sarki and his entourage, separately and together with me. Soon Sarki Abdul invited us into his palace for pictures with his wives. And when it became clear that Mike would be staying for the party the next day, the Sarki invited him to stay at his brother's compound across the square.

The next day I walked a few blocks to the large compound we'd been invited to use for the event. Boys perched on the top of the walls to view the hubbub inside where bending women attended the fires. Smoke and savory smells emanated from the yard. In the far-right corner Maimouna and Akwiya stirred two immense earthenware pots with paddles as long as walking sticks. A third woman fed the fires. Smoke drifted up and over the wall. "Lale Laouré, Lale Laouré," they greeted me, smiling, then quickly returned to their work, discussing the food with no need of my counsel. Knowing that their friendship with each other was largely due to each having been close to me in the old days, I wondered in what other small ways my living here with Rich had left an imprint.

Onion and garlic, tomato and chili melded in the one pot for the sauce that would go with rice in the second pot. I stood there feeling useless and foolish. Why hadn't I come earlier? I certainly could have at least done some of the massive amounts of prep work they must have done. I was chagrined to think I had so added to my friends' workload when my intention was to honor them!

Yet they seemed to be having a great time, excited to create such a feast and looking forward to the party. Maybe they considered my having financed the event enough. I was reminded of my sense of helplessness and confusion when I first arrived here as a twenty-year-old. All the etiquette my mother ever taught me just didn't quite cover the situations I found myself in.

Then my heart swelled with gratitude for what they were doing for me, and for having been so well taken care of in Aguié, by the

Sarki, neighbors, and friends. I realized that I'd never before felt myself such an integral part of any neighborhood or town, even Mill Valley where I grew up. Rich and I had been truly claimed by the whole village, and thirty years later I still felt a part of the fabric of this community. I wished, not for the first time, that Rich could be here to experience this.

"You two are amazing," I said, and they laughed. "Where is the sheep?"

"It's on the fire next door," Akwiya answered. "Haowa and her daughter are basting it and her son and husband will bring it over when it's done." Of course it was what I had intended, but it gave me a jolt to realize that the stubborn, shaggy white beast I had bought at the market was now transformed into our main course. I suddenly had more compassion for his resistance.

There was a commotion out on the street. The boys disappeared off the wall. A few drum beats told me that the musicians had arrived. They were setting up outside, further evidence that I was not in charge of my own party. I would have had them come into the spacious compound; but they knew better. Dust from the dancing wouldn't mix well with food. As the music warmed up, children gathered around the musicians, dancing and suddenly stopping when the music stopped. It reminded me of the musical chairs games of my childhood birthday parties.

I walked back home, gave myself a teapot bath, and dressed in my new *zani*, finishing my outfit with a tightly wrapped headscarf. Mike appeared at my door and together we returned to the venue. Guests had begun to arrive, men a few steps ahead of their wives, dressed in their best clothes. The women wore crisp matching *zanis*, blouses and scarves, and plastic flip flops on their feet. The men wore long white *riga* shirts, a few of them in voluminous grand boubous, the geometric embroidery like breastplates of frosting.

Dressed up for the party

I greeted the men first, with the traditional inquiries after their house and health. The women I greeted less formally, holding their hands in mine, smiling, conjuring up the names I remembered. The men entered the compound but the women stayed in the street and I stayed with them.

My invitees arrived, but so did others, who undoubtedly felt they should have been invited. I didn't recognize them all, but they all knew me. I hoped there would be enough food.

The drumming by now had begun in earnest and as the women formed a circle, children made way for them, stepping back into the shade of the wall. Soon there were at least twenty women dancing, each holding the shoulder of the woman in front of her. They were like bold color wheels turning slowly, their feet thrusting forward, hips and shoulders swaying in a dance so familiar to me that I had daydreamed about it long after leaving Niger. I was delighted to see that Mike had scaled a wall and was getting aerial photos of the dancing.

I knew I could recapture this dance! When Maimouna came out to the street, I took her hand and said, "Let's join the dance."

"No," she answered, "I'm too old to dance, and so are you." I was shocked. Since when was I too old to dance? How serious was this stricture? What if I danced anyway?

I did what I had done many times before in Aguié. I ignored tradition and joined the circle. As I caught the rhythm and fell into step with the other women, joy filled me. The younger women included me enthusiastically with smiles, heads thrown back, ululating as they made space for me in their chain. The drumming was so strong I could feel the vibrations in my bones. I danced until I was sweaty and muddy with dust. If I was transgressing, I had to trust they would forgive me, just as they always had.

Dancing with my young friends

When the signal came that food was ready, a wild rush ensued. Men and boys ripped meat off the whole roasted lamb, called *mishwi*, and took handfuls of rice as the women and children looked on. It was pandemonium and I was aghast. No *politesse* here: elbowing your way into the meat seemed to be the accepted protocol. Then the women and children got their turn. It was all over in a flash. No one else expressed dismay, so I hid mine and chalked it up to my naiveté.

The dancing recommenced, and this time the children joined in. My women friends, the "honorees", had worked all day and were still cleaning up when the musicians and guests departed. Except for that fact, I was well satisfied that the party had been a success. I heaped gratitude onto the cooks and the helpers they had recruited, paid some of them and then helped carry the large cooking pots back to Maimouna's compound.

As I left, Akwiya reminded me, "Don't forget tomorrow is the Bori ritual I told you about. If you want to come, Muman will pick you up. Late afternoon," she said, her arm raised to the mid-afternoon position of the sun.

"Definitely," I said. With more effusive thank yous, I took my leave and made my way home, where Mike was waiting with a couple of miraculously cold beers. We did a quick post-mortem on the party, both quite satisfied.

"It's so great to have someone to speak with in English!" I told him. He'd been in-country almost as long as I had and felt much the same. We were excited to share the stories of our exotic travels, and talked until exhaustion slowed us down. Maimouna's boys arrived to be my protection for the night, and Mike took his leave.

OVERSTAYED WELCOME

I was so enjoying my stay. The most ordinary things gave me delight, like watching a small boy carrying a red and yellow Chinese enameled bowl across the square, perhaps delivering food to a sick relative, then crossing back later, wearing the bowl on his head like a helmet. Judging from the slow pace he'd set for himself, he'd probably already eaten and was using the opportunity of being sent on this errand to have some free time; he was in no hurry. In fact, I realized, no one's in a hurry.

But in other ways, I was sensing it was time for me to go. My rusty Hausa was not good enough for deeper conversations with my renewed friends in Aguié. Our words and smiles had stretched about as far as they could go. And, despite lots of goodwill in both directions, I felt I was becoming a burden on my closest friends and the Sarki's wives, who were cooking for me every day.

My heart ached to think about saying goodbye, knowing how unlikely it was that I would ever see them again.

On the other hand, I hated to admit it, but minor irritations were mounting. Children continued to think it was fun to knock on my door. When I would ask who was there, there would be no answer. Adults, too, wouldn't answer. Was giving a vocal answer through the door some sort of taboo? Was there a taboo against saying one's own name? I sensed the difficulty was cultural, but still, I let it get to me. The knocking interrupted naps, writing, and visits with friends. My little private haven was anything but. The ever-protective Muman put a teenager guard outside my door from time to time, yet Muman's protectiveness itself was irritating. At times I felt trapped in my guesthouse. Late one morning when Muman returned me home, he ordered me to lock my door and not let anyone in until his return at 4:00. Excuse me? Was the town really so dangerous? Muman's tight rein had me chomping at the bit. He started so many sentences with '*Il faut..*: You must zip your money pouch. You must lock your windows. You must be sure to padlock your door each time you go out. You must not let the children in."

How could I tell him I wanted more independence when I was so grateful to him for so much? I held my tongue.

My bachelor neighbors were another annoyance. They were mending their roof, which meant that when they were up there they could look straight down into my patio and latrine. I was never sure of my privacy. They also blasted their radio for hours at a time. How I longed for the sound of roosters and muezzin calls and pounding millet. Anything but this!

Neighbors working on their roof

Questions began to plague me: What am I doing here? Have I worn out my welcome? What else is there to do here? What am I trying to prove? If I leave before I had planned, will I feel like a failure? Maybe I should start to think about saying goodbye to my friends in Aguié and hitting the road toward the capital.

When I ran into Phyllis, from the Mission school, she happened to mention that she was driving to Maradi the next day and said she'd be happy to give me a ride. That could save me at least one uncomfortable bus trip. Since Tal Hadji hadn't come to Aguié, I could go visit her in Maradi, which was on my way back to Niamey. There was a Peace Corps hostel where I could stay for a couple of days. How to find Tal in Maradi without Akwiya to guide me was a puzzle with no answer yet. But plans for my departure began to take shape in my mind, lessening my sense of frustration with my current situation.

Meanwhile, I looked forward to the Bori ritual Akwiya had invited me to that afternoon.

BORI RITUAL

Muman collected me in the early afternoon and led me through an ordinary door on an ordinary street. It was a home compound like any other, but today many people were there. I had never been to a gathering inside a compound; gatherings of unrelated people always took place in the street, square, mosque, clinic or marketplace.

About thirty people sat quietly on grass mats around the perimeter of the courtyard. It felt in some ways like a church. Muman and I found places to sit and soon the musicians, located behind us, began to play. Zig-zagging notes from a high-pitched string instrument carried the melody, while several drums tapped lightly. From an inner door Akwiya emerged, dancing slowly, bare feet placed carefully one after the other on the clean-swept dirt. She wore the regalia I had seen: the heavy beads swayed as she moved. Her arms curved through the air as if through matter. Her hands appeared to be touching and feeling unseen objects. Her body was bent forward at the waist, the beaded strands hanging from her headdress, clacking together as she swerved first left, then right, circling again and again in the empty space before us. Her eyes were closed and she seemed oblivious to our presence.

The fiddle and drummers increased their pace. I couldn't tell if she was responding to them or they to her, but both the music and the dancing intensified. Syllables, not in Hausa and not in her normal voice, a guttural and commanding cadence, came from deep inside her chest. Sweat beaded and trickled down her rapt face. She seemed to be seeing and speaking to forces unknown.

A young woman from somewhere behind the scenes was led into the dance. Seemingly in a trance, she moved in circles, slowly at first, then her movements became jerky and frenetic. She threw herself around, eyes closed, flailing her arms, as if struggling with a physical opponent. Akwiya's attention and movements were now riveted on this young woman. She encircled the girl in her arms but could not quell her hysterical movements. An assistant brought a large white length of fabric and helped Akwiya throw it over the head of the girl. The girl's body went limp, almost collapsing to the ground but Akwiya broke her fall, holding her tightly. Akwiya knelt and with one hand on the girl's limp body and the other raised above her head, incanted a phrase, many repetitions, eyes closed, her own body vibrating with energy.

I sat, feeling the oddness of the situation, uncomfortable to be witnessing an interaction that was so very private---something that in my own country might be more likely to take place in a therapy session behind closed doors. Yet I was enthralled to observe such an out-of-the-ordinary happening. Did seeing another person let go of control cause us all to free our own animal selves and bring on a catharsis? Did it open in us a door to an irrational world that lies carefully hidden, allowing fresh air into the dungeon where we keep our devils, thrilling us with the danger or the truth of it?

The whining fiddle bow strokes had gone from loud and frenzied to slow and soft. The drumming descended to a background heartbeat. The girl ripped off the white fabric covering her head and torso. The audience was curious, empathetic, not knowing the story of this woman's affliction, but pulling for her to cast off her physical or emotional burden and to emerge purged from her ordeal.

As the girl was lying limp and motionless on the ground, Akwiya, who had removed some of her priestess finery, moved vigorously above and around her in time to a guttural chant which leapt from her throat. Her hands described circles, palms facing out. The musicians followed her lead, pulsing with her chant. She smoothed her hands like a caress just above the girl's form, fingers opening in a sweeping gesture. Did she see tendrils of evil? I wondered. Or was it like a midwife clearing space for oneness to emerge? She stopped, her hands now lying still on the girl, soothing.

It appeared as though there had been a healing. The music slowed to one slow-fiddled melody line.

Throats cleared, people rearranged themselves, a collective breath was taken as we, one at a time, disconnected from our own trances. The girl stirred, her shoulders shaking off some unseen force. Akwiya gathered her up and helped her to stand. They shuffled through the crowd into the interior of the house.

Several other healings followed. What I remember most is the huge energy that Akwiya brought to each new case. She seemed, indeed, possessed, overwhelmed by a fierce vibrating energy. She exuded command and authority I'd never experienced in her presence before. I felt grateful that she had invited me, that she had wished to reveal herself to me. Muman and I walked home in silence. I found myself admiring Akwiya's courage. She had a calling and she was true to it even though her community marginalized her for it. She had pursued that calling all these years and had ended up honored and recognized as the high priestess she was.

I felt strangely exhausted that evening and, after packing for tomorrow's departure, I drifted off to sleep to the happy sound of the boys' cards slapping and thoughtfully whispered arguments.

FINDING TAL HADJI

Tal Hadji had been like a little sister to me during our time in Aguié, keeping me entertained, properly educated and fiercely protected. As lovely as it was to get to know her brother Muman as an adult, and as amazing as it was to see her mother as the high priestess she had become, Tal had always had my heart. I was determined to see her. But how?

She hadn't returned to Aguié and it didn't look like she would before my departure. So I was determined to go to her in Maradi. But I wouldn't be able to find her without help, as there were no street signs or house numbers. So I asked Akwiya if she would come to Maradi. Phyllis had offered me a ride and was fine with adding another passenger—or two, since Mike wanted to come along. He agreed to photograph my reunion with Tal Hadji, and then he would proceed to Niamey from there on his own.

On Wednesday morning, Mike arrived with his backpack right on cue. To my surprise Maimouna appeared at the door to announce that she was coming as well. She had gotten permission to take off a day of work at the clinic. I was delighted, and relieved to postpone our parting.

Akwiya met up with us out at the National Route. Phyllis was right on time and we set off together on the seventy kilometer ride to Maradi. I couldn't help but compare this ride to Rich's and my experiences of sitting alongside the highway for hours waiting for a hard, dusty uncomfortable journey on the back of a truck.

As the five of us traveled along, our conversation became limited by the complexities of translation so that neither Mike nor Akwiya would feel left out. Since we had already shared so deeply, one-on-one, our conversation felt unnecessary, so we settled into a companionable silence.

Maimouna and I nearing our parting

In anticipation of the upcoming reunion, I found my mind drifting into the past, recalling Tal Hadji when she was half my age and twice as wise. I thought about all the times she stayed overnight when Rich was out on *touré*. Tal never said so, but I imagined that sleeping on a mattress must have been a treat. Her small body curled next to me exuded the sweet smell of onions and bean cakes that filled her family compound when the women were cooking over the open fire. I smiled to think how she enjoyed introducing me to new words, songs and games; and policing how many kids could congregate in our yard, making sure none of them took advantage of my naiveté or hospitality. At the age of eleven, she had already seen births and deaths and was quite clear on the facts of life, since it all happened in the confines of a ten-foot-diameter hut where the whole family slept.

When Zach and Reina were about the ages Tal had been when I knew her, I couldn't help thinking what very different lives they had.

Sometimes I wished they could experience village life in the carefree unstructured way the children of Aguié did. Other times I wondered what bright little Tal would have done with a Western education.

Now I couldn't wait to meet the woman she'd become. I wondered if I would recognize her. Would she be as excited to see me as I was? Would I be welcome in her household?

After Phyllis let us off at the edge of the city, we caught a taxi, and Akwiya directed the driver through streets so changed that I had no clue where I was. Perhaps I had never been to this section of town, or more likely, this section had grown up out of nowhere during my absence. We followed a paved boulevard and turned right onto a rutted dirt street. Then we shifted left into a yet smaller road which boasted a mix of small businesses and homes amid contiguous walls. Household activities spilled out onto the street. Oxen were billeted on the edge of the road, hobbled to permanent stakes. We saw fenced areas for sheep and goats alongside a household wall. One house had a patio area outside its doorway, delineated by a screen of blue-flowering vines.

I tried to pay attention to the turns and outstanding landmarks in case I needed to find my way back to Tal Hadji's the next day. One barber shop would be unforgettable. It sported large, awkward images of male hair styles and in large letters above the door was the name of the establishment: TAMPON. I was glad I didn't have to explain to anyone why I chuckled.

At the next corner the driver opened our doors and we piled out; it was a typical Peugeot taxi with doors that didn't open from the inside. Akwiya smiled a conspiratorial smile, and Mike, Maimouna and I followed her, dipping into the darkness of a small auto parts shop. She spoke briefly with a man, who took a studied look at me and vanished through the curtained back door.

I heard women's excited voices, "It's her, it's her!" And then a woman stepped into the shop. It could not be Tal, but I was uncertain. The woman greeted Akwiya warmly and Akwiya introduced her as Fati, one of Tal Hadji's co-wives. Fati pulled aside the curtain and gestured us into a large well-swept compound with several huts around the edges. We followed her. Suddenly the city disappeared and it felt like we were in a village. A group of women sat together in the slanting afternoon shadow, one rising to stir a pot on the fire. Then they all rose to welcome me, taking turns gripping my hands in theirs, big smiles on their faces; they knew without a doubt who I was. Children began to congregate from around the edges of the compound, peering at me, amazed. As introductions proceeded, I gazed from one woman to another, trying unsuccessfully to recognize my old friend.

I heard her before I saw her. "Laouré, Laouré, Laouré," she yelled from the far side of the sloped compound. She ran towards me, yelling all the way, and jumped into my arms, kicking her heels up over and over again as though she was a child again, not the forty-two-year-old matron I saw before me. She finally stood back and looked deeply into my eyes, searching for the young woman I was thirty years ago. We evidently found what we were looking for, because tears rolled down our cheeks.

Akwiya, Maimouna and Mike, clearly caught up in the drama, were welcomed and offered mats in the shade, while Tal Hadji grabbed my hand and led me imperiously to her corner of the compound. Sitting together in her hut, we began to share where our lives had led us. She showed me a photograph of her grown daughter from her first marriage, and another of her daughter's five children. Then another picture of three school-age kids from her current marriage to Laowali. Between marriages she told me she had been single in Maradi. I showed her photographs of Zach and Reina, Rich with his second wife and son, and one of me and Bryan.

We reminisced about the things we both remembered best, my rusty Hausa only a small impediment to complete understanding. We laughed, remembering how surprised she had been when introduced to the miracle of bursting corn kernels into tasty popcorn. We talked about that other miracle: our kerosene refrigerator that produced ice she and the other kids loved. She reminded me about the tape recorder Rich and I had, and how much kids loved to sing into it and then listen to the playback. I said, "Remember how excited you all were when our families sent back developed film, featuring pictures of all of your own faces? You ran next door with them to show your parents."

Tal Hadji, finally

She told me that two of the other women in the household are co-wives. She was the third. She assured me that her husband was kind and generous and her life was good.

Satisfied with that information, we relaxed into our easy camaraderie. I admired a ring she was wearing. It was brass-colored and ornate, like a filigreed scarab, very unusual. I'd forgotten that anything you admire in Hausa culture you are likely to be offered. She urged me to put it on, and then she wouldn't let me give it back. "All right, If you won't take it back, you'll have to accept mine." I took off a silver ring I was wearing and gave it to her. Feeling the reaffirmed bond of our friendship, we again paused to wipe our tears.

Tal Hadji, found

I left her hut so she could get dressed for pictures. She returned in her finery, all white ruffles and scallops, like a wedding cake. I guessed that it might have been her wedding dress. Mike took pictures of the whole family, then of me and Tal and just Tal alone in all her finery. Then he left to find the Peace Corps hostel, where we agreed to meet up later.

It had already been emotional day, but I still had to say a final goodbye to Akwiya and Maimouna who would be catching a bush-taxi back to Aguié. Tal came with us, and she and Akwiya had some mother-daughter time as we walked, while Maimouna and I held hands, knowing our parting was near. To delay it a little, we all stopped at a sidewalk restaurant and had some rice and sauce and soft drinks.

Tal Hadji and other women of her household

We were subdued as we ate, unable to sustain our earlier joyful chatter. Then reluctantly we all walked to the bush-taxi lot and waited while a van filled with enough passengers. Our hugs were fierce and tears welled up as the van's engine started and two of my favorite women in all the world were ordered to get aboard. I watched as they settled in, and I held eye contact with Maimouna until the van turned the corner and was out of sight. I couldn't help but think back to our long ago parting, how she ran alongside our vehicle, holding my hand, crying as if her world was coming to an end. I didn't need to run alongside this van for her to know I loved her, but some part of me was with her and always would be.

Tal walked me to the Peace Corps hostel, where we said more tearful goodbyes. Exhausted, I took a nap and didn't wake up until morning.

Over breakfast with Mike and some volunteers, there was a discussion about that day's national election. There were reports of violent protests in Maradi and elsewhere. Peace Corps Headquarters had called and demanded that no volunteer should travel until further notice. They made it clear that that included *me*. My plan had been to stay in Maradi just one night and then proceed on to the capital. Now that plan would be imprudent and against direct orders from the Peace Corps, who considered themselves to be my hosts while in Niger. Mike, a free agent, was not bound by such an edict, and he decided to go ahead and travel to Niamey. We said our farewells.

The next day Maradi was filled with tension. Before the votes were all counted, the military came and confiscated the ballot boxes. The election had been annulled. The President's party lost everywhere.

I still had eleven days before my flight to Paris. I'd developed a bad cold. I hung around the hostel and was befriended by an African-American Peace Corps volunteer named Iffi who offered to let me stay at her house, and then nursed me back to health. While there I was surprised when the American Ambassador tracked me down by phone, inquiring about my safety and whereabouts. He too instructed me to stay in Maradi until the danger had passed.

Once I was sufficiently recovered to do more than sleep and moan, Iffi and I enjoyed relaxing into a typical conversation among vols, comparing notes, sharing honestly, knowing we'd be understood. But her main complaint surprised me. "People here can't believe I'm an American. They think all Americans are white. And at first they expect me to speak fluent Hausa. I'm always having to explain myself."

Well, she didn't have to explain herself to me. We cemented our friendship by exchanging clothes: my black cloth captain's hat for her loose dress with tie-dyed elephants on it.

When I had fully recovered, Tal Hadji and I went to the market together. Tal was still a good teacher, and shared information she thought was important for me to know, as if I would be setting up housekeeping in Maradi instead of shopping for a few gifts before heading home to California. But I enjoyed learning things, like the fact that the butchers always left a sheep's tail on the carcass while he butchered it in front of his customers. "That way," Tal explained, "the customer can be sure it's lamb and not goat. Goat is less desirable." Walking back together, I had a sense of belonging beside Tal, who balanced an immense striated green and orange squash on her head.

After five nights at the Maradi Peace Corps hostel, I finally received permission to travel to Niamey. Tracing the labyrinthine path from the hostel to her house, I both reveled in having learned my way through the unmarked streets of Maradi, and grieved at the likelihood that I would never again follow this route to see my dear friend.

After our brief visit, the women of her compound gathered around me to say goodbye, then ushered Tal and me to the street door with final wishes for a safe trip.

Tal walked me quietly to the bus station, holding my hand in a firm grip. When it came time to take my place in the bus, she squeezed me as hard as I squeezed her, tears welling in our eyes. Her sweet "*sai enjuma*", until we meet again, ricocheted in my chest, battling with knowing that we would not meet again. The bus revved and rolled, Tal waved until I couldn't see her anymore. I twisted the brass ring around my finger, already nostalgic.

RISING TO CHALLENGES

From Maradi by bus it was roughly a nine-hour trip to Niamey, not including stops. I decided to treat myself to a bush taxi instead. This worked out well except for one small but explosive moment when the driver stopped to let a few passengers off and then kept delaying taking off again until he found others to replace them.

This trip had been full of stressful nighttime arrivals, so I wanted to get to the capital while it was still daylight and early enough to get a decent bed at the Peace Corps hostel. The driver kept saying we'd be leaving "right away" then disappearing for thirty minute stretches. Finally, I'd had enough. I blew up. He was surprised at my rant, but not as surprised as I was to discover that in my fit of anger I had regained fluency in Hausa. I told him that I had paid him to take me to Niamey. It wasn't right that my trip was being delayed so he could snag another fare. This was not part of the deal. He finally agreed to leave lacking one rider if I would pay extra. Fine. At least we were on the road, and my Hausa was pretty damn good!

I woke the next morning refreshed and set in motion a plan. I called the recommended tour agency to sign up to visit Niger's only wild animal park, _Park W_, so called because of the _W_ shape of the river. They said they'd call when there were enough tourists signed up to share the cost.

While waiting to hear from the agency, I kept busy by going to the open market, buying gifts and souvenirs, taking in the last sights and sounds, and always learning something new. I remembered the way to Zeinabou's home from my earlier stay in the capital, so I dropped by and enjoyed seeing her and getting to know her little twins.

I had a lot of time on my hands, since the tour agency kept promising the tour would be ready soon but not yet. This was reminiscent of Rich's and my four week stay in the capital, where every day we thought we'd be leaving.

I remembered Maimouna mentioning that Somaila had a post with the National Health Service. Though I hadn't thought I would want to see him, it seemed petty not to at least try, as if I was holding onto an old grudge that just didn't hold up under scrutiny. And I seemed to have nothing but time. So one afternoon I took a taxi to the civic center and roamed around looking for the Health Service offices.

Before long I was knocking on a door with Somaila's name on it. A voice answered, inviting me to enter. His expression went from puzzlement to astonishment as he realized who I was. Suddenly he was up and rushing around his desk. He took my extended hand in both of his, smiling one of his amazing smiles—reward enough for my having taken the trouble to find him. Now with graying hair, he still had his good looks and charming manner.

We had had a rough start to our two years of working together. Now in retrospect, it was easier for me to recognize his viewpoint: Why was he suddenly having to deal with this young inexperienced *anasara* who had no understanding of the language and customs, let alone any real medical knowledge? And worst of all, a woman! Thankfully, I seemed trainable, so he gradually lowered his resistance to my using the clinic space to establish a well-baby clinic. This became clearer once Maimouna and I established regular Wednesday mornings for the clinic, and he could see that I was no threat to him, in fact an asset. Perhaps it was only this he was remembering as he gave me such a warm reception.

I left his office a half hour later feeling lighter for having thoroughly mended my one challenging relationship in Aguié.

Meanwhile, day by day it became clear that the tour agency was giving me the same kind of runaround as the driver had on my ride to the capital, stringing me along for the same reason: Not enough other paying customers. Apparently there was not even *one* other person who wanted to go to Parc W. After three days of phone calls, I took a taxi to their office. The price they quoted me for a single traveler was way beyond my budget. I left, so frustrated and disappointed that I was crying. The manager caught me as I was about to step into a taxi. Probably figuring that one customer was better than none, he offered me a significant discount. I went for it.

The next morning as I stood in front of the Peace Corps hostel gate, where just a few weeks before I had been rooted like a tree, overwhelmed and unsure of myself, now I felt high on a sense of confidence from having persevered. In following my heart in the matter, I had dissolved what seemed to be insurmountable barriers.

A Land Rover pulled up and I hopped in, the sole passenger on yet another African adventure. But this time instead of a night on the dunes, I was traveling along the Niger River, lined with green farms and lush trees and bushes. I saw few boats, but those in evidence were either laden with freight or were fishing boats plying lazily up or downstream.

On one of the many long stretches between towns, I saw what I assumed was a wedding or baptism party. Streams of men and women walked beside the road, dressed in their finest, the women with pots, calabashes and baskets on their heads, weighted with foods and gifts. Looking as far as I could in every direction, I saw no sign of a town. I figured most of these people were subsistence farmers, and yet they came up with enough money for new clothes and gifts and music for festivals and family ceremonies like this one. How did they have the time and resources? Who fed their animals and the children left at home? And, how far were they willing to walk to honor holidays? The magnitude of their sacrifices for one another seemed to far outdistance what we did for one another in my American community. But these communities relied on such reciprocity for their very existence. With every celebration came a deepening connection that was the very fabric of their lives.

At *Parc W* I felt like a warrior queen riding solo on the roof of the Land Rover, buffered by spare tires. Exhilarating to see warthogs, antelopes, springboks, and several varieties of monkeys and birds.

There were *dama* gazelles, the symbol of Niger; and a lonely little elephant, who had been imported from another country to represent what used to roam in these increasingly arid lands. I wondered if the park was more like a zoo than a preserve. But my guide pointed out that there were no fences to keep them in. "It's an oasis-like forest, rich with habitat. The terrain surrounding the park is inhospitable. Animals that range out usually return."

After four hours of being on high-alert, wanting to see everything, we drove through a crude but sturdy gateway over the road; "*Bienvenue à Parc W*" said the sign. We drove directly up to a white canvas tent, a small version of one you'd see at the circus. After a quick visit to the WC, I took my suitcase into the tent; I had my pick of beds. It was Africa's high tourist season, being the relatively cool time of year, but there were no tourists, either from Niger or the two adjoining countries. Evidently, none of the three countries had yet established themselves as popular tourist destinations.

As the sole visitor and four park employees in attendance, I felt pampered and a bit overwhelmed by so much attention to my every need. But they were delightful and the food was excellent. A special treat was going down to the river early the next morning to fish for my breakfast, and observing, from a polite distance, four hippos taking their morning bath. The guide caught a fish large enough for all of us to have for breakfast, fried up with bread and coffee. Delicious! And fortifying for the return trip to Niamey.

At the Peace Corps hostel I had a chance to have conversations with current Peace Corps volunteers. We enjoyed comparing our Peace Corps experiences. In some ways theirs seemed harsher than mine. For one thing, they didn't have kerosene refrigerators as Rich and I had. Also, these vols couldn't have their own homes, but were housed in compounds with their village hosts. Such total immersion surely would ramp up learning the local language, diet and customs; but I couldn't imagine how Rich and I would have managed as a pair of newlyweds rooming with any of our neighbors. We created a little haven where we could retreat into some semblance of American life for a few hours, even as we kept the door open to all who wanted to visit. We bought and cooked our own food, while I imagine these vols ate with their host families much of the time. Could we have survived on three millet-based meals a day?

What I knew for certain was that the Peace Corps experience Rich and I had could never be replicated. We had the good fortune of experiencing a traditional culture, quite insulated from the outside world. The villagers were going about their lives very much as they had for hundreds of years, almost completely self-sustaining. Yes, they knew about their French colonizers, but few had any direct experience of a French person, and even less opportunity to meet an American. A great majority of the villagers had no idea where America was. While we were there, we too were largely isolated from the outside world with no radio or periodicals. Living without a clock, we adapted our routines to those of our neighbors, rising early and going to bed early. We were happy we had meaningful work, not so much because what we had to offer was so important, but because work gave a structure for our lives and a sense of belonging. What we learned from them about true community, self-sufficiency, hard work, family and generosity of spirit far outweighed what we were offering with our presence.

The Aguié of 10,000 inhabitants I re-visited was not the same as the tiny village I once knew. I felt fortunate to be able to return after three decades and grateful to be remembered and welcomed by those who had known me before.

The Peace Corps withdrew volunteers from Niger in 2011 due to security concerns. More than 3,000 volunteers served in Niger in those 49 years.

HEADING HOME

Mounting the stairs to the plane with sweat-drenched clothes clinging to my body, I looked forward to air conditioning, but then remembered that I would likely miss the heat in Paris, where the temperature would be frigid.

Once again, I nodded off. And once again I woke to a view of the desert, the patterns as hypnotic as ever, though this time I had a relationship to the sand itself, having slept through a windstorm in the dunes, putting all my trust in a little bush that I too would survive. What a crazy but amazing thing to have done. I didn't regret it for an instant!

In fact, I realized I had no regrets whatsoever. I had reconnected with the people I cared so much about, people I never imagined I would have the good fortune to see again. And I had been received with such warmth and kindness from both old friends and new ones. Yes, the goodbyes with Maimouna and Tal had been painful, but what a gift to see how well they had done, and to be able to share once again that sweet closeness.

And what a gift that my body had not only stayed well, my whole being had strengthened. Even with that nasty cold that anyone could have contracted, I felt whole in a way I hadn't felt in over twelve years. Bryan had been right to encourage me to go on this adventure, and I couldn't wait to get home to share it with him.

I felt so grateful that I had followed my impulse. No, not an impulse. It was a deep calling from within me to reweave the threads of my life in just that way, to follow a vivid dream of Maimouna, to write to her not knowing if she was even alive, and to travel solo halfway around the world to reunite with her and the others.

But there was an even deeper reunion going on, one I didn't fully recognize until that moment: I had reunited Laurie with Laouré, rediscovering myself in the process. I was not the woman I had been when I landed in Niamey a few weeks before, so unsure of herself, doubting her abilities, and afraid of what kind of reception she would receive from people she'd known so long ago.

Reconnecting with Laouré, that twenty-year-old who became an intrinsic part of Aguié, meeting so many challenges, developing friendships deep enough to hold her every time she fell, every time she faltered, every time she doubted her worth, even inviting her to dance the inner circle.

Maimouna, Tal Hadji, Issaka, Akwiya, Sarki Brazaki and so many other villagers helped make me the strong woman I became. Later, laid low by that long illness, I thought I had lost her. But now she was found: Laouré walking me home again.

AFTERWORD - 2020

I look back on my history in Aguié with a wide-open heart. A few years ago, Maimouna stopped answering my letters, so I'm sad to conclude that she has passed away. Further letters to other friends in Aguié have also gone unanswered; perhaps because no one wants to be the bearer of bad news, or it's possible that my letters haven't reached them. Even if I wanted to return, the political situation there is too dangerous for me to want to risk it. My having lived and visited there have been highlights of my life. I have thoroughly enjoyed re-living my experiences through writing about them. My return trip confirmed for me that the friendships I cherished remained strong and vibrant. I hope that relating my impressions in this book will begin to give the reader a feeling for Aguié, the warm and generous Hausa villagers, and the determined efforts of Peace Corps volunteers from 1962 to 2011 when political discord dictated its departure.

I took liberties both consciously and unintentionally, I'm sure, with the people, and timing of events in this memoir. It is based on my recollections and any factual errors are my own, and I apologize if I have misrepresented anything.

ABOUT THE AUTHOR

Laurie Oman lives and gardens in San Rafael with her husband, Bryan Gould, a writer and a swing jazz band leader.

She is retired from a career in liberal politics both local and state levels.

Before entering into the Peace Corps, she joined Cesar Chavez and the National Farm Workers Association as a full-time volunteer working on the strike and grape boycott.

After leaving politics, she spent 15 years as a children's nature guide for Marin Audubon and Wildcare, San Rafael. She has two children, six grandchildren and 2 great grandchildren.

Please avail yourself of the Facebook page devoted to the book where these photographs and others can be viewed: www.facebook.com/peacecorpsmemoir.

Ms. Oman can be reached at: walkinghomeagain67@gmail.com

CPSIA information can be obtained
at www.ICGtesting.com
Printed in the USA
BVHW021729010321
601382BV00022B/681